W9-BUQ-777

BUILDER-TESTED | CODE APPROVED

THE ENERGY-SMART HOUSE

FROM THE EDITORS OF **Fine Homebuilding**

The Taunton Press

The Taunton Press
Inspiration for hands-on living®

The Taunton Press Inc., 63 South Main St., PO Box 5506, Newtown, CT 06470-5506
e-mail: tp@taunton.com

Editor: Alex Giannini
Copy editor: Seth Reichgott
Technical editor: Joseph R. Provey
Indexer: Lynda Stannard
Cover design: Alison Wilkes
Interior design: Cathy Cassidy
Layout: Cathy Cassidy

Library of Congress Cataloging-in-Publication Data

The energy-smart house / from the editors of Fine homebuilding.
   p. cm.
  Includes index.
  ISBN 978-1-60085-409-5
  1. Dwellings--Energy conservation. 2. Energy auditing. I. Fine homebuilding.
  TJ163.5.D86E545 2011
  644--dc23
                  2011023844
Printed in the United States of America
10 9 8 7 6 5 4 3 2 1

About Your Safety: Homebuilding is inherently dangerous. From accidents with power tools to falls from ladders, scaffolds, and roofs, builders risk serious injury and even death. We try to promote safe work habits through our articles. But what is safe for one person under certain circumstances may not be safe for you under different circumstances. So don't try anything you learn about here (or elsewhere) unless you're certain that it is safe for you. Please be careful.

Except for new page numbers that reflect the organization of this collection, these articles appear just as they did when they were originally published. You may find that some information about manufacturers or products is no longer up to date. Similarly, building methods change and building codes vary by region and are constantly evolving, so please check with your local building department.

Special thanks to the authors, editors, art directors,

copy editors, and other staff members of *Fine Homebuilding* who

contributed to the development of the chapters in this book.

CONTENTS

PART 1: ENERGY EFFICIENCY

PART 2: INSULATION

PART 3: WINDOWS

PART 4: HEATING AND COOLING

PART 5: LIGHTING AND APPLIANCES

INTRODUCTION

If there is one topic that has dominated the homebuilding field in recent years, it's energy efficiency. But for all the headlines and airtime dedicated to the topic of trimming home-energy use, many of the discussions they generate don't go any further than the admission that, yes, we need to work harder to save energy where we live.

What we really need to talk about is *how*.

At *Fine Homebuilding* magazine, we focus not only on what good, responsible builders should do to construct or remodel homes that don't waste energy, but also on *how* they do it. This book explains how you can, too.

In *The Energy-Smart House*, you'll be able to follow these builders step-by-step through critical energy enhancements that include air-sealing, insulation upgrades, and window replacement, as well as choosing the best low-energy fixtures and appliances.

Today, the opportunities for reducing the energy requirements of the homes we live in—no matter how old they may be—are tremendous. The evolution in building products alone, from housewraps to LED lighting to high-performance windows, has equipped builders with a wide array of options to make homes more durable and healthier as well as less costly to live in and maintain. Ever-advancing technologies enable new mechanical systems to deliver heating, cooling, and hot water more effectively and at a lower cost. All the while, a greater understanding of building science enables knowledgeable builders to craft efficient, long-lasting dwellings regardless of the climate in which they build.

The fact is, true energy efficiency can only be achieved through a multifaceted approach that takes the whole house, its site, structure, and systems, into account. A home is not made "energy efficient" by popping in a few new windows or loading up the attic with cellulose. Good builders know the path to energy efficiency is a multistep process, and that each improvement influences the steps that follow. And that the conscientious application of smart building techniques like the ones found here is the most reliable roadmap they can follow in their pursuit of an energy-smart home.

Debra Judge Silber, Managing editor,
Fine Homebuilding magazine

Every House Needs an Energy Audit

■ BY JEFFERSON KOLLE

In the bill from her gas company, Leslie MacKensie of Minneapolis learned that she could have a free energy audit performed on her house, so she made an appointment. After assessing the 1915 bungalow, the auditors showed her air leaks and other problems that resulted in a monthly bill of $110. The auditors left her with weatherstripping and foam-insulation pads to install, along with a list of other needed improvements.

Chipping away at the list has had dramatic results. Even after she expanded her home with a small addition, her current gas bill averages only $80 a month. "Almost as important," she says, "is that now our home is really comfortable to live in all year round."

Home-energy auditing—the process of diagnosing and recommending improvements to reduce a house's energy consumption—is not a new idea, but the reasons to get an audit are more pressing as concerns about costs, comfort, personal health, and the environment loom large.

Along with free or reduced-cost audits offered by utility companies, an increasing number of private companies perform audits. And while an old leaky house might be the obvious choice for an energy-waste diagnosis, new houses can benefit, too. The results can be an excellent marketing tool for builders and can help homebuyers qualify for an energy-efficient mortgage, which uses energy-cost savings to lower debt-to-income ratios.

The most important thing to note about energy audits, however, is that they don't save money or energy. Implementing the recommended improvements is how the savings happen.

There Are Two Types of Audits

Energy audits vary in complexity from an unscientific but learned assessment to one that uses an assortment of diagnostic equipment to measure the performance of a house and its systems. The unscientific assessment typically consists of a thorough two- to three-hour walk-through, during which the auditor makes a visual inspection; takes photographs; and records information about the

Locating leaks. One of the most valuable scientific tools an auditor can use is a blower door, which is mounted temporarily on an exterior-door frame. The blower door's calibrated fan pulls air through the building, measuring the amount of air leaks. While the fan is operating, an auditor uses a smoke stick to locate the leaks. Smoke pulls away from the leaky spot and toward the blower door.

size of the building and specifics about the assumed efficiencies of the insulation, the appliances, and the HVAC (heating, ventilation, and air-conditioning) system. (For instance, he might know how fiberglass batts should be performing but can't tell if they were installed properly.)

The scientific approach, which takes four to six hours to complete, uses diagnostic equipment to record and quantify a home's energy shortcomings. The auditor completes a walk-through of the house, but he doesn't stop there.

The first step is often a blower-door test. After closing windows, exterior doors, and often flues, the auditor turns on a calibrated fan mounted in an airtight frame temporarily set in an exterior door (see the photo on p. 5). The fan reduces air pressure inside the building, pulling air in through all the holes in the building envelope. Depending on the blower door's supporting software, the auditor quantifies the number of air changes the house goes through in an hour (expressed as ACH) as well as the combined size of all the air leaks. In an old house, those leaks can

easily equate to leaving the bottom sash of a double-hung window open all year long.

To pinpoint where air infiltration is happening, the auditor holds a smoke stick or smoke pen in front of doors, windows, or other suspect areas (see the inset photo on p. 5). The pen emits a chemical smoke that wafts away from the leak and toward the fan to identify air infiltration. The auditor makes a note of the location and later suggests how to seal the leak.

A blower-door test can find air leaks in heating and cooling ductwork that runs through unconditioned spaces, such as an attic or a crawlspace. But it can't find leaks in ducts that run through the conditioned space, such as walls and floors. A tool made specifically for that job is a calibrated airflow-measurement device called a duct blaster. After turning off the blower door and taping over the floor, wall, and ceiling registers, the auditor connects the blaster to a central return in the system and measures its airtightness. Leaky ductwork can lead to substantial energy loss, which can be espe-

Making the improvements. Sealing leaky windows and air ducts, and adding insulation are the most common improvements auditors suggest. Attics can be the largest culprits for air and energy loss.

cially costly when that loss is happening in an unconditioned space.

Perhaps the best qualitative scientific tool an inspector pulls out during a diagnostic audit is an infrared thermograph, a camera-style device that shows the relative temperatures of objects portrayed as a kaleidoscopic image (see the photos at right). The colors reveal heat loss or gain, which indicates if a wall or attic floor is insulated, for example, and how well that insulation is performing. It also can identify moisture problems and leaky pipes behind the walls.

The auditor might also use a combustion analyzer and flue-gas monitor to measure the efficiency of boilers and furnaces (see the left photo on p. 8). Finally, he plugs in an electricity-usage monitor near appliances like the refrigerator to determine their efficiency.

Proponents of these diagnostic audits say that scientific measuring allows individual house components to be assessed as part of a whole system in which change to one part affects another. For instance, extensive air-sealing could make the building too tight and result in a furnace's flue gases being sucked down a chimney and into the living space—something that might not be detected without testing. This system's approach might also show that increasing insulation levels would allow a home to be heated by a smaller boiler. Test equipment can measure these kinds of occurrences, whereas a strictly visual inspection results only in an educated guess. The other main reason to use testing equipment is that retesting can determine the success of the recommended improvements.

Steve Luxton, regional manager for CMC Energy Services® (www.cmcenergy.com), disagrees with the need for scientific testing. Luxton's company has trained more than 1,000 energy auditors, 90% of whom are working as home inspectors, the folks that mortgage companies require you to hire before they'll lend you money. "These guys already know what to look for in a house,"

Infrared imaging paints an informative picture. Auditors can use a thermographer, or infrared camera, to locate differences in the temperatures of a house's parts. The image in the handheld infrared camera shows cold spots in blue around the warmer crown molding, indicating insulation voids. In the inset photo, taken outside in the winter, heat loss from inside the house appears in red and yellow. Cooler areas of the exterior wall appear blue. An auditor will use images like this to indicate un- or under-insulated areas, air leaks, and even moisture problems.

says Luxton. "[They] don't need a fan to tell you where the leaks are."

His point is well taken; most experts agree that air infiltration is the No. 1 cause of energy loss in any house. Most buildings have common air-infiltration areas that are easy to spot if you know where to look.

A duct blaster is not quackery. Similar to a blower door, a duct blaster is a calibrated fan. It is used on buildings with forced-air heat or central air-conditioning. Leaking ducts can decrease the overall efficiency of your heating and cooling system by as much as 20%.

Tools for a furnace tune-up. Your heating and air-conditioning systems could be the third-largest energy-wasting devices in your home. An auditor can use a combustion analyzer and flue-gas monitor to measure the efficiencies of your systems.

New Homes Need Audits, Too

There are a number of reasons to have a new home audited as well, not the least of which is to ensure that the building envelope and mechanical systems are performing as they were designed to perform. The Residential Energy Services Network (RESNET®; www.natresnet.org), a not-for-profit membership corporation, has developed an index called the home-energy rating system, or HERS, that both predicts and confirms a new home's energy performance. The HERS index can be used to evaluate a home's plans and specifications before it is built, then assign it a number from 0 to 100. A house that scores a 0 is said to be "net zero," meaning it produces as much energy as it uses over the course of a year. A home that scores 100 is built to the energy specs of the 2006 *International Residential Code*® (IRC). Once the house is completed, it is tested by a RESNET auditor using scientific testing equipment to ensure the as-built house conforms to the as-planned HERS rating.

The reasons to get a verified new-house HERS rating are fourfold. Not only can a HERS-index rating help homeowners to qualify for an energy-efficient mortgage, but it also assures them that building efficiencies have been verified by an independent third party. The HERS rating is also an excellent marketing tool, and it helps builders to qualify in the Energy Star® program.

How to Hire a Qualified Auditor

As home-energy audits become a more important part of building and owning a home, more and more auditors are entering the field. Free audits are available from local utility companies, but this avenue has its pros and cons (see the sidebar on the facing page). Independent auditors tend to offer various packages that can be tailored to your home's needs and your goals. Look for an auditor who has been certified by CMC Energy Services, Building Performance Institute® (BPI; www.bpi.org), or RESNET.

Although they don't provide diagnostic testing of a home, CMC Energy Services auditors are screened and complete energy-inspector training. CMC-trained auditors pay $300 and spend two classroom days learning about energy fundamentals; they also receive instruction in how to use the company's proprietary reporting software. Online refresher courses keep inspectors up to date. CMC maintains a searchable database so that you can find an inspector in your area.

BPI in Malta, N.Y., trains auditors to use diagnostic-testing equipment. To get BPI accreditation, an auditor goes through "a rigorous, credible, and defensible written- and field-examination process administered to individuals by BPI or its affiliates," according to BPI's website. BPI affiliates, such as the Metropolitan Energy Center in Kansas City, Mo., are trained to give exams to prospective auditors. Then BPI awards certification to those auditors who pass the tests.

According to Dustin Jensen, associate executive director at Metropolitan Energy Center, a 40-hour auditor-training class costs $1,000, and the examination costs about $500, if there is no government subsidy involved, which there often is. Affiliates are allowed to set their own prices for training, so they vary across the country. A searchable database of all BPI-certified professionals is maintained on the Building Performance Institute's website.

RESNET has a similar teacher-mentor system. RESNET trains providers, who then train raters, who are the folks that do the audits. Certification requires a week of classroom time, and the cost varies from $1,200 to $1,500, depending on the provider. A list of providers and raters is available on the RESNET website.

The Department of Energy's Energy Star program is not involved directly in the certification of auditors, but Energy Star endorses both RESNET and BPI auditors in two separate programs. In the first program, Energy Star Qualified New Homes, houses must score at least an 85 on RESNET's HERS-index rating. The second program, Home Performance with Energy Star, currently has locally sponsored programs in 28 states that help homeowners to improve a home's energy efficiency cost-effectively. The contractors that participate in the program are BPI-certified and are listed at www.energystar.gov.

Regardless of certifications, ask any auditor you might hire for a list of customers that you can contact to find out if they were satisfied with the auditor's work.

Don't Give Free Audits the Cold Shoulder

President Jimmy Carter's 1977 Energy Policy Act required utility companies to provide energy audits to their customers. These programs have helped hundreds of thousands of homeowners to tune up their houses. One advantage of many utility-company audits is that they might also give you some free products, such as compact-fluorescent light-bulbs, or perform remedial work, such as air-sealing and weatherstripping.

Although it might seem contrary, utility companies want homes to save energy. It helps them to manage peak power loads, the times of day or season when energy use is at its greatest. Plus, it's not bad for a company's public relations. And an electric company can actually save money if it doesn't have to construct new power plants.

Don't be surprised if a so-called free audit comes with strings attached, though. An electrical utility in Connecticut, for example, has a great-sounding program. But for the program to be free, the house must be heated with gas or electricity; otherwise, the service costs $300.

Consultant or Contractor?

There are two schools of thought about whom to hire to perform a home-energy audit. One says that a disinterested third party is the most trustworthy opinion, while the other argues for the convenience of hiring someone who can pinpoint the improvements needed and then perform the work.

Brian Smith of Energy Saving Comfort Systems (www.escs1.com) prides himself on the fact that his company isn't selling anything other than testing services. When he sits down with customers to review what his blower door and infrared camera have detected, they know that "I'm not then going to try to sell them new windows or a furnace." CMC's Luxton concurs: "We feel strongly that an audit should be performed by an unbiased person."

John Jennings is an energy auditor with Steven Winter Associates, an architecture/engineering research and consulting firm in Norwalk, Conn. He favors the idea of independent auditors who can provide a list of vetted contractors that can make the recommended improvements.

Mike Rogers, senior vice president of business development for GreenHomes® America, a Syracuse, N.Y., firm that tests homes and then does improvement work, disagrees. "Would you take your car to one guy to tell you what's wrong with it and then to another to do the repairs?" he asks. Some companies, including GreenHomes, even have a financing program for energy-performance upgrades.

Costs and Reports Vary

Whether a basic inspection or an in-depth scientific test, an auditor's findings will likely be output from software that not only takes into account the physical data about the structure but also data about utility bills, the local climate, and, possibly, comparative information from other houses.

A CMC-trained auditor will generate a report about the existing house's needed improvements, including a cost-benefit analysis and payback time in years. CMC doesn't control what its inspectors charge, but Luxton says audits cost from $200 to $400, depending on the size of the house.

RESNET auditors are licensed to use company software that produces a HERS-index report. An audit with a HERS report (report fees can run around $150) costs from $1,000 to $1,500. While BPI doesn't supply its own software, there are independent programs available that auditors can choose.

An audit from BPI-accredited TerraLogos® in Baltimore costs $495, and though it is thorough in its assessment of and recommendations for the house's existing systems, it does not predict energy savings if the suggested upgrades are carried out.

On the other end of the scale is a soup-to-nuts audit done by a company such as Steven Winter Associates. Along with a basic inspection of a house up to 4,000 sq. ft., which includes no scientific testing, the a-la-carte audit menu could include a blower-door test, a duct-leakage test,

Online audits can help you save, too. Spend some time with online home energy-savings applications, and you could realize substantial savings on your energy bills (see the sidebar on the facing page).

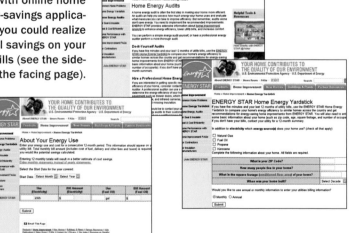

Before you schedule an audit, you might want to check out the many online do-it-yourself energy-audit programs. Although they don't require any scientific testing equipment and some suggest lots of behavior modifications—turn down your thermostat, take shorter showers—their computer applications will give you guidance and information about energy improvements. According to Energy Star's John Passe, "A homeowner who follows these programs to a T might save 20% to 30% on his energy bills." Along with your local utilities, here are some sites to try.

Home Performance with Energy Star, the branch of the organization that deals with existing homes, has three auditing tools you can complete online at www.energystar.gov. After entering data about your utility bills, the Home Energy Yardstick gives you a 1 to 10 rating on your consumption as compared to others in your area. The Energy Star Home Advisor gives you savings recommendations based on your ZIP code and utility use. Energy Star at Home offers room-by-room and lifestyle energy-saving tips.

The Home Energy Saver™ (http://hes.lbl.gov), developed by Lawrence Berkeley National Laboratory, is sponsored by several government agencies and is visited by about 750,000 people a year. To start, all you do is enter your ZIP code; hours later, you will have gathered tons of valuable information.

The Alliance to Save Energy, a nonprofit funded by private grants and government agencies, sponsors Home Energy Checkup (www.ase.org). According to the site, you can select from more than a dozen energy-efficiency measures, see how much money and pollution you can save, find out where to get energy-efficient products, and pick up tips on how to act on your choices.

---

appliance-combustion testing, infrared-imaging, energy-modeling, and a HERS rating. All this adds up to an audit that costs upward of $2,000.

What's Next for Energy Audits

The business of energy-auditing is getting huge. "It's at a tipping point," says Courtney Moriarta, senior engineer at Steven Winter Associates. "Not only do homeowners think it's a cool thing to do, but it's also being driven more and more by energy-efficient mortgages and potential tax credits." Both Massachusetts and California are working on legislation that will require house sellers to divulge energy-audit information to prospective buyers.

Also on the horizon is a joint energy-auditing standard between RESNET and BPI (which could be adopted by Energy Star, too). Currently in draft form and open to public comment, the new standard is intended to clear up confusion among homeowners, but the reciprocity between the two organizations will also help auditors, many of whom have previously felt the need to get accreditation from both nonprofit groups. Steve Baden, executive director of RESNET, says that the standard will recognize the efficacy of all types of energy audits and auditors from "the DIY type to the guy with the clipboard and flashlight to the guy who also uses a blower door and an infrared camera."

Jefferson Kolle is a former editor at Fine Homebuilding.

Home Remedies for Energy Nosebleeds

■ BY BRUCE HARLEY

My friend Terry Brennan told me that on his first job as a mason's tender he learned two things: "Whatever I did was wrong," and "If the work wasn't going to show, don't strike the joints" because it didn't have to be pretty. Now, not taking the time to smooth out a mortar joint that no one will see may not rank as a great offense. But the fact is, many things that go wrong in home building go wrong where sloppy work is done because "it's not going to show, so it doesn't matter." I know this because as an energy consultant, I plug the same nosebleeds in new and old homes alike. We're good at cutting construction costs but bad at building houses that serve their owners well, minimize operating costs, and also reduce pollution.

Gaps in the Construction Sequence Cause Many Problems

People think windows and doors are the biggest leaks in a house because windows and doors are the most visible holes. But even old windows and doors are relatively small holes. In reality, the majority of energy leaks happen in places you can't see, where one subcontractor's work ends and another's begins: behind the drywall, up in the attic, or down in the crawlspace. Even when each trade does its job well, problems can occur because nobody sees the big picture. The way the work fits together is as significant as the work itself.

The gaps between subs' responsibilities usually translate into gaps in a house's thermal boundary. These gaps are addressed in current building codes, but building inspectors can't always offer protection. Sometimes they don't understand; sometimes they just don't enforce energy codes. The architect, the general contractor, or the homeowner must take the responsibility for understanding and closing these gaps.

Amazingly, the two trades most concerned with energy efficiency—HVAC (heating, ventilation, air-conditioning) and insulation—rarely follow the minimum industry standards for their work. The reasons differ, but they share one common element: Their work is hidden behind drywall. The only feedback they get is when these systems fail, when our homes are uncomfortable (an issue that's often misdiagnosed) and high energy bills mount. Pressure to keep up-front costs low and underestimating the magnitude of these problems are also common to both trades. This standard of care isn't reasonable. Just because it has always been done this way doesn't make it right.

Some Holes Are So Big That Nobody Notices Them

It's not only insulation and HVAC contractors who are inadvertently sabotaging our houses. Framers often construct large holes that extend from the basement to the attic in the form of chimney, plumbing, and duct chases. These chases are hidden behind drywall or are covered by fiberglass-batt insulation. But insulation alone won't prevent conditioned interior air from escaping. Big holes should be sealed with plywood, rigid foam, or drywall and caulk or spray foam.

Kneewalls and rim joists are two more often-missed examples. Think of them as long holes in a house. Kneewalls are the short walls found in finished attics and in bonus rooms above the garage. Insulation is usually put in the kneewall and under the floorboards, but this insulation doesn't keep a room warm unless you block each

joist cavity or, better yet, insulate under the roof deck (see p. 16).

Rim joists also have multiple holes cut in them for dryer vents and outdoor water faucets. Rim joists are best sealed when the house is built. The top and bottom edges should be sealed with construction adhesive during framing and insulated with spray foam afterward.

Architectural Massing Can Often Mean Massive Leaking

Architects use features such as cantilevers and wraparound porches to break up the massing of a mundane facade. I have nothing against great-looking houses, but these architecturally interesting details can create giant energy nosebleeds.

Insulation and air-barrier details are often missed in cantilevered areas. The underside of a cantilever should be covered with solid sheathing (caulked in place) before finish materials are installed. Roof and wall sheathing is frequently left off below intersecting porch and garage roofs. The spaces below these roofs often connect to vented attics; they are just big air vents to the outdoors. Fancy details like tray ceilings and curved walls also can create big holes that open to attics.

Great-looking houses should also perform well. Architects should draw a line between inside and out on the blueprints, and make sure the house is built that way.

With Insulation, a Little Laziness Goes a Long Way

People naturally think that if you cover 98% of a surface with insulation, you'll get 98% of the performance. This thinking is horribly wrong. Gaps and missing insulation create a hugely disproportionate performance penalty. If you install R-38 batts in an attic but leave 0.5% of the surface area uncovered, you end up with R-32 (16% reduction in R-value). Leave 2% uncovered, and you drop to R-22 (42% reduction). So with 98% coverage, you get 58% of the performance.

If you run across information saying it's not cost-effective to add insulation, it probably assumes the initial R-value is what you say it is. In all likelihood, the R-value is less than half what you think, and the upgrade is worth much more—provided it's done right.

Uncover the Hidden Holes in Your House

When framing lumber shrinks, the gap between top plates and drywall can add up to a 5-sq.-ft. hole.

TWO BIG HOLES CAN COST YOU MONEY. Directly above a bathroom, this attic view reveals a dropped soffit and a large plumbing chase for the vent stack. The soffit connects the attic with the walls; the plumbing chase is a direct hole running through the house. These two leaks are like leaving a window open. **The Fix:** Cover the open framing with rigid foam or plywood, and seal small openings with spray foam. Finally, cover them with insulation. Loose-fill insulation such as cellulose is cheap and easy to install.

This dropped soffit connects the walls to the ceiling, making a path for air leakage.

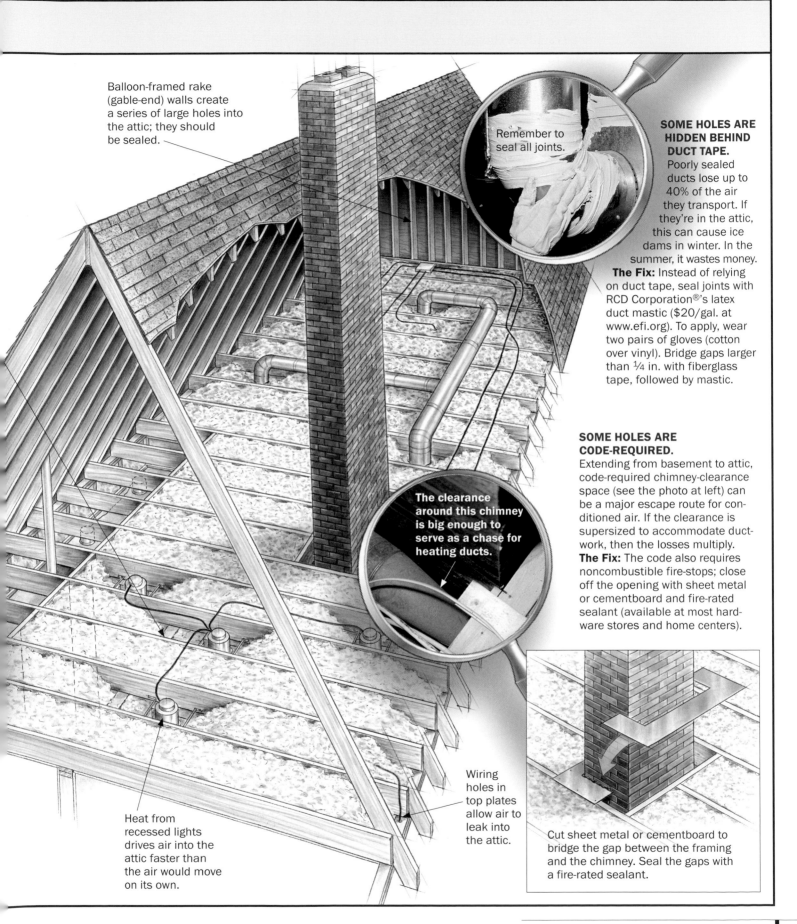

Balloon-framed rake (gable-end) walls create a series of large holes into the attic; they should be sealed.

Remember to seal all joints.

SOME HOLES ARE HIDDEN BEHIND DUCT TAPE.
Poorly sealed ducts lose up to 40% of the air they transport. If they're in the attic, this can cause ice dams in winter. In the summer, it wastes money.
The Fix: Instead of relying on duct tape, seal joints with RCD Corporation®'s latex duct mastic ($20/gal. at www.efi.org). To apply, wear two pairs of gloves (cotton over vinyl). Bridge gaps larger than ¼ in. with fiberglass tape, followed by mastic.

SOME HOLES ARE CODE-REQUIRED.
Extending from basement to attic, code-required chimney-clearance space (see the photo at left) can be a major escape route for conditioned air. If the clearance is supersized to accommodate duct-work, then the losses multiply.
The Fix: The code also requires noncombustible fire-stops; close off the opening with sheet metal or cementboard and fire-rated sealant (available at most hardware stores and home centers).

The clearance around this chimney is big enough to serve as a chase for heating ducts.

Heat from recessed lights drives air into the attic faster than the air would move on its own.

Wiring holes in top plates allow air to leak into the attic.

Cut sheet metal or cementboard to bridge the gap between the framing and the chimney. Seal the gaps with a fire-rated sealant.

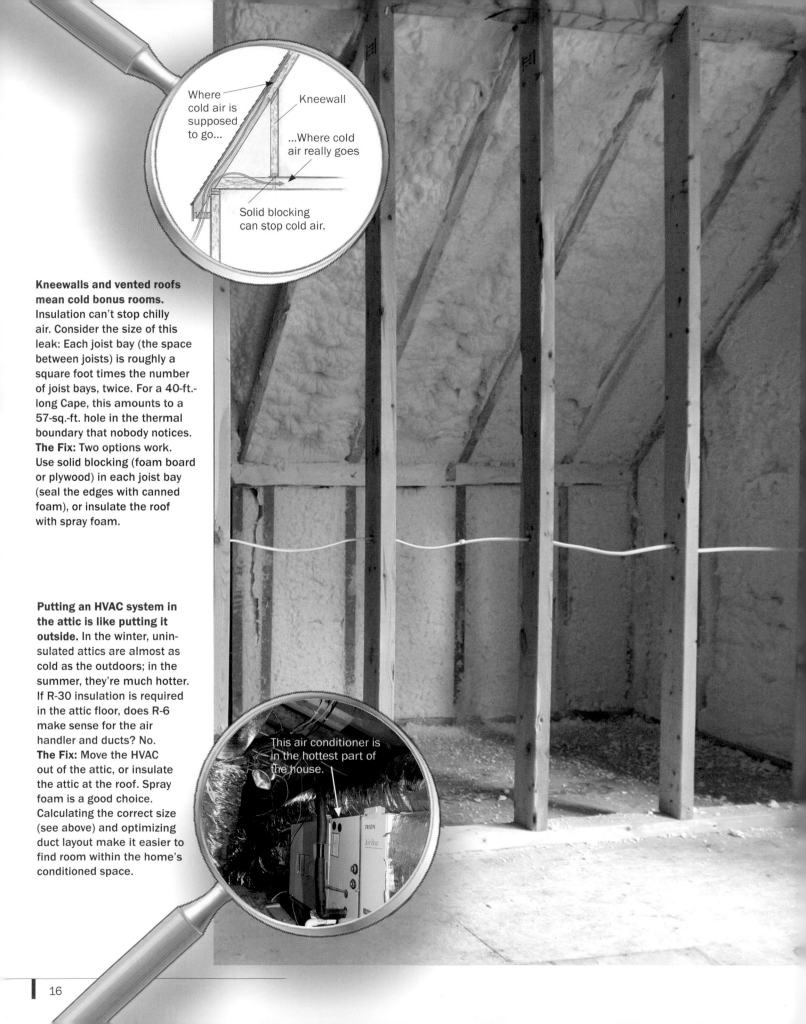

Where cold air is supposed to go...

Kneewall

...Where cold air really goes

Solid blocking can stop cold air.

Kneewalls and vented roofs mean cold bonus rooms. Insulation can't stop chilly air. Consider the size of this leak: Each joist bay (the space between joists) is roughly a square foot times the number of joist bays, twice. For a 40-ft.-long Cape, this amounts to a 57-sq.-ft. hole in the thermal boundary that nobody notices. **The Fix:** Two options work. Use solid blocking (foam board or plywood) in each joist bay (seal the edges with canned foam), or insulate the roof with spray foam.

Putting an HVAC system in the attic is like putting it outside. In the winter, uninsulated attics are almost as cold as the outdoors; in the summer, they're much hotter. If R-30 insulation is required in the attic floor, does R-6 make sense for the air handler and ducts? No. **The Fix:** Move the HVAC out of the attic, or insulate the attic at the roof. Spray foam is a good choice. Calculating the correct size (see above) and optimizing duct layout make it easier to find room within the home's conditioned space.

This air conditioner is in the hottest part of the house.

TRION
Air Bear

HVAC Ducts Can Leak One-Third of the Air They Transport

From 20% to 40% of the air that comes out of furnaces and air conditioners never gets to the rooms it's supposed to heat or cool. When you consider that most of the ducts are in attics, garages, and vented crawlspaces, the effect of that loss is huge: We're heating and cooling the outdoors. Sometimes whole rooms are disconnected, as when the ductwork isn't connected to the register and the duct spews conditioned air into the attic or crawlspace. Return ducts often leak more than supply ducts; although they cause less energy loss, these leaks lead to moisture problems and pressure imbalances that pose health and durability risks by contributing to mold, ice dams, and even carbon-monoxide poisoning.

Required by code, duct-sealing is rarely completed and even more rarely tested. Houses more than 10 years old didn't have this code requirement. Every connection in every duct run should be sealed with mastic (not tape), and the system should be pressure-tested, just like your plumbing. Holes in the air handler can be sealed with aluminum-foil tape because mastic would render the cabinet unserviceable. After you seal the ducts and the cabinet, insulate them carefully.

Retrofits can be more difficult. If you can access the ducts, you can use mastic under the insulation (put the insulation back when you're done). If the ducts are inaccessible, they can be sealed from the inside with a product like Aeroseal® (see www.aeroseal .com for local contractors), or you can move the insulation and the air barrier to bring the ducts inside the thermal boundary.

Putting the Air Handler Outside the House Is Not a Good Idea

Many air handlers and ducts are in attics. This location is a lot more costly than people realize. Putting an air handler and ductwork in the attic, garage, or crawlspace is like putting it outside the house. In winter, attics are almost as cold as the outdoors; in the summer, attics are much hotter than the outside temperature.

If you must place the air handler and ductwork in the attic, you can do a few things to minimize energy losses: Seal everything with mastic; insulate the air handler carefully; and keep the ducts low and covered with blown insulation. Even better, use spray foam on the whole roof and gable ends so that the attic space is within the house's thermal envelope.

The best idea, though, is to run the mechanical system inside the house. You can use smaller mechanical equipment with smaller ducts in shorter runs; it's easier to design space for them within the house. The payoff is a much more efficient HVAC system that increases comfort while decreasing operating costs. For more information, go to www.toolbase.org/Design-Construction-Guides/HVAC/forced-air-system.

This uncovered cantilever is somewhat unusual, but finished overhangs are often covered only with vinyl soffit.

Cantilevers can be like open windows. The same principle applies to cantilevers as to kneewalls: Cold air has a direct path to the living space through the insulation and floor framing. **The Fix:** Cover the underside with solid sheathing, caulked in place.

How Durable Is Spray Foam?

Q: Spray foam is touted as a "superior" insulation material. I've been building for nearly 20 years, however, and I've occasionally found spray foam that has settled in the wall cavity and/or disintegrated enough to lose all its effectiveness. How do we know today's spray foams won't do the same thing in 30 years?
—*Mike Connors, Beacon, N.Y.*

A: The failed foam you're describing is likely urea-formaldehyde foam insulation (UFFI). It was installed in many homes in the 1970s, but eventually was banned in Canada and the United States due to concerns about chemical off-gassing. UFFI also tended to become brittle, shrink, and crumble over time, affecting durability and performance.

The current generation of spray-polyurethane foams is based on a different chemistry, so the cured foam is much more stable. This quality suggests that spray-polyurethane foams will last much longer than UFFI and will retain their flexibility and mechanical integrity.

I wouldn't worry about the durability of the foams that are currently available. In fact, I believe that in some applications today's spray foams add to the durability of the overall structure by reducing air leakage and vapor diffusion.

—*Bruce Harley*

Oversize AC Units Can Hide Many Big Problems

Oversize air-conditioning systems are the norm, not the exception. It's easier to pick a huge system based on erroneous rules of thumb than to spend time designing a more suitable but smaller system. Oversize systems have the added problem of masking many of the problems I've discussed here. Poor insulation, duct leaks, and more can be covered up by blasting twice as much cold air through the ductwork as would be necessary if things were done correctly.

If you double the size of the AC unit, you can lose 50% of the performance and still provide enough comfort so that the homeowner won't call you back. But a behemoth AC unit short-cycles (turns on and off too

Oversize HVAC Is Overkill

When it comes to air-conditioning units, oversize air handlers waste energy, burn out faster, and leave the house cold and clammy. Unfortunately, many HVAC contractors still rely on rules of thumb to determine system size. The best way to get the right-size HVAC unit is to model your home's energy features with one of the many software programs available (such as the one at www.hvaccomputer.com; $49 for homeowner version).

To calculate whether an existing AC unit is too big, measure the number of minutes per hour that the AC unit runs on the hottest afternoons in the summer. Then divide 60 by the number of minutes to determine the amount that the unit is oversize. For example, $60 \div 30 = 2\times$ oversize; $60 \div 20 = 3\times$ oversize.

quickly), which hurts its energy efficiency, degrades its ability to dehumidify the air, and shortens its life. A larger unit is also noisier and costs more to install (both system and ducts). The solution is simple: Pay for the load calculations, and size the unit correctly. In fact, according to the Air Conditioning Contractors of America (ACCA), it's often better to undersize an AC system a little bit.

Water Heaters and Windows Are the Next Savings Opportunities

Water heaters store hot water all day long. They keep it hot on the off chance that you'll need it. Tankless, or on-demand, water heaters, on the other hand, convert cold water into hot water when you turn on the tap.

You'll notice that windows aren't on this list. Only after you correct all the things I've mentioned will your windows start to look bad. If you're building a home, upgrading the windows at the design stage to at least Energy Star (preferably beyond) is a lot less expensive than buying substandard windows now and replacing them later. Even so, windows are not usually the first place to start looking for big savings, because the other nosebleeds are running hard.

Bruce Harley is technical director of Conservation Services Group (www.csgrp.com) in Westborough, Mass.

Can a Vintage Home Be Energy Efficient?

■ BY BETSY PETTIT

In America, there are around 58 million houses that were built before the last energy crisis. Because these pre-1970s houses have little or no insulation, they are all ripe for energy-efficiency improvements. Houses eat up 20% of the energy used in this country and account for 21% of the carbon dioxide that contributes to global warming. This adds up to a huge opportunity.

America's old houses can be made much tighter and can even approach net-zero energy use. Here, I'll highlight three houses that my company, Building Science Corp., has renovated. Each house had different limitations and learning curves. I share one of the houses with my husband and business partner, Joe Lstiburek, and two of them have been used as our office space.

Renovating an old house is an expensive process. It's also a delicate process because the end product must retain its charm. Most old houses are still around because people love their timeless form, floor plan, trim, details, and historical significance. Renovating an old house is a surprising and challenging process because many of them have undergone numerous renovations over the years. You never know exactly what you'll find.

In Old Houses, Most Systems Are at the End of Their Useful Life

A hundred years can take its toll on infrastructure, and this is often the case with old houses. The water line from the street, electrical wiring, plumbing, mechanical systems—all are often nearing the end of their life. It would be foolish to renovate a house without replacing these basic systems. Windows often no longer function as intended, either. Their ventilation properties are hindered by layers of paint, or they simply became swollen shut years ago. If neglected, siding can need repair or replacement, too.

While the shape, floor plan, and details of an old house allow it to endure, people often think they need an addition to provide another bathroom, bedroom, office, or better views. Then they spend money building an addition, only to spend all their time in this new space because the rest of the house is uncomfortable. They don't really get more space in this deal; they get a smaller space that's comfortable.

Energy Upgrades Are Cheaper Than You Think

While the cost of fixing wet basements and adding bathrooms can add up quickly, energy upgrades can be folded in without putting projects out of reach. In fact, they don't really cost that much more because they're integral to the decisions and choices made in the renovation process.

If you consider your renovation from a whole-house approach, you might find that you can add modern conveniences (an extra bathroom, bedroom, or office space) and comfort without building an addition, and reduce energy costs in the process. The basement and attic are already built; you just need to use them. By adding rooms in the basement and attic, you often can reconfigure the floor plan to accommodate an extra bathroom, a larger kitchen, or a master suite.

Replacing the furnace, the boiler, or the HVAC system might cost $10,000 before you are done. But the upgrade could easily save $1,000 a year in heating and cooling costs. Even in simple payback terms, this new system would pay for itself after 10 years. Amortized into a 30-year mortgage, it costs $27 per month; the savings works out to $83 per month for a net gain of $56 per month. Because we know energy costs are rising, these numbers will only get better.

A TRICKY VICTORIAN

OUR FIRST RENOVATION

THIRD TIME IS A CHARM

Case Studies Illustrate Real-World Challenges

The three homes featured in this chapter have several things in common. First, they are all more than 90 years old. Two of them were built in 1860 and the third in 1916. Second, they all had their major systems totally replaced: new wiring, light fixtures, plumbing, and mechanical systems, including the addition of central air-conditioning. Third, they all had attic spaces that were incorporated into the living space of the house by moving the insulation from over the second-floor ceiling to under the roof. Fourth, they all had insulation added under

Seven Steps to Net-Zero Energy Use

In renovating old homes into superefficient ones, there is a definite path to success: Start where you can get the most bang, and work your way down the list. After you get past item 5, the house will be efficient enough to downsize the mechanical equipment, which you replaced in step 1. If you're planning to go at least through step 5, keep that in mind before buying a new boiler or HVAC unit.

1. Upgrade the mechanical systems

An old furnace or boiler is often the worst energy user in an old house. Many houses built prior to 1920 still have old coal-fired boilers that were converted to gas or oil. These units are workhorses, but use a lot of energy. A new furnace or boiler can save energy dollars right away. Replacing window air conditioners, which we did in all these houses, with a central system also can save energy right away, as long as the ductwork has been placed in the conditioned space. Solar water heating is a good option to add here if you can afford it, but at the very least, upgrade the efficiency of hot-water production by coupling the tank to the boiler.

2. Bring the basement and crawlspace inside the house

Warm, dry basements and crawlspaces can extend living and storage space. Wet basements are the source of high humidity levels and discomfort in the summertime in old houses. They also can be the source of mold growth that gets distributed around the house. Spray foam is a fast, effective way to bring these areas into the conditioned space while sealing the leaks between foundation and floor framing.

3. Superinsulate and air-seal the roof

If air leaks in at the bottom of the house, it leaks out at the top, which makes a house cold and drafty in winter. A poorly insulated roof also can make a house hot in summer. Air-sealing is a by-product of good insulating, so it's really a one-step process. Using spray foam under a roof also can eliminate the need for roof venting, which is tricky in complicated roofs.

4. Replace the windows

With the bottom and top of the house sealed and insulated, a new basement slab, as well as insulation applied to the inside of the exterior foundation wall. Fifth, they all had at least some windows replaced, and all had new window openings added in critical areas to provide better views of the yard and better daylighting to the home. Sixth, all the homes had bathrooms and bedrooms added. Finally, we replaced inefficient window A/C units with central A/C systems in each house.

Because of the work in the basements and attics, all the homes had increased living area without increasing the footprint of the home. And while the living space increased by 30% to 100%, all of them saw a reduction of energy use that ranged from 30% to more than 100%. While the renovations cost more than $100 per sq. ft. for each home, all were appraised at values exceeding that cost after the renovations were complete.

Some things are different in each case, too. The two oldest homes had major structural issues that needed to be repaired before other work could be done. Foundations needed to be rebuilt, and additional columns and beams were added for support. One house, the Greek revival, had frequent basement flooding that had to be stopped, and its attached barn was leaning enough to fall down. The Victorian was in a historic the next opportunity is the walls. Old windows are like big holes in the walls. They often leak both air and water into the house while functioning poorly. They might not open and close properly, and can be obscured with storm windows and screens that diminish the amount of light that can enter. Properly installed, Energy Star (or better) windows seal the holes in the walls to keep out water and weather extremes. (For more, see "A Buyer's Guide to Windows" on pp. 91–103.)

5. Insulate the walls

Filling empty wall cavities with cellulose is a cheap, easy, effective way to warm up an old house. Blowing cellulose into existing wall cavities is an art, to be sure, but there are many contractors who have been doing it for years. In fact, there are now inexpensive ways to check with infrared cameras to make sure that all voids have been filled without disturbing the existing plaster or sheathing on outside walls.

Because siding or shingles on old houses might also have worn out, we take the opportunity to install foam sheathing on the outside of the house before re-siding.*

6. Buy Energy Star (or better) fixtures, appliances, and lighting

Once you have reduced your space-conditioning and water-heating loads, the lighting, appliance, and plug load will be your next big energy item. A new Energy Star refrigerator will use 20% less energy than a standard model. Replacing old light fixtures with pin-based compact-fluorescent fixtures ensures that your electric bill will stay lower (up to 30%).

7. Add a renewable-energy source

Once your energy consumption has been reduced significantly, it becomes reasonable to produce your own energy with systems such as photovoltaics, wind power, or hydro, if you happen to have a stream nearby.

Until you slash the energy usage, though, it's not worth the investment in renewable power sources. Conservation is still the cheapest game in town.

*Go back to step 1 and reduce the size of the mechanicals. An airtight house with insulation on all six sides of the cube and good windows provides predictable performance, so the mechanical contractor won't have to guess at the quality of the enclosure. Downsized mechanical equipment can defray the cost of steps 2-5.

district, so even though the chimneys were structurally unsound and the old slate roof was beyond its useful service life, they had to be repaired (at a great cost) rather than replaced.

Durability and Energy Efficiency Are Intertwined

Making a flooded basement livable is a great example of how one type of repair is directly related to another. On one of these projects, we needed to stop water from leaking into the old rubble foundation with a perimeter drain and a new slab. Adding insulation under the slab and inside the walls keeps the space free of condensation and also saves energy.

The durability and functional upgrades illustrated on the following pages cost a lot. By spending a bit more, we were able to reduce energy costs tremendously. After cutting energy consumption, the stage is set for the installation of affordable, renewable power sources to offset the remaining energy needs. And that 21st-century step could transform these vintage homes to net-zero energy houses or even energy producers.

3-in. closed-cell spray foam (R-21)

3-in. fiberglass batts (R-10)

2-in. XPS foam (R-10)

Tar paper

Wood sheathing

Housewrap

Blown-in cellulose (R-16)

3/4-in. furring strips create a drainage plane behind the siding.

1-in. XPS foam (R-5)

Wood siding

FOR THE HOUSE, THREE INSULATIONS UNDER ONE ROOF
To get a high R-value (R-40) without disrupting the roof or increasing the 2×6 rafter size, we combined insulation types. We could have used only closed-cell spray foam to fill the rafters, but at the time, it was too expensive. Instead, we used 3 in. of spray foam to create an air barrier and fiberglass batts to fill the rest of the rafter bay. A layer of rigid foam under the rafters is a thermal break.

SPECS

Built: 1860s
Renovation completed: 2,000
Conditioned space: 2,600 sq. ft. before; 5,240 sq. ft. after, including the barn
Bedrooms: 4 before; 6 after
Bathrooms: 2 before; 4½ after
Cost of renovation: $125 per sq. ft.

Annual utility cost:
- **Before:** $1.90 per sq. ft.; after: 86¢ per sq. ft.
- **Gas:** $3,000 a year before; $2,400 a year after
- **Electric:** $1,950 a year before; $2,100 a year after

Our First Renovation

Built in the 1860s, this house was a typical New England Greek-revival farmhouse. It had a basement prone to flooding, sagging floors, a leaning barn, and old, inefficient mechanical equipment. The structural and water issues were expensive to fix, so we looked for ways to save on energy upgrades. We took different approaches to fixing the house and the barn (see the drawings at left and on the facing page). Because we wanted to keep the barn's timber-framing visible, all insulation went to the outside of the wall sheathing on the barn. On the house, we aimed to maintain interior finishes wherever possible.

Overall, our strategies worked. The house's Energy Star rating for homes was 91 out of a possible 100 points (www.energystar.gov). We doubled the living area by bringing the barn and attached shed into the conditioned space while increasing power consumption by only 8%. We used

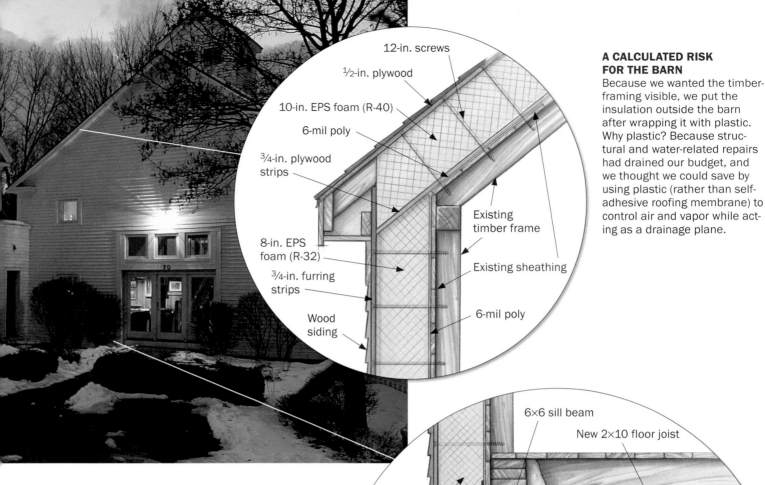

12-in. screws

½-in. plywood

10-in. EPS foam (R-40)

6-mil poly

¾-in. plywood strips

8-in. EPS foam (R-32)

¾-in. furring strips

Wood siding

Existing timber frame

Existing sheathing

6-mil poly

A CALCULATED RISK FOR THE BARN
Because we wanted the timber-framing visible, we put the insulation outside the barn after wrapping it with plastic. Why plastic? Because structural and water-related repairs had drained our budget, and we thought we could save by using plastic (rather than self-adhesive roofing membrane) to control air and vapor while acting as a drainage plane.

the renovated barn as our office space for 10 years while fighting a zoning battle to allow this "commercial" use. In the end, we lost the zoning battle, and now the barn is a huge guest house with full kitchen and bath.

We did what we thought we could afford at the time, but in trying to save money, we scrimped in ways we would not do again. The 6-mil polyethylene (see the drawing above) was a risky control layer for the barn and has been working except for some areas where the roof leaked at the intersection of the new cupola that we installed. Today, we would use a peel-and-stick roofing membrane rather than plastic and be very diligent with the flashing and counterflashing around the cupola.

The waterproof membrane covering the basement wall was meant as a drainage plane for the granite-block foundation. We've learned that this is probably an unnecessary and expensive extra layer; the surface of closed-cell foam forms a hard skin that sheds water.

6×6 sill beam

New 2×10 floor joist

8-in. EPS foam (R-32)

Dense mesh drainage mat

Roofing membrane

Granite-block foundation

Embedded perimeter drainpipe leads to sump pump.

2-in. metal stud wall with drywall

2-in. closed-cell spray foam (R-14)

2-in. XPS foam

4-in. concrete slab

4-in. crushed stone (no fines)

FIX FOR A FLOOD-PRONE BASEMENT
The granite-block foundation in this 150-year-old barn quit blocking water many years ago. The solution? Pump it out. Peel-and-stick roofing membrane acts as a drainage plane, directing water to the perimeter drainpipe leading to a sump pump. Closed-cell insulation keeps the basement warm and dry.

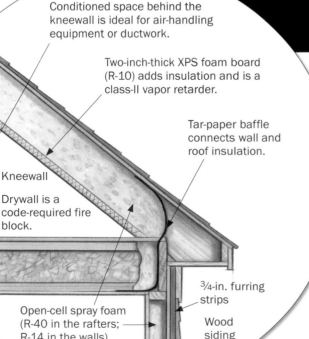

SPECS

Built: Circa 1860
Renovation completed: 2003
Conditioned space: 2,150 sq. ft. before; 2,750sq. ft., after, plus 1,000 sq. ft. of dry warm basement space
Bedrooms: 2 before; 4½ after
Bathrooms: 2 before; 4½ after
Cost of renovation: $125 per sq. ft.

Annual utility cost:
- **Before:** $2.34 per sq. ft.; after: 83¢ per sq. ft.
- **Gas:** $3,600 a year before; $1,474 a year after
- **Electric:** $1,440 a year before; $830 a year after

A DEEPER ROOF IS CHEAPER TO INSULATE

Because the 2×4 rafters were sagging under the weight of the slate, we sistered 12-in.-deep rafters to them. Deep rafter cavities such as these mean that the more-economical open-cell foam can be used and still get high R-values. Along with 2 in. of XPS (extruded polystyrene) under the rafters, we got an R-value of 50.

Conditioned space behind the kneewall is ideal for air-handling equipment or ductwork.

Two-inch-thick XPS foam board (R-10) adds insulation and is a class-II vapor retarder.

Tar-paper baffle connects wall and roof insulation.

Kneewall

Drywall is a code-required fire block.

Open-cell spray foam (R-40 in the rafters; R-14 in the walls)

¾-in. furring strips

Wood siding

Housewrap

A Tricky Victorian

This two-family Victorian house (circa 1860) was difficult to upgrade because we weren't allowed to remove siding, replace the windows, or dig into the slate roof.

The historic commission did, however, allow us to remove and replace the siding and windows on one wall where the siding was damaged and needed replacement, so we injected open-cell foam, added housewrap and furring strips, and replaced the siding on that wall.

Historic commissions all over the country favor historical authenticity over durability and energy efficiency with regard

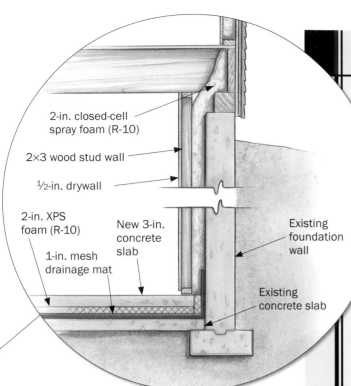

2-in. closed-cell spray foam (R-10)

2×3 wood stud wall

½-in. drywall

2-in. XPS foam (R-10)

New 3-in. concrete slab

1-in. mesh drainage mat

Existing foundation wall

Existing concrete slab

A DRY BASEMENT TO BEGIN WITH
This house had no standing water in the basement, nor was there evidence of previous flooding. Because the basement had historically been dry, we didn't install a perimeter drain and sump pump. Rather, we installed a drainage mat on top of the existing slab (to trap errant seepage) and placed 2 in. of rigid-foam insulation on top of that. We then topped the assembly with a new slab to make a warm, dry storage area.

to windows, chimneys, roof finishes, and other elements. Faced with these restrictions, we compromised and used all-wood simulated divided-lite replacement sashes for two-thirds of the window units. Because the openings were so far out of square, the sashes never fit quite right.

We weren't prepared for the battle over siding replacement. In the future, we'd like to replace the rest of the siding. When we do that, we'll insulate with cellulose and foam sheathing.

How Much Insulation Do You Need?

Because the earth is such a great buffer to heat loss and gain, the insulation needs in a house grow as you get farther from the ground. Naturally, they're greatest at the roof, which is baked by the sun all day and chilled by the sky at night.

We specify significantly higher levels of insulation than are required by the International Energy Conservation Code, and we think it is money well spent. When you're attempting to approach net-zero energy use in homes, energy that isn't used is always the cheapest energy.

R-10 under the Basement Slab

It is easy to add 2 in. or 3 in. of extruded (or expanded) polystyrene under a new slab before pouring the concrete. This could cut into headroom a bit, but the benefits outweigh the cost.

R-20 Basement Walls

Warming basement walls is often the best protection you can get from mold growth. Additional living space is an added benefit. Energy codes in most cold climates call for at least R-10, but if you can afford the additional insulation at this time, it is well worth it. Both closed-cell spray foam and rigid-foam insulation are good choices.

R-40 in the Walls

By warming above-grade walls, you eliminate chilly convection currents inside a room, which can increase your actual living space because furniture no longer needs to be moved away from exterior walls. While the building code asks for at least R-19 in most cold climates, it is worthwhile to use as much insulation as you can afford.

R-60 in the Roof

Adding insulation to the roof (rather than the attic floor) brings extra living and storage space into the home at little cost. It also reduces summer cooling loads. It's often easy to provide more than the code minimums because of deep rafter cavities. If you're reroofing the house, consider putting rigid-foam board insulation on top of the sheathing as we did in two of the case studies here. After judging the performance of the first two houses, we increased our recommendation from R-40 to R-60.

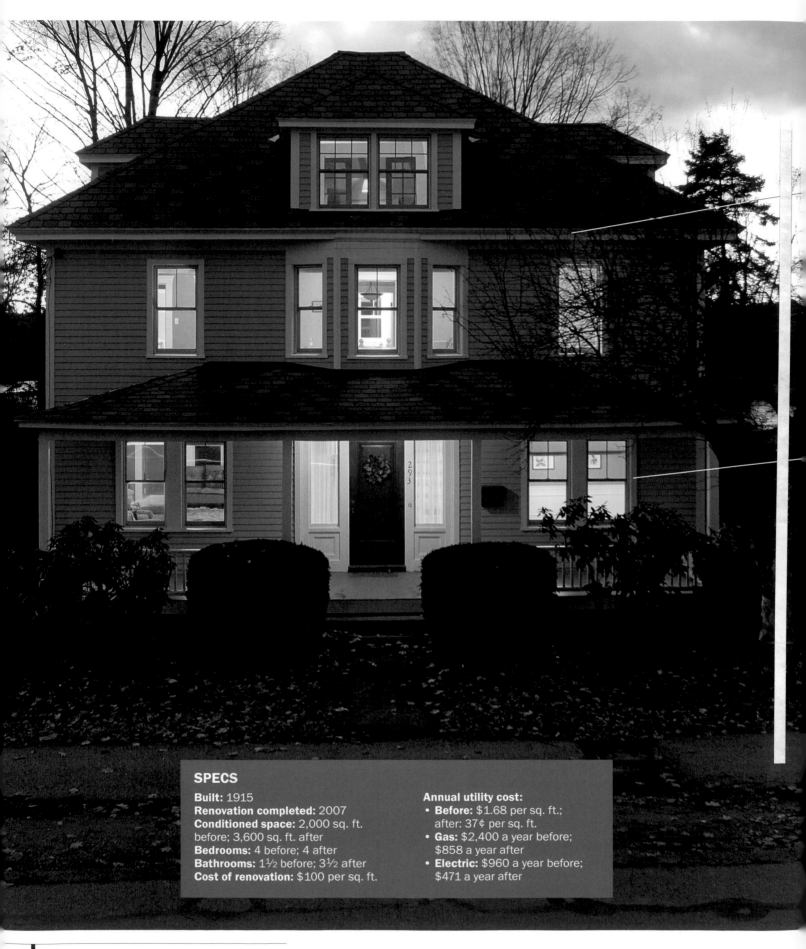

SPECS

Built: 1915
Renovation completed: 2007
Conditioned space: 2,000 sq. ft. before; 3,600 sq. ft. after
Bedrooms: 4 before; 4 after
Bathrooms: 1½ before; 3½ after
Cost of renovation: $100 per sq. ft.

Annual utility cost:
- **Before:** $1.68 per sq. ft.; after: 37¢ per sq. ft.
- **Gas:** $2,400 a year before; $858 a year after
- **Electric:** $960 a year before; $471 a year after

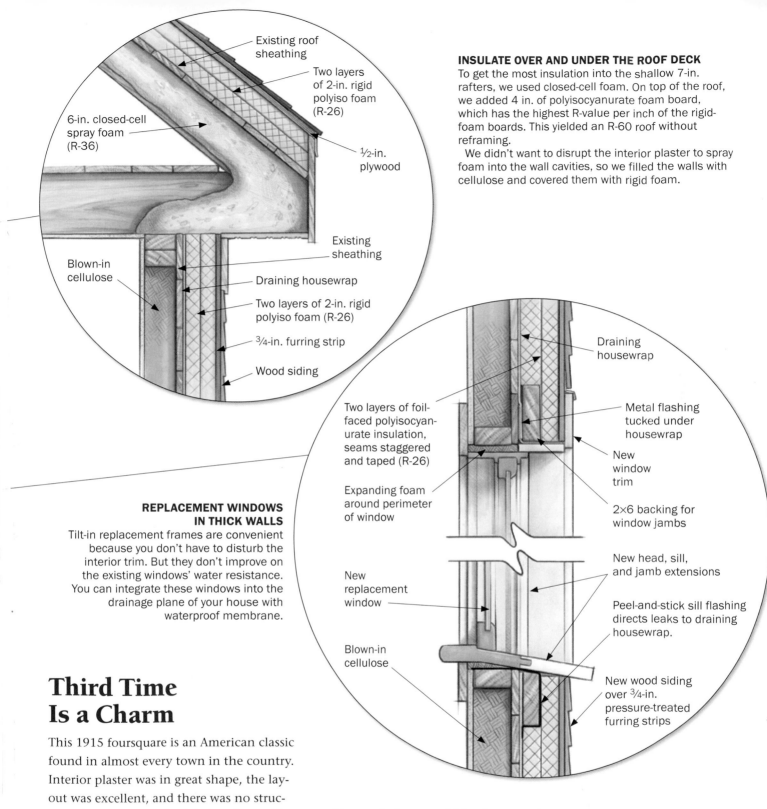

Existing roof sheathing

Two layers of 2-in. rigid polyiso foam (R-26)

6-in. closed-cell spray foam (R-36)

½-in. plywood

Blown-in cellulose

Existing sheathing

Draining housewrap

Two layers of 2-in. rigid polyiso foam (R-26)

¾-in. furring strip

Wood siding

Two layers of foil-faced polyisocyanurate insulation, seams staggered and taped (R-26)

Expanding foam around perimeter of window

New replacement window

Blown-in cellulose

Draining housewrap

Metal flashing tucked under housewrap

New window trim

2×6 backing for window jambs

New head, sill, and jamb extensions

Peel-and-stick sill flashing directs leaks to draining housewrap.

New wood siding over ¾-in. pressure-treated furring strips

INSULATE OVER AND UNDER THE ROOF DECK

To get the most insulation into the shallow 7-in. rafters, we used closed-cell foam. On top of the roof, we added 4 in. of polyisocyanurate foam board, which has the highest R-value per inch of the rigid-foam boards. This yielded an R-60 roof without reframing.

We didn't want to disrupt the interior plaster to spray foam into the wall cavities, so we filled the walls with cellulose and covered them with rigid foam.

REPLACEMENT WINDOWS IN THICK WALLS

Tilt-in replacement frames are convenient because you don't have to disturb the interior trim. But they don't improve on the existing windows' water resistance. You can integrate these windows into the drainage plane of your house with waterproof membrane.

Third Time Is a Charm

This 1915 foursquare is an American classic found in almost every town in the country. Interior plaster was in great shape, the layout was excellent, and there was no structural damage to speak of. Other than adding a few new windows to the back (for better views to a pond) and updating the kitchen, we didn't disrupt the interior too much. By insulating the basement and roof, we almost doubled the living space of this house without adding an inch to the footprint. And the utility bills were cut by 60%.

Better windows would be the next place to reduce energy loads in this house. A triple-glazed unit with heat-mirror technology might further reduce the heating load, allowing us to get closer to zero.

Betsy Pettit, FAIA, is an architect and a principal of Building Science Corp., now located in the Victorian house featured here.

Efficient Houses Need Fresh Air

■ BY MAX H. SHERMAN

I hear it all the time: "Houses are too tight." "Houses didn't used to make people sick." These assertions seem well founded: The most serious chronic illness of American children is asthma, and the Environmental Protection Agency lists poor indoor-air quality among its top five environmental threats. Are tight houses poisoning us?

There's no disputing the cause-and-effect relationship between tight houses and indoor-air pollution. In theory, the solution is simple: If you build tight, you must ventilate right. In practice, though, ventilating right is complicated and controversial. In 2003, I chaired an American Society of Heating, Refrigerating and Air-Conditioning Engineers (ASHRAE) committee that passed the country's first residential ventilation standard. It gives builders and designers guidelines for providing good indoor air while keeping utility costs low (see the sidebar on p. 37).

Houses Require Ventilation

Before I go farther, let me define *ventilation*. The word *ventilate* comes from the Latin *ventuilare*, and it means to expose to the wind. Although this might sound like some creep in a raincoat, the real story is more complex. *Ventilation* is used many ways when describing how a house works: There's crawlspace ventilation (often bad), ventilated siding assemblies (good), and roof ventilation (sometimes bad, sometimes good). We're not talking about that stuff. Here, we're talking about mechanical ventilation, using fans to blow out old air (exhaust), suck in new air (supply), or both (balanced ventilation).

Leaky Houses Are Not the Answer

On average, the air in older homes is replaced once every hour (1 ACH, or air change per hour) because older homes have a built-in ventilating method that's simple and reliable: leaks (or infiltration). The average house in the United States has about 3 sq. ft. of holes in it, but infiltration is a pretty bad way to ventilate because it wastes a tremendous amount of energy. You could plaster that 3 ft. of holes with $20 bills, and the work would pay for itself in less than a season.

Since the oil shock of the 1970s, houses are tighter and better insulated. Even conventionally framed new houses can be 5 times tighter than the general stock. Many builders and designers are tempted to take the Goldilocks approach and to look for a level of leakage that is just right, neither too little nor too much. Unfortunately, there is no hole for all seasons. The best a leaky house can do is waste energy much of the year and be underventilated the rest of the year.

Won't open windows provide the ventilation we need? In principle, yes, but in practice, no. People are pretty bad at sensing exactly how much, how often, and for how long to open a window to provide optimal ventilation. Furthermore, noise, dirt, drafts, and creeps in raincoats dissuade people from opening windows.

Indoor Air Usually Is Dirtier Than Outdoor Air

Because indoor air starts as outdoor air, then grows more polluted from contaminants in a house (see "Indoor Air Pollutants," p. 32),

Tight houses are energy efficient, but they need to breathe to be healthful and comfortable

indoor air needs to be cleaned. Flushing a house with fresh air removes much of the indoor pollution.

The most obvious way to control some contaminants is to isolate them. Paint thinner and other poisons can be stored in a garden shed. Another way to control contaminants is to eliminate them from the construction process: Use low-VOC paint, low-emitting carpet, and solid wood, rather than particleboard, in furniture and cabinetry. A third way to control the pollution level in a house is to exhaust spaces where contaminants are produced, such as kitchens, laundries, utility/storage rooms, and bathrooms. But even after you've isolated, eliminated, and exhausted, there are still pollutant sources that are most practically diluted with controlled whole-house ventilation.

Pressurized/Depressurized

When the inside of a house has a higher pressure than the outside, the house is pressurized (think of a balloon). This happens when air is blown into a tight house. The effect is to push interior air into openings in the walls and ceiling. When the inside of a house has a lower pressure than the outside, it is depressurized. This happens when a lot of air is exhausted from a tight house (such as with a large range hood) without any makeup air. The effect is to suck air through openings in the walls or ceiling (chimneys being the biggest and most obvious), potentially causing backdrafting.

Backdrafting

When air flows opposite the direction of its intended path, often through a flue or chimney, backdrafting occurs. This can happen if a house is depressurized. In backdrafting, contaminants are pulled into the house instead of being expelled, which can cause sickness or death.

Indoor Air Pollutants

Air pollution typically makes us think of smokestacks and exhaust pipes, but indoor air is usually dirtier than outdoor air. Listed below are some of the common pollution sources that argue for good whole-house ventilation.

Moisture
Moisture is not a contaminant in the usual sense because water vapor itself is not an air-quality issue. But if the humidity is too high (as can happen easily in a tight house in a cold climate), it can lead to condensation, which can cause problematic mold and fungi to grow.

Consumer products
Toxic chemicals (such as pesticides, paint supplies, and cleaning supplies) that are stored around the house can cause health problems. These items aren't limited to the garage and the cleaning-supply cabinet; many consumer products such as cosmetics and "air fresheners" also can cause indoor-air pollution.

Building materials
Volatile organic compounds (VOCs) may or may not be considered toxic, but they are the largest class of chemicals found in indoor air. The most common VOC is formaldehyde from glues used in engineered-wood products, such as particleboard. Synthetic carpet and oil-based paint are other sources of indoor VOCs.

Biological sources
Pets, dust mites, mold, and other nano-critters are not contaminants by themselves, but the particles they shed can cause various kinds of allergic reactions and/or asthma. Mites and mold require specific moisture and temperature conditions to grow and usually can be controlled by controlling the humidity. Bioeffluents from pets can be difficult to control.

Smoke
Smoke from candles, tobacco, and frying fish contains particles (soot and ash), VOCs, and other gaseous contaminants in addition to semi-VOCs, many of which can cause health problems.

Good Ventilation: Different Paths to the Same Place

When ventilation removes contaminants, it's your friend, but in doing so, it usually brings in outdoor air that must be heated, cooled, or dehumidified, which costs money. Just because it costs money, though, doesn't mean ventilation is your foe. The energy savings of a tight house more than offset the operating cost of a small fan, not to mention the costs of asthma and allergy medications. The trick is to design a ventilation system that provides acceptable indoor air as efficiently as possible. The system's design depends on where you live, but the ASHRAE ventilation standard can guide you through alternatives. Every ventilation system likely will be a little different. In general, though, there are three approaches to whole-house ventilation—exhaust, supply, and balanced systems—each a little more involved and more expensive than the last.

Exhaust Ventilation Clears Pollutants at Their Source

The simplest system, exhaust only, provides mechanical ventilation with a continuously operating exhaust fan (see the drawing on the facing page). This fan can be as simple as upgrading your bath fan or as complex as installing a multi-room exhaust fan. The exhausted air is replaced by air infiltrating through leaks (in humid climates, this can cause moisture problems). But rather than doing so at the whim of the weather, it is being done at a steady level with the fan. With the quiet, energy-efficient fans available today, this option is cheap and easy. Because its makeup-air requirements are small, a low-volume exhaust fan won't depressurize your house enough to cause backdrafting. This system also has the advantage that it can be used in homes without ductwork.

An Exhaust-Only System Removes the Bad Air

The simplest way to make sure contaminants don't build up in a house is to suck them out with one or more continuously running exhaust fans. This approach is the least expensive, is the least invasive, and has the advantage of working in houses without existing ductwork. For whole-house ventilation, existing kitchen and bath fans must be left running, a noisy prospect unless you have super-quiet models. A better solution is to use a multiport fan (see the drawing on p. 36) in the attic to exhaust many rooms simultaneously.

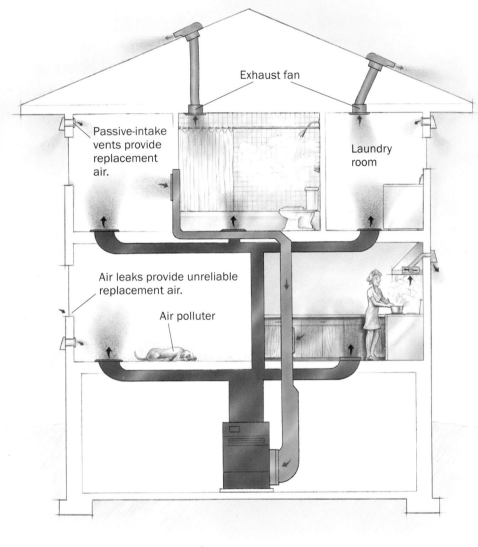

Exhaust fan

Passive-intake vents provide replacement air.

Laundry room

Air leaks provide unreliable replacement air.

Air polluter

Pull cord opens and closes vent.

PASSIVE INTAKE

In this exhaust-only system, makeup air comes in through open doors and windows, or through leaks if you have a leaky house. If you have a tight house, passive vents serve the same purpose. The Therma-Stor® fresh air inlet pictured here comes from www.efi.org and costs about $37. Similar vents are available from American Aldes Ventilation (www.americanaldes.com).

In a hot, humid climate, drawing fresh air into a house can be a problem. You can inadvertently introduce 8 gal. of water a day from ventilation air. When combined with internally generated moisture sources, this is way too much. There are three design options to consider or combine.

1. Tolerate

You can accept periods of high moisture levels if you use moisture-tolerant materials. Hard, cleanable surfaces are better choices than fuzzy ones. Use hardwood floors instead of carpet, or tile, plaster, or brick rather than paper-faced drywall.

2. Desiccate

Get the extra moisture out of the air by condensing it and draining it. Air conditioners can remove moisture, but they usually are sized and designed for controlling temperature. In some climates, they won't dehumidify enough under normal use. A better option is a standalone dehumidifier or enhanced dehumidification gear.

3. Procrastinate

Some humid climates have dry seasons. It might be possible to use reservoir-type buffer materials that store moisture during hot, humid periods, then release it during dry ones. Examples of such materials are brick interior walls, cellulose insulation, and solid-wood exposed beams.

A downside is that this system blows out heated (or cooled) air and, therefore, wastes energy. Another downside is that you don't know where the ventilation air being sucked in is coming from (or where it has been). Air from a garage or other polluted space shouldn't be inadvertently brought into a house. Passive-intake vents are a simple way to offset this problem (see the photo on p. 33).

Supply Ventilation Dilutes Pollutants Throughout the House

A supply system has the advantage of allowing you to select where the air comes from and how it is distributed throughout your home. For example, fresh air can come from a duct run connected to the return plenum of an HVAC system (see the drawing on the facing page). This way, outdoor air is pulled into the house through the air handler whenever it operates. Such an air intake must have controls (such as a timer or cycler) to turn on the air handler to make sure there is enough ventilation air. This system also should have a damper to prevent overventilating when the heating or cooling system is operating most of the time (very hot or very cold weather). Without these controls, this supply system is just a hole in the return duct, worse than a leaky house.

Supply systems must temper ventilated air to moderate temperatures in all but the mildest climates. When there is no heating or cooling call, the system above does this by running the air handler and mixing unconditioned outside air with large volumes of conditioned indoor air. While this process tempers the outside air, it uses a lot of electricity because the air-handler fan is overkill for the amount of ventilation air being sucked in.

Houses with a forced-air heating system or with central air-conditioning have a built-in air-distribution network. A supply system uses it to distribute fresh outside air through the existing ductwork. But you still need exhaust fans in wet rooms. The best approach is a quiet, continuously running multiport vent fan in the attic that draws from several rooms (see p. 36).

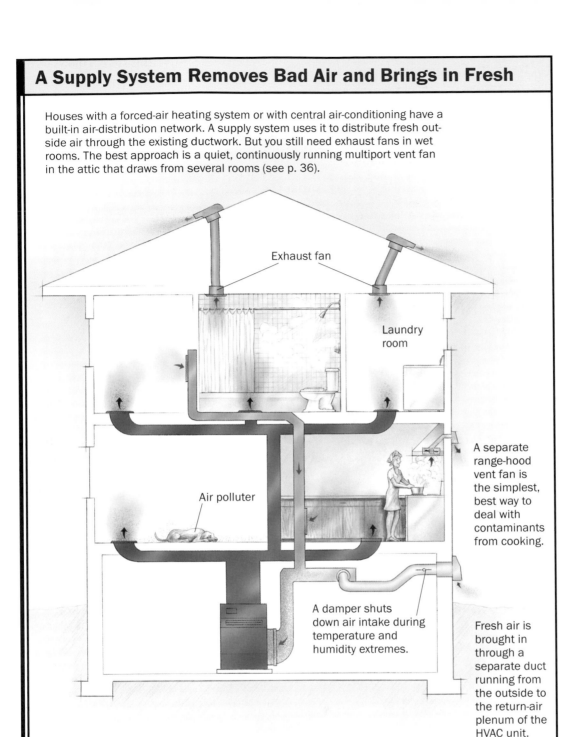

Exhaust fan

Laundry room

Air polluter

A separate range-hood vent fan is the simplest, best way to deal with contaminants from cooking.

A damper shuts down air intake during temperature and humidity extremes.

Fresh air is brought in through a separate duct running from the outside to the return-air plenum of the HVAC unit.

ACTIVE INTAKE
With a duct from outside the house to the furnace's return-air plenum, fresh makeup air is drawn into the house by the furnace fan. A temperature- and humidity-sensing damper system (pictured at left) installed in the duct curtails airflow during very hot and humid or very cold weather.

A Balanced System Removes Bad Air, Brings in Fresh, and Can Save Heat (or Cold)

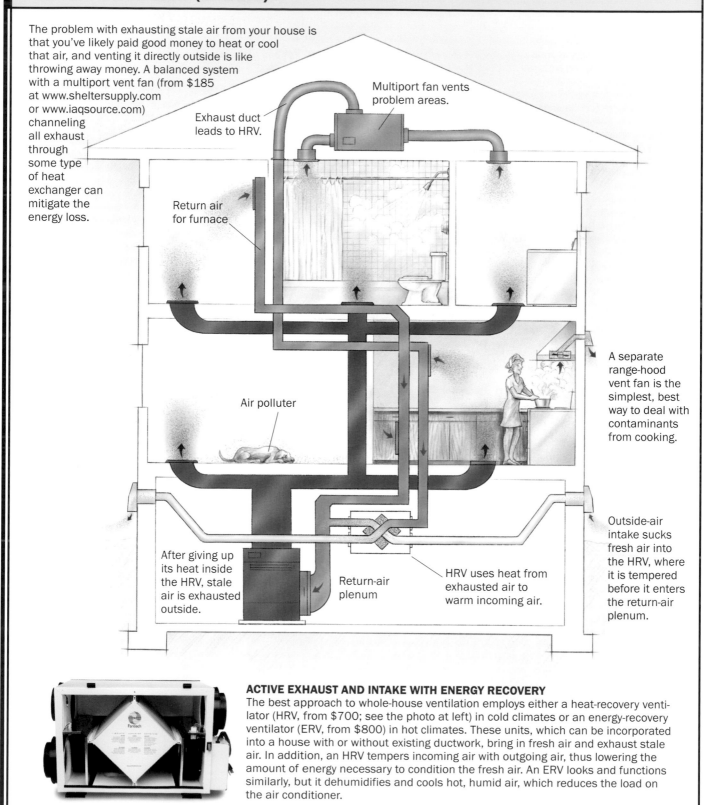

The problem with exhausting stale air from your house is that you've likely paid good money to heat or cool that air, and venting it directly outside is like throwing away money. A balanced system with a multiport vent fan (from $185 at www.sheltersupply.com or www.iaqsource.com) channeling all exhaust through some type of heat exchanger can mitigate the energy loss.

Exhaust duct leads to HRV.

Multiport fan vents problem areas.

Return air for furnace

Air polluter

A separate range-hood vent fan is the simplest, best way to deal with contaminants from cooking.

After giving up its heat inside the HRV, stale air is exhausted outside.

Return-air plenum

HRV uses heat from exhausted air to warm incoming air.

Outside-air intake sucks fresh air into the HRV, where it is tempered before it enters the return-air plenum.

ACTIVE EXHAUST AND INTAKE WITH ENERGY RECOVERY

The best approach to whole-house ventilation employs either a heat-recovery ventilator (HRV, from $700; see the photo at left) in cold climates or an energy-recovery ventilator (ERV, from $800) in hot climates. These units, which can be incorporated into a house with or without existing ductwork, bring in fresh air and exhaust stale air. In addition, an HRV tempers incoming air with outgoing air, thus lowering the amount of energy necessary to condition the fresh air. An ERV looks and functions similarly, but it dehumidifies and cools hot, humid air, which reduces the load on the air conditioner.

Until recently, not much had changed since 1631, when England's King Charles I passed the first ventilation code (your dwelling had to have operable windows taller than they were wide). Because today's houses aren't leaky enough to provide fresh air, the American Society of Heating, Refrigerating and Air-Conditioning Engineers wrote a ventilation standard. ASHRAE 62.2 is a minimum standard applicable to both new and existing homes (including small multifamily ones). Keep in mind that 62.2 is a standard, not a code. Think of it as a recommendation that might lead to a new code requirement.

THE MAJOR REQUIREMENTS OF 62.2:

• **WHOLE-HOUSE MECHANICAL VENTILATION**

Ventilation can be achieved with an exhaust, supply, or balanced ventilation system. Ventilation airflow, measured in cubic feet per minute (cfm), must increase with the size of the house and the number of occupants. The 62.2 standard recommends minimum ventilation rates of 45 cfm for 2- to 3-bedroom houses up to 1,500 sq. ft.; 60 cfm for 2- to 3-bedroom houses between 1,500 and 3,000 sq. ft.; and 75 cfm for 4- to 5-bedroom houses between 1,500 and 3,000 sq. ft.

• **MECHANICAL EXHAUST IN KITCHENS AND BATHROOMS**

In addition to the whole-house ventilation requirement:
Kitchen: a user-operable vented range hood of at least 100 cfm; or a fan giving 5 kitchen air changes per hour of continuous or intermittent exhaust.
Bathroom: a user-operable fan of at least 50 cfm; or a continuously operating 20-cfm exhaust fan.

• **MINIMUM PERFORMANCE STANDARDS FOR FANS**
Volume: Fan's airflow rates must be rated by a third party.
Noise: Continuously operating fans should be 1 sone or less; intermittent-use kitchen and bath fans cannot exceed 3 sones.

• **AIRTIGHT GARAGE DUCT SYSTEMS**

Air handlers or return ducts in an attached garage must be tested for tightness. While tight ducts save energy, 62.2 sets only minimum requirements to protect indoor-air quality.

• **PARTICLE FILTRATION UPSTREAM OF AIR HANDLERS**

Dirty ducts and coils can become a pollution source, so 62.2 requires pleated furnace filters (MERV 6 or better). To clean the air inside a house, more-aggressive filtration is needed.

Balanced Ventilation Brings in the Good Air, Banishes the Bad, and Conserves Energy

The best way to temper incoming air while reducing HVAC energy consumption is to use a heat-recovery ventilator (HRV) or an energy-recovery ventilator (ERV). These systems (see the drawing on the facing page) are balanced approaches that use the temperature and humidity of an exhaust-air stream (which otherwise would have been wasted) to temper the air of a supply stream, thereby reducing the HVAC energy cost. An HRV heats or cools incoming fresh air and can recapture up to 80% of the energy that would be lost without it. ERVs are better suited for hot, humid climates because they dry incoming air, thus reducing the work that the air conditioner has to do.

You Still Need to Clean Up

Ventilation is good at diluting gaseous compounds and small particles because small particles act like gases. They mix quickly in the air and follow air currents when air is expelled. But large particles such as pollen, pet dander, and dust mites must be cleaned up or vacuumed rather than exhausted or diluted because they're too heavy to mix with air. Other large particles, called semi-VOCs, are solids or liquids at room temperature. While they're not gaseous, as with VOCs, they are volatile enough to emit lots of gaseous vapor. This is important, because if you filter out SVOC particulates you haven't really done anything until you clean the filter; the SVOCs keep emitting gaseous vapor from the filter. If you don't replace filters on your HVAC system regularly, the system itself becomes a contamination source.

The three ventilation systems discussed here are by no means comprehensive; they can be combined in various recipes to meet particular conditions. In addition to climate and house tightness, cost can be a big consideration, but it shouldn't be the major one. Be sure to consider long-term durability and maintenance requirements. Systems with heat recovery (HRV/ERV) require a lot more maintenance than those without. Systems with multiple filters or requiring seasonal adjustment can be confusing.

Tight Houses Are Good, and They Should Breathe

Excessive leaks are one way for a house to breathe, but not the best. While there's a lot of ongoing research and a robust scholarly debate on the best way to achieve acceptable indoor-air quality, building scientists all agree that houses need to breathe.

As houses become higher and higher performance, they need to breathe in a steady, reasonably controllable way. We cannot afford to let them breathe at the whim of the weather or with windows only. We also sometimes need to be able to have them hold their breath when conditions outside are exceptionally bad. Only with designed ventilation systems can we make sure that indoor-air quality and energy efficiency advance hand in hand.

Dr. Max H. Sherman is a consulting building scientist and physicist at Lawrence Berkeley National Laboratory in Berkeley, Calif.

A Practical Look at Deep-Energy Retrofits

■ BY MARTIN HOLLADAY

If you pay any attention to building science, you have probably seen the term "deep-energy retrofit"—a phrase being thrown around with the colloquiality of "sustainability" and "green." Like the word "green," the term "deep-energy retrofit" is poorly defined and somewhat ambiguous. In most cases, though, "deep-energy retrofit" is used to describe remodeling projects designed to reduce a house's energy use by 50% to 90%.

Remodelers have been performing deep-energy retrofits—originally called "superinsulation retrofits"—since the 1980s. Most deep-energy retrofit projects are predominantly focused on reducing heating and cooling loads, not on the upgrade of appliances, lighting, or finish materials.

While a deep-energy retrofit yields a home that is more comfortable and healthy to live in, the cost of such renovation work can be astronomical, making this type of retrofit work impossible for many people. Those of us who can't afford a deep-energy retrofit can still study the deep-energy approach, using it to shed light on more practical and cost-effective measures to make any home tighter and more efficient.

How Deep?

No standard-setting agency has established a legal definition of a deep-energy retrofit, but the term generally refers to retrofit measures that reduce a home's energy use by 50% to 90% below that of a code-minimum house—or, according to a more lenient definition, below preretrofit levels. Probably fewer than 100 homes in North America have completed deep-energy retrofits that conform to the strictest definition of the term.

A house that has undergone a deep-energy retrofit typically ends up with R-20 basement walls, R-40 above-grade walls, R-60 roofs, and U-0.20 windows. A typical airtightness goal, determined by a blower-door test, is 1.2 ACH (air changes per hour) at 50 pascals.

A deep-energy retrofit doesn't make sense in all climates, and not every home is a good candidate for the work. Cold-climate homes often have higher energy bills than homes in more moderate climates, so a cold-climate

An old house with a new shell. This deep-energy retrofit in Somerville, Mass., received 4 in. of spray polyurethane foam on its exterior. (For more information, see the case study on p. 45.) However, not all energy upgrades have to be so elaborate.

home may be a better candidate than a home in a moderate climate or a home that already has low energy bills. A house with a simple rectangular shape and a simple gable roof is easier and less expensive to retrofit than a house with complicated exterior elevations, bay windows, dormers, or a roof full of hips and valleys. Most of the deep-energy retrofits include the installation of a new layer of exterior insulation. Intricate architectural details add to the difficulty of such retrofit work, driving up costs. Homes with simple exterior trim and uncomplicated cornice details are much easier to work on than Victorian homes with gingerbread trim. Because many deep-energy retrofits require existing roofing and siding to be replaced, the best candidates for deep-energy retrofit work are houses that are in need of new roofing and siding.

The Payback

Homeowners who undertake deep-energy retrofits are usually motivated by environmental or energy-security concerns rather than a desire to save money on their energy bills. These jobs are so expensive—in the range of $50,000 to $150,000 per house—that a homeowner would have to wait decades before the investment could be recouped. "In a retrofit situation, it can cost a lot of money to save a small amount of energy," says energy consultant Michael Blasnik. "Going from R-19 to R-40 walls or R-30 to R-60 ceilings doesn't save a whole lot of Btu—and the cost of that work is potentially tremendous."

There's no easy way to calculate the payback period for many deep-energy retrofits, in part because a major overhaul of a building's shell inevitably includes many measures (for example, adding new siding or roofing) that aren't energy-related. Although these elements don't make a significant con-

Phases

1. Get an energy audit. An auditor will evaluate your home and develop a list of energy-retrofit measures (see "Every House Needs an Energy Audit," pp. 4–11).

2. Perform air-sealing work, using blower-door test results to direct you.

3. Install a mechanical ventilation system once you've tightened up the building envelope.

4. Start insulating the home from the top, because a lot of heat is lost through ceilings and roofs.

5. Insulate the interior side of basement walls, a relatively easy task because basement walls are accessible.

6. Install dense-pack cellulose insulation into any empty stud bays of above-grade walls. This work is affordable and cost-effective.

7. Install thick rigid foam on the exterior of the sheathing and new high-performance replacement windows.

8. Finally, install a new heating system. This should be done last, because the unit should be sized for your new high-performance home. If a new heating unit is installed earlier in the project, it's likely to be too big.

tribution to a home's energy performance, they may greatly enhance the home's aesthetics and value.

Those of us without a Midas budget will need to settle on a less ambitious approach to energy savings than a full-blown deep-energy retrofit, and that's OK. Less expensive and less invasive retrofit measures, typically referred to in the industry as weatherization, have payback periods of 15 years or less.

Energy Retrofits of All Levels

Paul Eldrenkamp is a Massachusetts remodeler who has performed several deep-energy retrofits. When his clients balk at the high cost of a full retrofit, he sometimes advises them to work in phases. Although it is common to perform energy improvements over time as finances permit, it's also important to take advantage of upgrade opportunities even if they seem to fall out of sequence. For example, if you have to install new siding or roofing and you do so without installing thick rigid foam underneath, you may regret your shortsighted decision in time. Here's a general overview of the work to be done, the order in which it should be completed, and the practical alternatives to going deep.

ROOF INSULATION

Deep-energy retrofit Many deep-energy retrofits call for insulating a roof to R-60, which can most easily be done by adding 4 in. of rigid polyisocyanurate foam on top of the roof deck and then filling each rafter bay with loose fill or batt insulation. Exterior foam sheathing has the added benefit of reducing thermal bridging through the rafters.

Practical approach It's much less expensive to install cellulose on an attic floor than to install rigid foam and new roofing. Address air leakage before dragging a cellulose hose into the attic. Seal all ceiling leaks under the existing insulation (for example, at electrical and plumbing penetrations, at utility chases, and at the gaps between partition drywall and partition top plates). It's also important to be sure that there are no air leaks at the perimeter of the attic, where the ceiling air barrier meets the wall air barrier.

Performance comparison While there is no upper limit on the R-value that can be achieved when installing foam on top of the roof sheathing, the maximum R-value of attic-floor insulation depends on the available height at the perimeter of the attic. Achieving R-60 requires about 16 in. of cellulose.

Cost comparison Attics with easy access are easier and cheaper to retrofit than cluttered attics with lots of penetrations that need to be sealed. From a material standpoint, the practical approach is almost always more economical. For any given R-value, polyisocyanurate costs from three to five times as much as cellulose insulation. Needless to say, adding rigid foam on top of the roof sheathing includes significant expenses for roof demolition, new roof sheathing, and new roofing—costing between $3 and $5.80 per sq. ft.

BASEMENT INSULATION

Deep-energy retrofit After addressing any moisture issues in the basement, many deep-energy retrofits call for basement walls to be insulated to R-20, requiring the addition of 4 in. of XPS insulation or about 3 in. of

Pile it on. If adding rigid foam on top of the roof sheathing isn't an option, a less expensive option is blowing cellulose on an air-sealed attic floor. The more insulation, the better.

Stop the leaks. If a full basement-insulation job isn't in the budget, attack the rim joist. Spray polyurethane foam works best, but a more affordable option is to seal rigid-foam panels in each joist bay with canned spray foam.

closed-cell spray polyurethane foam. The rim joists are also insulated with either spray foam or rigid foam.

The basement floor is insulated with 2 in. to 4 in. of XPS foam over the slab. A new subfloor is applied over the foam.

Practical approach Adding insulation to the basement walls and rim joists is cost effective in all northern climates. However, the payback period for basement-floor insulation is much longer than for basement-wall and rim-joist insulation, so it's often eliminated in projects with a limited budget.

Performance comparison Since the temperature of the soil under a below-grade slab is higher than the average outdoor-air temperature in winter, heat loss through a basement slab is much less than through a basement wall. In many homes, basement slabs are responsible for less than 1% of a home's total heat loss.

Cost comparison Not insulating your basement floor saves you from $1.80 to $2.50 per sq. ft. in materials.

Retrofit Results

Location: Arlington, Mass. **Size:** 3,000 sq. ft. (duplex) **Renovation cost:** $47 per sq. ft.; $140,000 total

Cost: $140K
Annual savings: $2,300

While planning a deep-energy retrofit of his 3,000-sq.-ft. two-story duplex in Arlington, Mass., owner Alex Cheimets got a lucky break: He was eligible to participate in a pilot superinsulation program sponsored by the Massachusetts Department of Energy Resources and his local utility.

Construction

Basement: Ceiling sprayed with open-cell spray polyurethane foam (adds thickness and R-value)

Walls: 2×4 construction filled with cellulose; 4 in. of foil-faced polyisocyanurate foam outside of sheathing for a total of R-39

Roof: 6 in. of polyisocyanurate insulation installed above the existing roof sheathing, topped with a layer of plywood; 8 in. of open-cell spray polyurethane foam (Icynene) installed between the existing rafters for a total of R-59

Windows: Double-pane (U-0.33) windows by Pella®

Mechanicals

Heating: Oil-fired steam boiler in each unit

Water: Main boiler in unit 1; on-demand gas water heater in unit 2

Ventilation: Heat-recovery ventilators (one for each apartment)

Results

Energy reduction: 65% (heating fuel)

Annual savings: $2,300 per year

Payback period: 61 years. If the cost of the roofing and siding are subtracted, payback is reduced to a little over 35 years.

Air-seal, then insulate. If you can't afford to add insulation to your walls, address simple air-sealing measures such as filling the gaps around windows, electrical boxes, doors, and recessed lights in the ceilings.

WALL INSULATION

Deep-energy retrofit A typical 2×4 wall insulated with fiberglass batts has a whole-wall R-value of about 10. Many deep-energy retrofits aim to insulate walls to R-40, which typically requires all of the siding to be removed and the addition of 4 in. to 5 in. of polyisocyanurate rigid insulation or spray polyurethane foam.

Practical takeaway Unless your home's existing siding is in bad shape, it's hard to justify the cost of installing exterior wall foam. If your existing siding is sound, your best retrofit option is careful air-sealing work from the interior with canned spray foam. Typical leakage areas include the gap between the baseboard and the finished floor; electrical boxes; and cracks behind window and door casing.

Performance comparison Above-grade walls represent most of a typical house's thermal envelope, and an R-10 wall leaks heat at four times the rate of an R-40 wall. Although air-sealing an R-10 wall will surely increase its performance, it will not rival an R-40 wall.

Cost comparison Installing thick exterior-wall foam and new siding on a typical house costs tens of thousands of dollars. Blower-door-directed air-sealing work might cost $700 to $1,000 per house.

WINDOWS

Deep-energy retrofit Single- or double-glazed windows are usually replaced with new triple-glazed windows with full-thickness (1⅜ in.) glazing. This glazing is better than thin ⅞-in. or 1-in. glazing.

Practical takeaway The cost of installing high-quality replacement windows can be staggering; as a less expensive alternative, consider installing low-e storm windows over tuned-up windows in good working order and that have been weatherstripped.

Performance comparison Good triple-glazed windows have a U-factor of 0.17 to 0.20. A low-e storm window won't achieve the same performance. Installed over a single-pane wood window, a low-e storm window provides a total U-factor of 0.40, while a low-e storm window installed over a double-pane wood window provides a total U-factor of 0.34. (The lower the U-factor, the better.)

Cost comparison The cost to install a low-e storm window ranges from $120 to $160. The installed cost of a new triple-glazed window is about $800 to $1,200.

HVAC

Deep-energy retrofit Most deep-energy retrofits include air-sealing measures. Once infiltration rates have been reduced, an older house requires a good mechanical ventilation system. Options range from low-sone bathroom exhaust fans controlled by timers to heat-recovery ventilation systems with dedicated ductwork.

A new heating unit is also a quintessential upgrade in many deep-energy retrofits. New furnaces or boilers are most often efficient sealed-combustion models. The fuel type is relatively unimportant, because the fuel demands of the newly renovated home will be low.

Practical takeaway If you've done any air-sealing work, a mechanical ventilation system is essential. Exhaust-only systems are much less expensive than a system with a heat-recovery ventilator. If you can't afford an HVAC overhaul, you should at least have ducts tested for leakage and sealed.

Performance comparison Replacing an 80% AFUE (annual fuel utilization efficiency) furnace with a 92% AFUE furnace will cut energy use 13%. Sealing ducts may save an additional 5% to 20% of your energy use.

Cost comparison The installed cost of a new 92% AFUE furnace ranges from $3,000 to $6,000. Duct sealing and repair costs between $250 and $500 per house.

Martin Holladay is a contributing editor to Fine Homebuilding.

Tight ducts save money. Sealing leaky ductwork can be done in several ways, but mastic and fiberglass-mesh tape are among the best options.

Retrofit Results

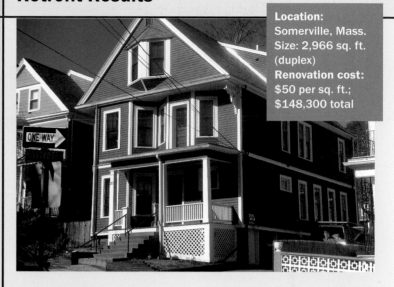

Location: Somerville, Mass. **Size:** 2,966 sq. ft. (duplex) **Renovation cost:** $50 per sq. ft.; $148,300 total

Cost: $148K
Annual savings: $2,490

Alarmed by the implications of the global climate-change crisis, Cador Price-Jones embarked on a major retrofit of his Massachusetts duplex (also pictured on p. 40).

Construction

Basement: 3 in. of closed-cell spray foam (R-18) applied between the studs of a 2×4 wall built against an 8-in. block foundation

Walls: Existing 2×4 walls filled with dense-pack cellulose; new 2×2 frame installed on exterior and filled with 4 in. of closed-cell spray foam for a total of R-37

Roof: Attic floor air-sealed and filled with 17 in. of loose-fill cellulose for an R-value of 60; 2 in. of spray foam used to air-seal the eaves

Windows: Main house windows are double-glazed, low-e, argon-filled units by Jeld-Wen®; basement windows are double-glazed hopper units by Harvey Industries

Mechanicals

Heating: Modulating condensing gas boiler, 22,700- to 75,200-Btu rated output, 95% AFUE

Water: 60-gal. Superstor® indirect hot-water tank

Ventilation: Heat-recovery ventilators (one for each apartment)

Photovoltaic: 5.25kw package system by Nexamp™

Results

Energy reduction: From $5,650 per year to $3,160 per year

Annual savings: $2,490

Payback period: 60 years

Upgrade Your Attic Insulation

■ BY MIKE GUERTIN

Saving money on heating-fuel costs is a lot simpler than negotiating with OPEC or your local utility. Here's how: On a recent upgrade in the attic of a 1950s-era house (one of two projects that is featured here), I air-sealed and spread a 12-in.-deep layer of cellulose throughout 1,500 sq. ft. of space in about a day. As a result of this and other energy-saving improvements that were made to the home, the owner saw his heating and cooling costs reduced by half compared to the previous year, even in the face of higher electricity and heating-fuel costs.

I typically focus my efforts to improve the energy efficiency of an attic in two areas: sealing air leaks in the ceiling and increasing the amount of insulation in the attic itself.

The payback period for tightening a leaky ceiling can be as short as a month. Adding insulation might take a few heating or cooling seasons to pay off, but the wait is relatively brief. I estimate the payback for air-sealing and upgrading attic insulation to be realized in three years.

On these projects, I often chose to install a radiant reflective membrane. Besides reducing radiant-heat gain from the roof, the membrane makes the attic more attractive and dust-free for storage use, and it keeps the blown-in insulation I use from blocking the rafter bays. While radiant barriers can reduce peak attic temperatures by 10°F to 30°F, they haven't proved to be cost effective in all geographic regions or in attics that are adequately insulated, that are air-sealed, and that have well-insulated, wrapped air-handling equipment and ductwork. In these cases, you may be better off spending the money on more insulation and air-sealing than on a radiant barrier.

Stop the Air Leaks, Stop Losing Heat

Air leaks can account for 30% of a home's energy loss, so it pays to seek out and seal every penetration between the living (conditioned) space and the attic (unconditioned) space before adding insulation. Don't leave any batt unturned when hunting down air leaks. Dust deposits in leaking air stain insulation brown or black, so you can start by looking for discoloration in the insulation.

I treat the drywall ceiling as the air barrier and seal all penetrations, joints, and holes. The open framing for soffits and chases is a highway for air leaks from wall cavities into the attic. Another gaping hole is the attic-stair bulkhead (see the sidebar on p. 53).

I install an insulated and gasketed cover for the attic access panel or pull-down stairway. You can buy a ready-made access cover or make your own. The cover can be fit within the riser or on top of it. When the cover sits on top of the riser, apply the gasket material (usually adhesive-backed foam tape) to the cover (not the floor) so that it's not damaged when someone accesses the attic.

Next, I seal recessed-light cans and ceiling-mounted light-fixture boxes. Both are often overlooked, but when combined are one of the biggest sources of air leaks. The holes and the perimeter of ceiling-mounted

Attic Work Safety

Working with insulation is about balancing safety and comfort. Although official health warnings are ambiguous at best, it's a good idea to err on the side of caution, especially regarding fiberglass. You might see photos of me without a long-sleeved shirt or, occasionally, gloves, but not without a mask; when it's 100°F in an attic, I'll sacrifice some itching to stay cooler.

- **A respirator** and safety glasses are necessary in any situation.

- **When handling fiberglass,** it's a good idea to wear long pants and a long-sleeved shirt, or a one-piece work suit. If your hands are sensitive, wear gloves.

- **Step only on ceiling joists,** never on the ceiling. Use kneeboards that span between ceiling joists for more freedom and stability.

- **Work in the cool of the day,** early morning or evening when the sun isn't beating on the roof (in the summer, of course).

electrical boxes should be sealed to the drywall with a fire-resistant sealant or foam (see the sidebar on p. 49). Gaps around ducts, wires, and pipes that penetrate into the attic must be located and closed, too. Most inexpensive and old bathroom exhaust-fan boxes have open seams and holes that should be covered with mastic or duct-sealing tape. The fan-box perimeter should be sealed to the drywall with caulk or foam.

Another typical area to block off and seal is the 2-in.-wide space between framing and masonry chimneys. Combustible materials aren't allowed to contact the masonry, so it's best to use sheet metal to block the space.

I also seal the joint between the drywall and the wall plates. The thin joints between

Potential Air Leaks in the Attic

If air leaks aren't properly sealed, the insulation typically placed between the ceiling joists of a conventional attic is only partially effective. These leaks can range in size from a pinhole to the gap surrounding the typical 3-ft. by 4-ft. access hatch. For the contractor or homeowner who wants to create a tighter building envelope, the hardest part of the task is finding the air leaks; sealing them is relatively easy.

Below is a checklist.
1. Recessed lights and electrical boxes
2. Holes for wires or pipes in drywall and framing
3. Attic hatchway
4. Spaces between the framing and the chimney
5. Plumbing or electrical chases
6. Framed soffits that are open to the attic
7. Drywall joints between ceiling and wall plates
8. Leaky joints in ductwork

A word of caution: Air-sealing a house can lead to backdrafting of natural draft combustion appliances like water heaters, furnaces, or boilers. To avoid creating a carbon-monoxide hazard, have a combustion-safety assessment done before tightening a house, and add a fresh-air intake duct to each burner.

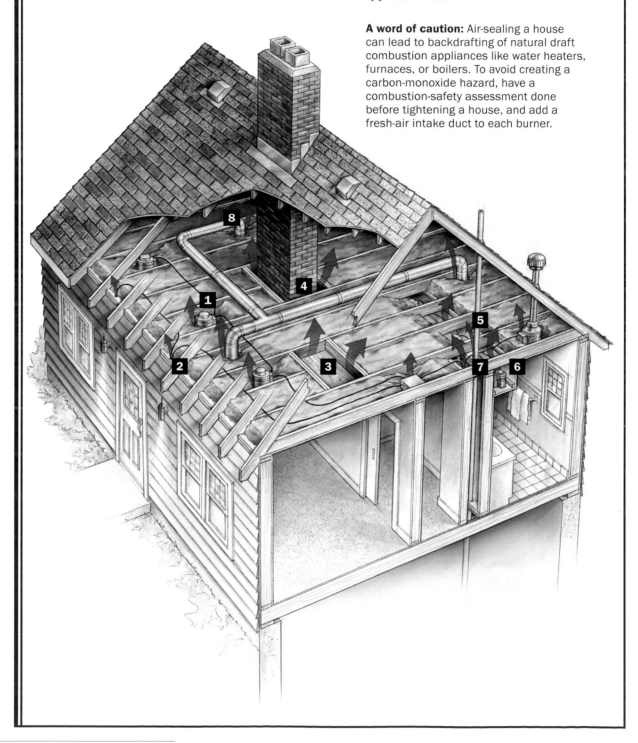

the ceiling drywall and the wall top plates might seem insignificant, but they add up when you figure the linear footage of walls. Expanding foam or sealing caulk easily fills the gaps.

Address Wiring Issues

Because old knob-and-tube wiring can't be buried under new insulation, have an electrician replace any old wires in the attic before adding insulation. Ideally, all junction boxes should be raised above the level of the insulation. When elevating the junction boxes isn't an option, you should install clearly marked permanent tags that can be seen above the insulation level.

While I am working in the attic, I like to install two electrical conduits (one line voltage and one telecom/low voltage) between the attic and the basement or the crawlspace to make any future wiring upgrades easier to accomplish.

Tune Up Existing Insulation

The two types of insulation that are usually found in older attics are fiberglass batts and loose-fill cellulose. For batt insulation to perform at its rated level, it must be installed snug to the ceiling surface and to the edges of the framing. Any gaps or voids reduce the insulation's effectiveness. If the existing insulation is in good condition, it can be reused.

I tune up the insulation by tightening end joints, making sure batts are tight to the ceiling drywall, and filling in any voids with new pieces of insulation.

If I've decided to increase the amount of insulation with more batts, I like to bring the level of the older batts flush with the top of the joists and then install a new layer of unfaced batts running perpendicular to the joists. Placed above the joists, the cross-

(continued on p. 53)

Choose the Right Air Sealant for the Job

When I'm air-sealing an attic, I use four or five different types of sealants. I use caulk when I need precision: caulking a recessed-light can to the ceiling drywall, for instance, or sealing some pieces of rigid foam to framing. Where gaps around pipes or wires need filling, I use expanding urethane foam.

Fire-blocking foam
DAP®
www.dap.com

The distinctions become finer when I'm sealing leaks that come under the code heading of draft-blocking or fire-stopping. (In many areas, local fire codes supersede the *International Building Code*, so be sure to check them first.) Draft- or fire-blocking refers to stopping smoke or fire from passing from one area to another through perforations in floors, walls, and ceilings. These caulk or foam sealants typically are used to seal holes and gaps in top plates, for example, that could compromise the integrity of the wall's fire-blocking.

Fire-blocking caulk
3M®
www.3m.com

Fire-stopping or fire barrier refers to sealants classified as intumescent: When exposed to direct flame or heat, they expand to fill the cavity and are rated to withstand direct flame.

Fire-barrier caulk
3M

The Space around the Chimney Needs a Fire-Resistant Seal

There's usually a 2-in.-wide gap, required by code, between framing and masonry chimneys. To close the gap, I first stuff it with rockwool (**1**), then apply a bead of adhesive caulk to the framing (**2**). Next, I screw down wide strips of metal (recycled drip edge) along the perimeter (**3**). I seal the metal to the chimney with fire-rated intumescent caulk (**4**). For continuity, you need to seal the ceiling joists to the drywall below and at inside/outside corners of the rough opening with expanding foam.

Small Leaks Add Up, So Seal Them All

Usually, the greatest number of leaks comes from small perforations in the ceiling: metal electrical boxes, drywall seams, and any place a wire or pipe comes through from below. Use expanding urethane foam to seal holes around PVC vent pipe (**1**), in electrical boxes (**2**), and especially at ceiling-corner drywall seams (**3**). If any of the sealing comes under local regulations for fire-stopping or draft-stopping, then use fire- or smoke-rated foam or caulking.

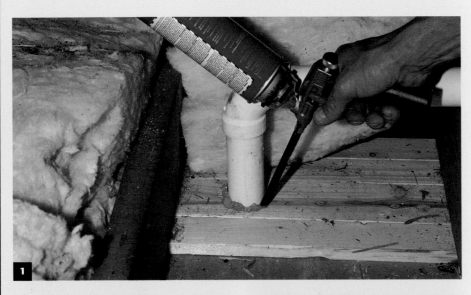

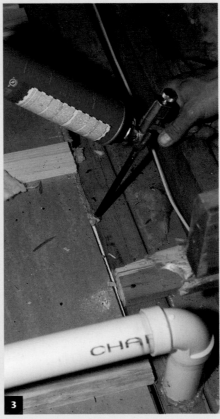

Replace, Seal, or Enclose Recessed Lights

Recessed lights are one of the most overlooked sources of air leaks into attics. The best choice is to change old can bodies (**1**) for airtight insulation-contact-rated (IC-rated) models (see the photo at right) and then seal the rim to the drywall with foam or caulk. IC-rated lights that aren't airtight can be sealed by covering the fixture with an airtight box made from rigid-foam insulation (**2** and **3**), metal, or drywall, or by sealing holes in the can body with spray-foam insulation (**4**).

Remember that non-IC-rated cans need an airspace around them and can't come in contact with the insulation. Some sources recommend installing a sealed box over non-IC-rated cans, but recessed-light manufacturers frown on this practice. The best practice is to replace non-IC-rated cans with air-sealed IC-rated models.

IC-rated light. An airtight insulation-contact-rated recessed light.

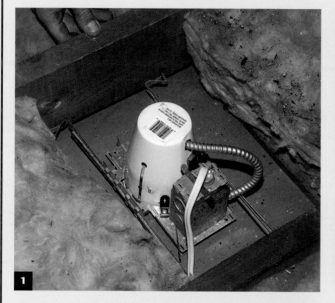

Block the Biggest Offenders

The attic access is a big leak that can be fixed quickly: Build or buy an insulated cover for the access bulkhead. The key is to provide a rim to connect to the sealing cover. The rim can be made from strips of sheathing, framing lumber, or rigid foam; then the cover sits on top or fits around the rim. On this job, I added a deck of leftover ½-in. plywood and OSB after the insulation was added.

Interior soffits that are framed before the drywall is hung can leak huge quantities of air. Fill in the openings between the ceiling joists above the soffits with solid materials like rigid-foam panels, drywall pieces, or sheathing scraps, then seal the edges with expanding foam or caulk.

Joist bays should be sealed with rigid blocks to keep insulation where it belongs. Cut rigid foam into strips the width of the joist bays, and slip them out over the top wall plate (photo at top right). The panels block the loose-fill insulation that's to be installed from clogging the soffit-to-ridge air channel and add a higher R-value to the short space over the plate.

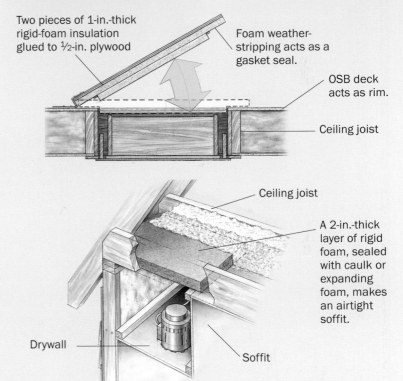

Two pieces of 1-in.-thick rigid-foam insulation glued to ½-in. plywood

Foam weather-stripping acts as a gasket seal.

OSB deck acts as rim.

Ceiling joist

Ceiling joist

A 2-in.-thick layer of rigid foam, sealed with caulk or expanding foam, makes an airtight soffit.

Drywall

Soffit

layered batts can be tight together to minimize heat loss through the joists and to maximize performance.

If I'm upgrading to loose-fill insulation, I keep it from falling into eave soffits and maintain channels for roof ventilation by installing a layer of blocking made from rigid insulation in the rafter (or truss) bays over the exterior-wall plates. I notch the rigid insulation around the rafters so that I get a tight fit in the bay.

Blowing Insulation is a Two-Person Operation

Blown-in loose-fill cellulose or fiberglass isn't as common as batt insulation, but both are installed quickly and completely cover the attic floor. Loose fill can be blown in over any existing insulation that's been tuned up first. Comparisons in R-value between the two are similar (around R-3.2 per in.). Over the first year, cellulose tends to

Blowing Insulation Is a Team Effort

A division of labor keeps insulation flowing. One person handles the hose, and the other feeds the blowing machine. The most critical job is at the machine (see the top left photo below and the bottom right photo), where the steady rate of insulation flow is controlled by the operator. At the other end of the hose, it's best to start at the farthest point and work back to the attic access. A slight upward hose angle helps to spread the insulation more evenly.

Fiberglass made easier

Owens Corning® (www.owenscorning.com) has introduced AttiCat®, a rental system that processes and distributes bales of fiberglass. The packaging is stripped as the bale is pushed into the hopper. Then the machine agitates the fiberglass and blows it out through the hose. The blowing fiberglass (top right photo below) is not as dusty as cellulose.

settle more than fiberglass. Of the two materials, cellulose is generally more available to homeowners; both can be installed with the same basic techniques. A two-person crew is the absolute minimum. The machines used to blow in insulation vary in power and features, but rental machines are typically the most basic.

Pick a blower location as close to the attic access as possible. Cellulose and blowing fiberglass are messy to handle, so the loading area will be covered quickly. I prefer to set up outside, but a garage is an ideal place to stage the bales and blower when the weather doesn't cooperate. I lay down a large, clean tarp and place the machine in the middle with the bales close by. Insulation that falls onto the tarp is easy to gather up and reload. Don't let any debris get mixed into fallen insulation. Nails and sticks can jam the blower or plug the hose.

Route the delivery hose through the shortest, straightest distance to the attic. Runs of 50 ft. or less are ideal. Runs longer than 100 ft. or runs with a lot of bends reduce airflow and can lead to a plugged hose.

All blowing machines have an agitator that breaks up the insulation bales and a blower that drives air and insulation through a hose. The person feeding the machine breaks up the bales and drops them through a protective grate on top of a hopper. It takes a little practice to know how fast and how full to feed the machine, especially when using a basic blower. Fill too fast, and you run the risk of slowing the flow through the delivery hose. After a little practice, the loader understands the sounds the blower makes and can adjust loading speed for optimal delivery.

The insulation dispenser handles the hose and works from the far ends of the attic toward the access hole. Good lighting is a must. If hard-wired attic lighting isn't enough, run a string of work lights or wear a high-powered headlamp. Discharge the hose at a slight angle upward, and let the insulation fall into place. This helps it to spread more evenly. Shooting the hose directly at

Cost and Labor for an Attic Upgrade

The project was a 1950s ranch with 1,500 sq. ft. of attic space. Here's a breakdown of the costs. It's mostly labor, and relatively little money for materials.

Air-Sealing
One tube of fire-barrier caulk: $7
Two cans of polyurethane foam: $20
Scrap pieces of rigid foam and recycled metal drip edge: $30
Labor: About three hours

Insulation
Cellulose bales and blower rental: $500
Labor: About eight hours to tune up existing insulation. Also, two people for three hours to blow in cellulose and clean up.
Optional: Seven hours to lay a new floor deck.

Total
Materials: $557; optional floor deck: $170
Labor: 17 hours

the ceiling causes the insulation to mound up. If high spots occur, use a long stick or broom to even them off. Although high spots aren't really a problem, low spots don't perform as well.

Once insulation covers the ceiling joists, there's little way to know the depth of the insulation. Insulation distributors sell paper gauges marked in inches that you staple to rafters or ceiling joists. I make gauges by cutting 1½-in.-wide cardboard strips about 1 in. to 2 in. longer than the target depth; I draw a line across each strip at the final insulation grade. Expecting the insulation to settle 1 in. or 2 in. over time, I mark the strips at 14 in. and staple them to the sides of the ceiling joists every 6 ft.

Mike Guertin (www.mikeguertin.com) is a builder, remodeling contractor, and writer in East Greenwich, R.I.

Beef Up Your Old Insulation without Tearing into Walls

■ BY JUSTIN FINK

When it comes to insulating floors, walls, and ceilings, nothing makes it easier than working with the blank canvas of a newly framed house. The walls are wide open, so contractors can add any type of insulation they want to achieve the best possible thermal performance.

What about the rest of us, though? Those of us living in houses built with minimal insulation, or none at all? The ones who don't have the luxury of gutting their walls? The ones who work on or live in houses that hemorrhage heat in the winter and bake like an oven during the summer? What can we do to improve the thermal performance of these homes?

A lot. Techniques and materials for retrofitting insulation in old walls have improved

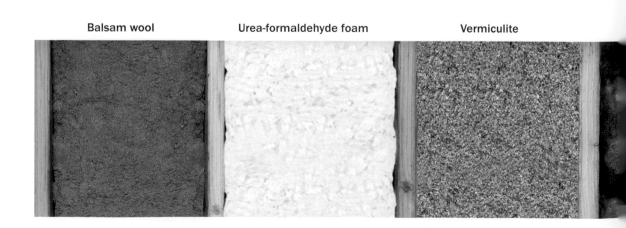

Balsam wool   Urea-formaldehyde foam   Vermiculite

over the years. Many times, insulation can be added from the interior or exterior of the house without gutting the walls. Even so, I'm not going to sugarcoat this: Adding new insulation to closed walls is a hassle.

Pick the Low-Hanging Fruit First

Before thinking about adding insulation to your walls, you should have already tackled your home's other major weak spots. If you haven't, you should, and your efforts should begin in the attic, where the most heat loss typically occurs (see "Upgrade Your Attic Insulation," pp. 46–55). If, however, after air-sealing and insulating the attic and plugging some other common energy trouble spots (see "Home Remedies for Energy Nosebleeds," pp. 12–19) your house still feels drafty and your energy bills are still too high, it's time to consider the walls.

There's a lot to consider when it comes to adding new insulation to old walls. The first step is to find out what type of insulation, if any, is already in the walls. Once that is determined, you can assess the thermal performance of the walls and then make a more informed decision about the potential benefits of an insulation upgrade. You might find that the existing insulation is astonishingly inferior and that a small outlay of cash would mean a significant decrease in your energy bills. Or you could be surprised to find that a high-cost retrofit will offer only a minuscule return on investment.

What's in My Walls?

The first step to determining your upgrade options is to learn the type and amount of insulation, if any, in your walls. Houses built before 1930 often were left uninsulated, so you will find either empty stud bays or insulation that was added later. Houses built in the '40s, '50s, and beyond typically were insulated, but often with thin batts that didn't fill the wall cavity.

The possibilities shown here represent the most common types of early insulation, but it's not a comprehensive list. Many of the earliest forms of insulation were driven by the local industry. If the town was home to sawmills, the surrounding houses could be insulated with sawdust. If the town was an agricultural hub, rice hulls were fairly common. What you find in your walls is limited only by the whim of the builder and the previous homeowners.

Fiberglass   **Rock wool**   **Cotton batts**

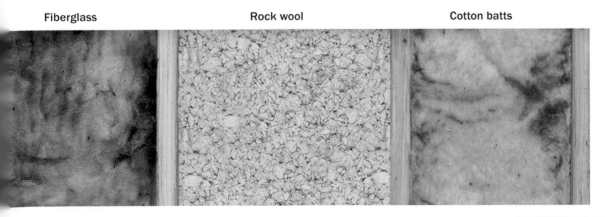

BALSAM WOOL, 1940s

What is it? "Wool" is a bit misleading because this insulation is essentially chopped balsam wood fibers.

Positive ID Although some installations may have been loose fill, this tan/brown insulation was most often packaged and installed in black-paper-faced batts. The tan fibers look similar to sawdust.

Health note Balsam wool is not a health hazard, but take care when investigating this insulation; wear a dust mask. Because the paper batts are likely to be brittle to the touch, disturbing them too much may leave holes that will decrease thermal performance.

Upgrade outlook This insulation was typically fastened to wall studs similar to fiberglass batts. Balsam wool should still yield an R-value of between R-2 and R-3 per in. if installed correctly, but the batts are likely only a couple of inches thick. Consider filling the remaining empty space in the stud cavities with blown cellulose or fiberglass. Some manufacturers of pour foam also recommend their product for this type of installation.

UREA-FORMALDEHYDE FOAM, 1950 TO 1982 (MOSTLY IN THE LATE 1970s)

What is it? Also known as UFFI, this once-popular retrofit option is a mixture of urea, formaldehyde, and a foaming agent that were combined on site and sprayed into wall cavities.

Positive ID Lightweight with brownish-gold coloring, this foam is fragile and likely to crumble if touched (hence the smooth chunks shown at left).

Health note Because this open-cell foam was banned in 1982 and most of the off-gassing happened in the hours and days following installation, chances of elevated levels of formaldehyde are slim.

Upgrade outlook Although it's rated at R-4.5 per in., UFFI rarely performs at this level. This foam is well known for its high rate of shrinkage and tendency to deteriorate if in contact with water, and it also crumbles if disturbed during remodeling. The result is walls that likely have large voids, but this insulation isn't a good candidate for discreet removal. The best option here is to add rigid foam to the exterior to help to make up for the large air voids that are likely hidden in the wall.

VERMICULITE, 1925 TO 1950

What is it? This naturally occurring mineral was heated to make it expand into a lightweight, fire-retardant insulating material.

Positive ID Brownish-pink or brownish-silver in color, these lightweight pellets were typically poured into closed wall cavities and into the voids in masonry blocks.

Health note Seventy to eighty percent of vermiculite came from a mine in Libby, Mont., that was later found to contain asbestos. The mine has been closed since 1990, but the EPA suggests treating previously installed vermiculite as if it is contaminated. If undisturbed, it's not a health risk, but if you want to upgrade to a different type of insulation, call an asbestos-removal professional.

Upgrade outlook Vermiculite doesn't typically settle and should still offer its original R-value of between R-2 and R-2.5 per in. This low thermal performance makes it an attractive candidate for upgrade, especially because it's a cinch to remove: Cut a hole, and it pours right out. But the potential for asbestos contamination makes the prep work and personal protection more of a hassle, and the job more costly as a result.

If cavities are not filled to the top, consider topping them off; fiberglass, cellulose, or pour foam will work if there is access from the attic.

FIBERGLASS, LATE 1930s TO PRESENT

What is it? This man-made product consists of fine strands of glass grouped together in a thick blanket.

Positive ID Most often yellow, though pink, white, blue, and green types are used. Older products were typically paper-faced batts.

Health note Official health information on fiberglass is ambiguous; the argument over whether it's a carcinogen continues. Even if it's not a cancer-causing material, it will make you itchy and irritate your lungs if disturbed. Be on the safe side if you plan to remove this insulation; wear gloves, long sleeves, goggles, and a respirator.

Upgrade outlook Fiberglass has a decent thermal performance of between R-3 and R-4.5 per in., but early products were typically only about 2 in. thick. Consider filling the remaining empty space in the stud cavities with blown cellulose or blown fiberglass. Some manufacturers of pour foam also recommend their product for this type of installation.

ROCK WOOL (MOSTLY IN THE 1950s)

What is it? Rock wool is a specific type of mineral wool, a by-product of the ore-smelting process.

Positive ID This fluffy, cottonlike material was typically installed as loose fill or batts. It usually started out white or gray, but even the white version will likely be blackened or brown from decades of filtering dirt out of air flowing through the cavity.

Health note Research indicates that this is a safe material. It's still in use today, and it's gaining popularity among green builders.

Upgrade outlook Rock wool is fairly dense, so it's less likely than other materials to have settled over time. If installed correctly, it should still yield a value of R-3 to R-4 per in., about the same as blown fiberglass or cellulose insulation. If anything, consider adding housewrap or a thin layer of rigid foam to the outside of the wall to air-seal the structure. If more insulation is desired, go with rigid foam.

How to Find Out

Inspector's Tricks

Electrical Outlets
You often can get a peek at what's in walls by removing electrical-outlet coverplates and shining a flashlight into the space where the drywall or plaster meets the electrical box.

Look Up or Down
Drilling a hole up into the wall cavity from the basement or down through the top plate from the attic may be helpful. A piece of wire bent into a hook is a helpful probing tool.

Cut a Small Hole
This last resort should be done in a location that will go unnoticed once patched up. Cut a neat hole with a drywall saw—a small square or rectangle will be easiest to replace—and keep the piece to use later as a patch.

Out with the Old

If your walls are filled with old insulation and your remodeling plans don't involve gutting the house, then you can either add rigid insulation to the exterior of the house (see the sidebar on the facing page) or, in some cases, surgically remove the old insulation.

Vermiculite can be removed by drilling a hole through the wall at the bottom of the stud cavity and letting gravity empty the stud bays. In balloon-framed houses, which have wall studs that run continuously from the foundation to the roofline, blocking in the basement can be removed to access the stud cavities above.

Batts or dense fibrous insulations can be removed by cutting a "bellyband," in which a narrow strip of wall is removed about 4 ft. from the floor (this can be done from the exterior as well). With this strip of wall open, the batts can be pulled out—a homemade hook helps—and new insulation can be blown or poured into the cavities through the same openings before they are patched.

COTTON BATTS, 1935 TO 1950

What is it? Made of a naturally grown material, cotton batts are treated to be flame resistant.

Positive ID This white insulation is dense, but still fluffy. It's not as refined as cotton balls; instead, it's likely to have more of a pilly, fuzzy appearance. Although several companies manufactured cotton batts, one of the most popular seems to have been Lockport Cotton Batting. Look for a product name (Lo-K) and company logo on the batts' paper facing.

Health note Cotton is all natural and is perfectly safe to touch, but don't remove the batts or otherwise disturb the insulation without wearing at least a nuisance dust mask or respirator to protect your lungs. Also, cotton by nature is absorbent, so if it gets wet, it will take time to dry.

Upgrade outlook The growing popularity of green-building materials has sparked renewed interest in cotton batts. Although these modern versions of cotton batting, often referred to as "blue-jean insulation," have an R-value of R-3.5 to R-4 per in., there is some controversy over the R-value of the old versions. Some sources claim the old products perform similarly to the modern versions, and others estimate the R-value to be as low as R-0.5 per in. Considering the density of the old cotton batts, such a low R-value seems unlikely.

Justin Fink is a senior editor of Fine Homebuilding.

Upgrade Options: Foam

Rigid Foam Always Works

It doesn't matter how the walls were built, what type of insulation they have now, or how many obstructions are hidden in the wall cavities: Rigid-foam panels installed over the exterior side of the walls are always an option. However, installation is not as easy as cutting the lightweight panels with a utility knife and nailing them to the framing, though that's part of it.

Rigid foam must be applied directly to the framing or sheathing, or on top of the existing siding, then covered with new siding. In any case, you are faced with a full re-siding job and maybe a siding tearoff. Also, depending on the added thickness of the panels, windows and doors might need to be furred out, and roof rakes and eaves extended. As long as the installation is detailed carefully, though, the result is wall cavities that stay warm and dry, allowing your existing insulation to perform its best.

Panels are available in 2-ft. by 8-ft. or 4-ft. by 8-ft. sheets, and range from ½ in. to 2 in. in thickness. Vapor permeability is determined by the type of foam and the presence of a facing. Panels faced with foil or plastic are class-I vapor retarders (also called vapor barriers) and should not be used if the house has poly sheeting or an equivalent vapor retarder under the drywall. Unfaced or fiberglass-faced panels allow water vapor to pass and won't be problematic in combination with a class-I retarder.

EXPANDED POLYSTYRENE (EPS)

These white, closed-cell panels are made from the same polystyrene beads used in disposable coffee cups. EPS is the least expensive option (45¢ per sq. ft. for 1-in. thickness) and has the lowest R-value of the group (about R-4 per in.). Some EPS is unfaced, which makes it more fragile to handle but also allows the passage of water vapor. Unfaced EPS should be installed in combination with #15 felt paper or housewrap.

EXTRUDED POLYSTYRENE (XPS)

XPS falls in the middle of the three types of rigid-foam insulation in terms of cost and performance. Easy to spot by its blue, pink, or green color, XPS is slightly more expensive than EPS (50¢ per sq. ft. for 1-in. thickness) and also offers better performance (about R-5 per in.). Panels are commonly unfaced, and though water-vapor transmission slows on thicker panels, all XPS panels greater than 1 in. thick are considered class-II vapor retarders, which allow water vapor to pass.

POLYISOCYANURATE (POLYISO)

This is the most expensive type of rigid foam (about 80¢ per sq. ft. for 1-in. thickness), but also the best insulator (about R-6.5). Polyiso is a popular choice for retrofit applications because it packs more insulation into a thin package—less hassle for detailing windows and doors. All polyiso boards are faced, most with foil, which retards the flow of water vapor.

SOURCES

www.owenscorning.com
www.polarcentral.com
www.styrofoam.com

Pour Foam Is the Most Thorough

This water- or HFC- (hydrofluorocarbon) blown mixture is injected into the wall cavity from either the interior or the exterior through two or more ¾-in.- to 1-in.-dia. holes. The foam flows to the bottom of the stud cavity, where it slowly expands upward, surrounding even the most complicated plumbing and electrical obstructions, and filling every gap to create an airtight wall assembly.

Pour foam follows the path of least resistance as it expands, so the bottoms of stud cavities (in the basement or crawlspace) need to be sealed in balloon-framed houses. Old houses with siding installed directly over the studs will likely have foam squeeze-out between siding courses, which must be removed with a paint scraper once cured.

Blowouts or distortions in drywall, plaster, or siding are also possible, although this is typically not a concern if the foam is installed by trained professionals. Still, this is the reason why most pour-foam companies don't sell directly to the public, instead relying on a network of trained installers. Tiger Foam®, on the other hand, sells disposable do-it-yourself kits to homeowners.

Pour foam

Although there are videos on the Internet showing pour foam being injected into wall cavities that have fiberglass insulation—compressing the batts against the wallboard or sheathing—most manufacturers do not recommend this practice. The pour foam could bond to individual strands of fiberglass and tear it apart as it expands, creating voids. Tiger Foam is the exception, but the company recommends the use of a long fill tube to control the injection.

Installation from the exterior requires removal of some clapboards or shingles. Installation from the inside is easier, but requires more prep work (moving furniture, wall art, drapes, etc.). Homeowners can expect a slight odor after installation and for the day following; proper ventilation is a must.

Homeowners can plan to spend from $2 to $6 per sq. ft. of wall area for a professional installation, depending on job specifics and foam choice. Tiger Foam's do-it-yourself kits sell for about $4 to $7 per sq. ft., depending on quantity. Open-cell foams—which are more permeable to water-vapor transmission—are about R-4 per in.; closed-cell, around R-6 per in.

SOURCES
www.demilecusa.com
www.fomo.com
www.icynene.com
www.polymaster.com
www.tigerfoam.com

Rigid foam

Upgrade Options: Blown-In

The Most Common Approach

This method begins with compressed packs of dry cellulose or fiberglass, which are dumped into the hopper of a blowing machine, where they are agitated and loosened. A 1-in.- to 2-in.-dia. hose runs from the blowing machine through a hole in the interior or exterior side of the wall and is lowered to the bottom of the stud cavity. The installation process usually involves either one hole at the top of each cavity and a long fill tube that is withdrawn as the insulation fills the space, or a "double-blow" method, where two holes are used—one about 4 ft. from the floor and a second near the top of the wall.

Both cellulose and fiberglass do a good job of surrounding typical plumbing and electrical utilities routed through the wall, but the finished density of the insulation is crucial. Cellulose that's installed too loosely will settle and create voids in the wall, and fiberglass that's packed too densely will not offer the performance you paid for.

Cellulose

Cellulose

This insulation is made from 80% post-consumer recycled newspaper and is treated with nontoxic borates to resist fire and mold. It's a good choice because of its balance among cost, thermal performance, and environmentally friendly characteristics. Also, unlike fiberglass insulation, cellulose doesn't rely only on its ability to trap air to stop heat flow. Cellulose can be packed tightly into a wall cavity to resist airflow—a practice called "dense-packing"—yielding an R-value of R-3 to R-4 per in.

Although blowing loose-fill cellulose into attics is a pretty straightforward process (and is touted as a good do-it-yourself project), dense-packing is more complicated. As the material is blown into the cavity, the blowing machine bogs down, letting the installer know to pull back the hose a bit. This process repeats until the wall is packed full of cellulose. Although it is possible to pack cellulose too densely, the more common problem is not packing it densely enough. Most blowing machines that are available as rentals are designed for blowing loose cellulose in an open attic. These machines aren't powerful enough to pack cellulose into a wall cavity, and unpacked cellulose can settle and leave voids. The Cellulose Insulation Manufacturers Association (www.cellulose.org) recommends that dense-pack cellulose be installed only by trained professionals with more powerful blowing machines. Material prices are about 25¢ per sq. ft. of wall space.

Finally, if soaked with water, cellulose is likely to settle, leaving voids. Then again, if there's liquid water in the wall cavity, voids in the insulation will be the least of your worries, and the least of your expenses.

Fiberglass

Fiberglass

This loose-fill insulation is made from molten glass that is spun into loose fibers. The material is available in two forms, either as a by-product of manufacturing traditional fiberglass batts and rolls, or from "prime" fibers produced especially for blowing applications. In either case, the material is noncombustible, will not absorb water, and is inorganic, so it will not support mold growth.

Fiberglass resists heat flow by trapping pockets of air between fibers, so the insulation must be left fluffy to take advantage of the air-trapping nature of the material. The R-value (typically between R-2.5 and R-4) is dependent not only on the thickness of the wall cavity but also on the density at which the insulation is installed. For information on ensuring that the fiberglass is installed to provide the stated R-value, visit the North American Insulation Manufacturer's Association (www.naima.org) for a free overview.

Because fiberglass doesn't need to be blown to such high densities, it's a more user-friendly installation for nonprofessionals. On the other hand, loose fiberglass is not as readily available as cellulose, which is often a stock item at home-improvement centers. Finally, fiberglass advocates contend that their product won't absorb water and that cellulose will—though fiberglass will still sag if it becomes wet. Material prices are about 45¢ per sq. ft. of wall space.

SOURCES
www.certainteed.com
www.greenfiber.com
www.johnsmanville.com
www.knaufusa.com
www.owenscorning.com

All You Need to Know about Spray Foam

■ BY ROB YAGID

I recently spent a day pulling wire with a friend who's an electrician in New York. Late in the afternoon, our conversation turned to a client and friend of his who was seeking advice about insulating her new home. The topic caught the interest of some other guys on site, most from different trades, who gathered around and offered their opinions on which material she should use. After a brief debate, everyone seemed confident that spray foam would yield the best performance. That was until I threw out the question, "Which type?" Sure, they all knew there were two types of spray polyurethane foam, open cell and closed cell, but no one knew enough about them to step up and defend the use of one over the other. The truth is, neither did I.

Spray polyurethane-foam manufacturers have a relatively easy job when it comes to marketing their products because of one key statistic. According to the U.S. Department of Energy, 30% or more of a home's heating and cooling costs are attributed to air leakage. Spray polyurethane foam, or spray foam as it's most often called, is an effective air barrier and significantly reduces energy loss. Combined with a higher R-value than most other forms of insulation, it's no wonder spray foam is often relied on to help make houses ultraefficient. Choosing to insulate your home with spray foam doesn't guarantee that it'll perform to its full potential. Different climates, construction practices, and wall and roof assemblies benefit from different types of foam. The installation of foam at specific thicknesses is critical when you're trying to get the most performance for the money.

It Won't Settle, and It Doesn't Off-Gas Toxic Chemicals

Because of the urea-formaldehyde foam used to insulate homes in the 1970s, which could degrade and off-gas unsafe formaldehyde, spray foam is often perceived as being un-healthful and poorly performing. Installers that look as if they're outfitted to survive a

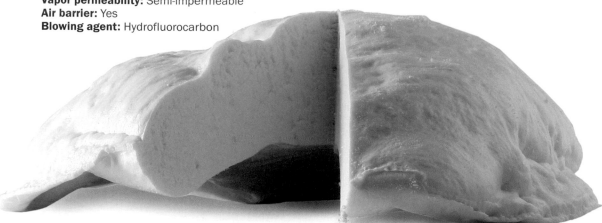

CLOSED CELL
Density: 2 lb. per cu. ft.
R-value: 6 per in. (aged)
Vapor permeability: Semi-impermeable
Air barrier: Yes
Blowing agent: Hydrofluorocarbon

To get the full benefit of this superinsulation, you must understand the difference between open- and closed-cell foams, how they perform, and which to use.

nuclear catastrophe perpetuate the misconception that spray foam is toxic.

The fact is that when it's installed properly, spray foam is more physically stable than the studs and sheathing it's adhered to. The oxygen-supplied respirators and head-to-toe protective suits installers wear are necessary only to keep the chemicals that make up spray foam out of their lungs and off their skin during installation.

The blowing agent, a gas that expands the foam's cells to give it volume, receives a lot of scrutiny. Over time, from three months to a year, a portion of the blowing agent in closed-cell foam evaporates into the air. Prior to 2003, chlorofluorocarbon and hydrochlorofluorocarbon blowing agents were in widespread use. These gases are damaging to the atmosphere. The U.S. Environmental Protection Agency has banned the use of those chemicals and recognized the current hydrofluorocarbon (HFC) blowing agent as a safe alternative.

Open-cell foam, which uses water as its blowing agent, emits carbon dioxide as it expands. But manufacturers claim that the amount of carbon dioxide released from the foam has a limited impact on the environment. The Spray Polyurethane Foam Alliance is currently testing this issue.

The Open-Cell vs. Closed-Cell Debate

In most closed-cell foams, such as those made by Corbond®, an HFC blowing agent is captured in the foam's cell structure. This gas has a better thermal performance than the air-filled open-cell foam and gives it a higher overall R-value. However, while HFC-blown closed-cell foam might initially have an R-value as high as R-8 per in., its R-value diminishes as the blowing agent evaporates through cell walls and is replaced by air. Closed-cell foam's "aged" R-value is roughly R-6 per in. Some manufacturers produce water-blown closed-cell foams. These foams have the same performance properties as HFC-blown foam, but slightly lower R-values, at around R-5.5 per in.

Closed-cell foam's greater density, 2 lb. per cu. ft. compared with open cell's ½ lb. per cu. ft., also increases its R-value and offers it the rigidity that open-cell foam lacks. Tests at the National Association of Home Builders research center confirmed that closed-cell foam can actually increase the shear strength of conventionally framed walls by 30%. Closed-cell foam also has a low vapor-permeability rating (roughly 0.5 perms at a thickness of 3 in.) and is considered a class-II vapor retarder, meaning it's semi-impermeable.

OPEN CELL
Density: ½ lb. per cu. ft.
R-value: 3.5 per in.
Vapor permeability: Permeable
Air barrier: Yes
Blowing agent: Water

Open-cell foam, made by companies such as Icynene® and Demilec®, has a greater expansion rate than closed-cell foam. It expands 100 times its initial volume (closed-cell foam expands only 30 times its initial volume), so less of the foam is needed to insulate a house.

Open cell's one major weakness is its lower R-value, roughly R-3.5 per in. This means that when used in a 2×4 exterior wall, it will create an assembly that's approximately only R-12, which won't meet code in most parts of the country.

Installing Lots of Foam Isn't as Effective as You Think

A lot of energy-conscious architects and builders shoot for the highest R-values they can possibly attain: R-40 walls and an R-60 roof. However, R-values aren't necessarily an accurate reflection of overall thermal performance. For example, you would think that an R-40 wall full of spray foam would perform twice as well as a wall sprayed to R-20 with the same foam, but that's not the case.

Chris Porter, the building-science and code manager for BioBased Insulation®, explains that "open-cell foam reaches a point of diminishing returns at around

Proper prep yields the best installation. While spray foam is installed by a pro, it's your responsibility to prep the site. Masking windows, electrical boxes, and even floors is important if you want the foam contained to wall, roof, and floor cavities. Anyone on site during the installation should be outfitted for optimum protection.

5 in. That threshold is even lower for closed-cell foam, which experiences diminishing returns at around 3 in. or 4 in." Those thicknesses create assemblies between R-20 and R-24, which by the numbers seem a little weak. Each additional inch of spray foam

More Than One Way to Use Spray Foam: Two Experts Weigh In

Most experts agree that spray polyurethane foam is a revolutionary product. What they don't always agree on is the way it's installed and integrated into a building assembly. To shed some light on this debate, energy-efficient building expert Bruce Harley (Westborough, Mass.) and architect Peter Pfeiffer (Austin, Texas) explain how they use spray polyurethane foam to insulate the homes they build.

BRUCE HARLEY

Spray foam can be a great material, but understanding its use is often hindered by overeager installers who emphasize the magic rather than the real properties of the products.

Too often, I hear from clients that "my dealer said that I only need 2 in. to 4 in. of foam in my walls because it performs just like R-40 fiberglass and prevents any possible moisture problems." It's just not true. An R-12 wall is an R-12 wall, no matter what the material is. Cutting air leakage saves energy, but it doesn't make up for a low R-value.

For best performance, I use spray foam in a variety of ways when designing the shell of a home. Here's one example.

Bruce Harley of Conservation Services Group is an energy-efficient construction expert and author of Cut Your Energy Bills Now *(The Taunton Press, 2008).*

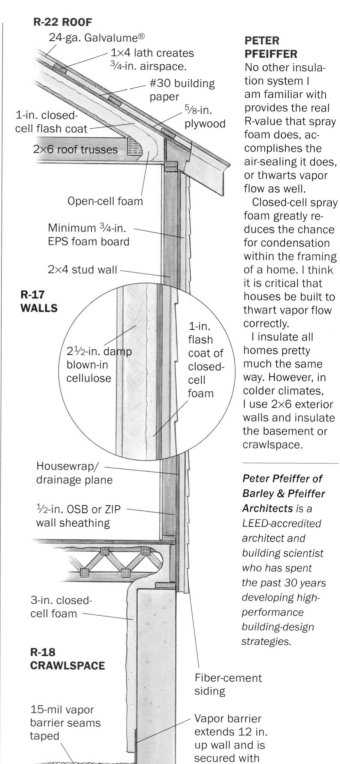

R-42 ROOF
2×10 rafters
⅝-in. OSB
#30 building paper under asphalt shingles
6-in. closed-cell foam
Mineral-wool batts
2×6 stud wall
½-in. OSB
⅜-in. furring strips over housewrap
R-19 WALLS
Fiber-cement siding
Insulated rim joist
Non-paper-faced drywall over 2×4 stud wall
R-19 BASEMENT
2-in. space
5½-in. layer of open-cell foam
Damp proofing
Concrete slab over 2-in. XPS foam

R-22 ROOF
24-ga. Galvalume®
1×4 lath creates ¾-in. airspace.
#30 building paper
1-in. closed-cell flash coat
⅝-in. plywood
2×6 roof trusses
Open-cell foam
Minimum ¾-in. EPS foam board
2×4 stud wall
R-17 WALLS
2½-in. damp blown-in cellulose
1-in. flash coat of closed-cell foam
Housewrap/drainage plane
½-in. OSB or ZIP wall sheathing
3-in. closed-cell foam
R-18 CRAWLSPACE
15-mil vapor barrier seams taped
Fiber-cement siding
Vapor barrier extends 12 in. up wall and is secured with mastic.

PETER PFEIFFER

No other insulation system I am familiar with provides the real R-value that spray foam does, accomplishes the air-sealing it does, or thwarts vapor flow as well.

Closed-cell spray foam greatly reduces the chance for condensation within the framing of a home. I think it is critical that houses be built to thwart vapor flow correctly.

I insulate all homes pretty much the same way. However, in colder climates, I use 2×6 exterior walls and insulate the basement or crawlspace.

Peter Pfeiffer of Barley & Pfeiffer Architects is a LEED-accredited architect and building scientist who has spent the past 30 years developing high-performance building-design strategies.

Spray Foam for the Eco-Conscious

Consuming fossil fuels to make products intended to conserve fossil fuels makes little sense to a lot of people. All spray foams contain a certain level of petroleum in their A component and in their B component. Manufacturers such as BioBased Insulation, Demilec, and Icynene have created more environmentally benign spray-foam products by reducing the amount of petroleum used in their B component. They replace a portion of the polyol resin, which makes up 20% to 30% of the B component, with a renewable resource such as soybean or castor-bean oil. Apex even has a sucrose-based polyol. Manufacturers say that the transition to bean oil or sucrose doesn't alter the look or the performance of open- or closed-cell foam in any way.

The amount of soybean, castor bean, or sucrose found in foam varies by manufacturer, so identifying the "greenest" foam might not be so easy. According to the U.S. Department of Agriculture, only 7% of a spray-foam product needs to be made of a renewable resource to be labeled as a bio-based foam. This, of course, doesn't factor in the petroleum fueling the crop-cultivation process.

Hardworking crops. The oil from soybeans, which is also being considered to create alternative forms of energy, is replacing the petroleum in some spray foams.

Sources

Although this is not a complete list of spray-foam manufacturers, it is representative of the larger national companies. For assistance in finding a spray-foam insulation contractor, visit the Spray Polyurethane Foam Alliance at www.sprayfoam.org.

BASF®:
www.basf.com

BioBased:
www.biobased.net

CertainTeed®:
www.certainteed.com

Chemical Design:
www.chemicaldesign
corp.net

Corbond:
www.corbond.com

Demilec:
www.demilecusa.com

Foametix®:
www.foametix.com

Fomo Products:
www.fomo.com

Great Stuff™:
www.greatstuff.dow
.com

Icynene:
www.icynene.com

NCFI:
www.ncfi.com

Tiger Foam:
www.tigerfoam.com

Touch 'n Seal®:
www.touch-n-seal.com

**Urethane Soy
Systems:**
www.soyol.com

**Versi-Foam®
Systems:**
www.rhhfoamsystems
.com

yields little performance. In fact, while the cost of an R-40 wall is indeed double that of an R-20 wall (not factoring in the construction materials used to create deeper cavities for the extra foam), it reduces the heat flow through a wall by only an additional 2%. For this reason, Porter says that in most parts of the country, 6 in. of foam—be it open or closed cell—is perfectly adequate.

Spray foam is priced based on board feet. Manufacturers don't price their product. Instead, cost is determined by installers. The spray-foam market is extremely competitive, and spray-foam prices can be astonishingly inconsistent. North Carolina builder Michael Chandler recommends getting as many bids as possible. "I've received quotes from $6,800 to $13,500 for the same exact job," Chandler says. "Prices vary so much that it may actually pay to have a truck drive two hours to do the job rather than have the local guy spray it." The message: Search far and wide for the installer that suits your needs and your budget.

Rob Yagid is an associate editor at Fine Homebuilding.

Making Sense of Housewraps

■ BY FERNANDO PAGÉS RUIZ

When I started building houses nearly 30 years ago, we lapped lightweight #15 asphalt- or rosin-impregnated building paper directly over the stud framing before installing the siding. Nowadays, concerns with energy-efficient construction and moisture infiltration have focused a great deal of attention and no small amount of high-tech chemistry on this thin layer of paper. Although some builders still advocate the felt-paper barriers of yesteryear, most have switched to plastic-based housewraps, products designed to stop air infiltration and wind-driven rain while allowing water vapor to evaporate—a great concept.

However, like everything high-tech, new solutions come with new problems. The range of choices and the precise installation requirements of modern housewraps challenge builders with terms like spun-bonded, polyolefin-based moisture, and air-infiltration fabric. Even if the technical terminology is hard to remember, learning how to install these products correctly is important. Yet a quick look around a construction site reveals that most builders, with thirty years or with three behind the hammer, are having a hard time handling this new technology.

There's plenty of confusion surrounding weather-resistive barriers. Many homeowners and builders don't know which product to choose, some builders never learned how to install it correctly, and many have no idea what housewrap does in the first place.

What Does a Housewrap Do?

Placed beneath the siding, housewrap is a second layer of defense for your home. When installed properly, it performs three basic functions (see the drawing on the facing page).

First and foremost, housewrap acts as a backup barrier that keeps water off the structural sheathing and framing. Properly installed siding is the first line of defense, but sometimes wind-driven rain and snow still find a way through. Housewrap also functions as an air barrier that stops hot- and cold-air movement through the wall cavity. As long as joints are sealed properly, housewrap is designed to cut utility costs and increase comfort by reducing air infiltration and potential drafts.

The real magic of housewrap lies in its third function: allowing the free passage of water vapor so that wall cavities and framing lumber can dry to the outside of the building, reducing the threat of mold and rot. Without this feature, installing housewrap would be like putting a thick raincoat over your house: great for keeping out the rain, but terrible at releasing water vapor from within. Instead, housewraps are designed to act like a Gore-Tex® jacket, allowing water vapor to pass through the building envelope in case moisture problems arise.

A Side-by-Side Comparison Is Often Pointless

Nowadays, any approved weather-resistive barrier, from #15 felt to high-tech housewrap, touts the dual benefit of being a weather-resistive drainage plane that also allows the passage of water vapor. But not every product balances these two features equally. To add to this confusion, housewraps are now available in dozens of varieties, so how do you choose? Unfortunately, there's no easy answer.

The American Society for Testing and Materials (ASTM) is working to standardize the tests used to evaluate weather-resistive barriers. For now, when trying to gain code approval, manufacturers can choose from at least two dozen different tests. Even if two manufacturers choose the same test, though, there is nothing to regulate the way in which the test materials are set up. This variability makes it nearly impossible to compare one product's performance to another's.

According to Paul Fisette, director of building materials and wood technology at the University of Massachusetts, one tested value that usually stands up to side-by-side comparison is a material's permeance rating, but sometimes even that can be misleading.

The Three Functions of Housewrap

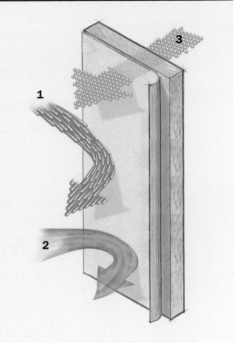

1. Create a **secondary weather barrier** behind the siding, preventing wind-driven rain and other water from reaching the sheathing.

2. Serve as an **air barrier** to prevent air infiltration, helping to reduce heating and cooling costs.

3. Provide a **vapor-permeable membrane** that allows moisture in framing lumber or insulation to escape.

Perm Ratings Tell Part of the Story

Permeance ratings, or perms, reflect the measure of a material's ability to transfer water vapor; the higher the perm number, the more permeable the material. For instance, 6-mil polyethylene sheeting has a very low perm rating of 0.06, which means that it prevents the passage of nearly all water vapor. Current building codes require a weather-resistive barrier to match or exceed grade-D building paper, which has a perm rating of about 5.0. To meet this requirement, perm ratings for commonly available brands of housewrap range from about 5.0 for Dow®'s Weathermate™ to 58.0 for Tyvek®'s HomeWrap®.

Materials with higher perm ratings speed the escape of trapped moisture. But higher ratings do not necessarily equal better housewraps, because the methods of achieving a high perm rating can be different.

For instance, some low-tech housewraps achieve their high perm ratings with mechanically punched perforations in the membrane. These perforations increase the passage of water vapor, but they also make the housewrap more susceptible to bulk-water leakage.

On the other hand, more-advanced non-perforated housewraps, such as HomeWrap and R-Wrap®, offer even greater moisture-vapor transmission (higher perms) than their perforated counterparts. They are also more effective at preventing the movement of bulk water.

Independent Tests Yield Clear Performance Comparisons

Fisette conducted independent testing of housewrap not to establish quantifiable data that mimicked real-world performance, but rather to subject the products to a set of simple laboratory conditions to see how they compared. For more on Fisette's testing, see www.umass.edu/bmatwt/publications.

According to Fisette's research, the best housewraps (those that resist water infiltration and also permit water vapor to evaporate) include Tyvek HomeWrap, R-Wrap by Berry Plastics™ Corporation, Typar® (manufactured in 2003 or later), and—believe it or not—traditional #15 felt paper (see the sidebar on p. 75).

I prefer Tyvek, which scored well for resisting water penetration in the Massachusetts study while also having one of the industry's highest perm ratings for water-vapor diffusion. Although #15 felt paper costs less and scores well in all categories, I like housewrap products because the variety of sizes available (3-ft. to 10-ft. widths) really speeds up the installation process. Also, the compatible sealing tapes and accessories make housewrap a superior air barrier compared to felt paper.

Housewrap

Nonwoven

Woven

HomeWrap
(DuPont™)

Type: Nonwoven polyolefin
Perm rating: 58.0
Notes: The first housewrap on the market more than 30 years ago; accounts for 70% of total house-wrap sales; highest perm rating. 800-448-9835; www.tyvek.com

PinkWrap®
(Owens Corning)

Type: Perforated, woven polyolefin
Perm rating: 14.0
Notes: Translucent membrane makes it easy to see where to nail siding. 800-438-7465; www.pinkwrap.com

StuccoWrap®
(DuPont)

Type: Nonwoven polyolefin
Perm rating: 50.0
Notes: Designed specifically for use under traditional- and synthetic-stucco applications; helps to reduce cracking because it won't absorb water or expand and contract. Surface texture channels water. www.tyvek.com

Typar (Fiberweb®)

Type: Nonwoven polyolefin
Perm rating: 11.7
Notes: Excellent protection against surfactants, making it ideal for use under stucco or cedar siding; guaranteed to be tear-resistant. 800-284-2780; www.typarhousewrap.com

Siding Often Determines the Type of Housewrap

When you're using vinyl siding, which comes with built-in drainage holes and fits on the wall loosely, an ordinary smooth-faced housewrap provides good drainage. But with tightly fastened board siding, any water trapped between the siding and a smooth housewrap will sit and eventually could make its way through the housewrap and into the framing. Remember, although many housewraps are good at resisting bulk water, they should not be considered waterproof.

In these cases, it's a good idea to choose a furrowed rain-screen housewrap. Its embossed texture provides just enough airspace for liquid water to drain away before it has a chance to penetrate the membrane (see "Rain screen and housewrap combined," p. 76).

When applying stucco, choose a housewrap designed specifically for stucco and masonry, such as DuPont's StuccoWrap or Benjamin Obdyke's Mortairvent®, which not only provide a corrugated surface but also are compatible with the chemicals in stucco.

Housewrap Choices continued

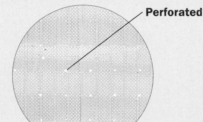

Perforated

Weathermate Plus (Dow)
Type: Nonwoven polyolefin
Perm rating: 6.7
Notes: Membrane has a more substantial, foamlike texture compared to other housewraps.
866-583-2583;
www.dow.com/styrofoam

Weathermate (Dow)
Type: Perforated, woven polyolefin
Perm rating: >5.0
Notes: Translucent; perforated products are less resistant to water intrusion; does not meet the air-barrier requirement of the National Building Code of Canada.
866-583-2583;
www.dow.com/styrofoam

Barricade® (Berry Plastics Corporation)
Type: Perforated, woven polyolefin
Perm rating: 9.0
Notes: Translucent; perforated products are less resistant to water intrusion; resists UV-degradation for 12 months.
877-832-0333;
www.berryplastics.com

I Still Prefer Felt Paper

Based on my lab testing at the University of Massachusetts, if I were buying housewrap today, I likely would choose a nonperforated product because it displays the best water resistance.

As it happens, I have felt paper on my own home. If I could do it over again and choose between felt and housewrap, I'd still choose felt. That's because I believe that under certain circumstances, felt paper outperforms housewrap.

For example, an ice dam or a roof leak might allow liquid water to get behind the felt or housewrap. It's also possible for the sun's heat to drive water vapor through the housewrap from the outside, where it can condense on the sheathing. In either case, you have liquid water on the wrong side of the wrap. Under these conditions, the liquid water is trapped by the housewrap, which is permeable only to diffusion of water vapor. Felt, on the other hand, absorbs water and dries more quickly to the outside.

**Paul Fisette** is director of building materials and wood technology at the University of Massachusetts.

R-Wrap
(Berry Plastics Corporation)
Type: Nonwoven polyolefin
Perm rating: 56.0
Notes: Membrane can be installed with printed logo in or out without change in performance; manufacturer will replace product if damaged by wind. 877-832-0333; www.berryplastics.com

GreenGuard® Value
(Pactiv® Corporation)
Type: Perforated, woven polyolefin
Perm rating: 15.0
Notes: Low-cost housewrap for the value-conscious builder. Resists UV-degradation for 12 months; translucent membrane makes it easy to see where to nail siding. 800-241-4402; www.green-guard.com

GreenGuard Classic
(Pactiv Corporation)
Type: Perforated, woven polyolefin
Perm rating: 15.0
Notes: Resists UV-degradation for 12 months. Highly tear-resistant; translucent, glare-reducing green color. 800-241-4402; www.green-guard.com

GreenGuard Ultra
(Pactiv Corporation)
Type: Nonwoven polyolefin
Perm rating: 48.0
Notes: Uses a reinforcing scrim that makes it highly tear-resistant. Translucent membrane makes it easy to see where to nail siding. 800-241-4402; www.green-guard.com

Housewraps Are Susceptible to Certain Chemicals

Builders have debated the chemical compatibility of housewrap for years. Studies have found that certain types of wood siding, like cedar and redwood, leach surfactants (surface-active contaminants) that can affect the water resistance of housewraps. The surfactants reduce the surface tension of water, easing its ability to pass through microscopic openings in the membrane. To combat the problem, manufacturers recommend back-priming potentially troublesome wood siding with a water-repellent primer. In a limited study, Fisette found that the newest version of Typar had superior resistance to surfactants compared to the performance of similar products.

In addition to the water-soluble extractives found in wood siding, the water resistance of housewrap also can be compromised by soaps, power-washing chemicals, and even some types of latex paints. The perforated variety is most susceptible, so consider choosing a high-quality, nonperforated housewrap.

It's also important not to leave housewrap exposed for longer than necessary. Housewrap left uncovered for longer than its intended UV-rating will deteriorate and decline in performance, and should be

---

Housewrap Choices continued

Rain screen and housewrap combined

No matter how tight the joints, how thorough the flashing installation, or how far the roof overhangs the walls, water always finds a way behind the siding of a house.

Housewrap or felt paper is a good safeguard for protecting sheathing and framing, but many builders also add a ¼-in. to ⅜-in. drainage plane between the housewrap and the siding by tacking up vertical furring strips. This vented space allows moisture to dissipate naturally so that paint won't peel prematurely, surfactants from the siding won't be in contact with the housewrap, and bulk water won't be trapped behind the siding with nowhere to drain.

Several manufacturers have started combining the water-shedding benefits of rain-screen-wall construction with the ease of installation and the added benefits found in typical housewrap, creating a separate category sometimes referred to as "drainscreen."

To the right are a few different designs that aim to accomplish the same basic task.

DrainWrap™ (DuPont)
Type: Nonwoven polyolefin
Perm rating: 50.0
Notes: Uses accordion-style vertical grooves to channel water. Because the product behaves like wrinkly housewrap, it isn't as rigid as other rain-screen products. 800-448-9835; www.tyvek.com

Weatherproofing Comes with Workmanship

Here's the bottom line: Installation is more important than material choice. No matter what brand of housewrap you choose, you will be wasting money unless the stuff is installed carefully.

Poorly installed housewrap will cause more problems than it solves. Getting the installation right is not hard, but it requires a basic understanding of how housewrap

covered with a fresh layer before siding is installed.

works. Detailed installation instructions can be found on manufacturers' websites and often at the lumberyard or home center where housewrap is purchased.

The basic installation premise is to think like a raindrop. Imagine a drop of water hitting the side of your house at the top of the wall. Gravity pulls the drop down along the face of the wall, and as long as all the courses, joints, tears, and penetrations are sealed and lapped in shingle fashion, the drop eventually will reach the ground. The moment that raindrop finds a puncture, a reverse lap, or an unflashed component, it will seep behind the housewrap and into the framing.

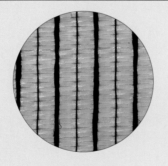

**Weather Trek®
(Berry Plastics
Corporation)**
Type: Perforated polyethylene
Perm rating: 6.5
Notes: A clever nondirectional surface pattern (reminiscent of the texture of a basketball) ensures that water drains easily, regardless of orientation to the sheathing. 877-832-0333; www.berryplastics.com

**GreenGuard
Raindrop®
(Pactiv Corporation)**
Type: Woven polyolefin
Perm rating: 10.0
Notes: Relies on drainage channels woven into the surface to direct water down and out. Channels must run vertically to be effective. 800-241-4402; www.green-guard.com

**Home Slicker®
(Benjamin Obdyke)**
This bound-nylon three-dimensional meshlike rain screen physically separates the housewrap and the siding. Three different versions are available (above, left to right): Home Slicker, Home Slicker Plus Typar (polyolefin housewrap), and Mortairvent (polypropylene matrix for masonry and stucco). 800-346-7655; www.benjaminobdyke.com

Seam Tape and Fasteners Are Vital to the System

It never ceases to amaze me how many builders omit seam tape from housewrap installations. Although proper lapping is enough to create a watershed, all seams must be sealed to stop air infiltration. Taping the seams also helps to preserve the housewrap's integrity throughout construction and makes the membrane less likely to catch the wind and tear.

Seam tape also provides a means to repair cuts, but every cut or penetration should always be treated like a horizontal or vertical seam. Seam tape is never used to make up for improper lapping. In fact, assume that the tape adhesive will fail eventually, allowing water to penetrate the drainage plane and wet the framing. In contrast, a proper lap can last forever.

Almost every housewrap manufacturer provides a seam tape for their product. Generic building tapes such as duct tape should be avoided because they might fail sooner.

Housewrap can be attached with plastic cap nails (see the photo, near right), 1-in.-wide crown staples, or large-head roofing nails. Many builders use a hammer tacker to fasten the wrap with staples, but this type of fastener is much more likely to pull through the housewrap before the siding is installed.

For a better installation, manufacturers recommend the use of plastic cap nails or cap screws, which are available for manual fastening or collated for use in pneumatic nailers (see the photo, far right). Cap nails also act as a gasket to keep water from leaking through the nail holes.

Whatever fastener is used, the manufacturer's recommendations for spacing are important. The most common spacing is 8 in. to 18 in. vertically, and 16 in. to 24 in. horizontally. Fasteners should be driven into studs or sheathing such as plywood or OSB.

Hitachi NV50AP3
800-706-7337;
www.hitachipowertools.com
Cost: $400

Bostitch N66BC-1
800-556-6696;
www.bostitch.com
Cost: $320

Housewrap installation starts from the bottom and works its way up. All horizontal joints should overlap at least 6 in., and all vertical joints 12 in. If housewrap is applied to the sheathing before the wall is raised, there needs to be enough material left to cover the band joist. Horizontal laps are as important as vertical laps because wind-blown rain can travel sideways.

Housewrap should always be installed with the same care and attention devoted to siding. Although no one will see good work underneath the siding, correctly installed housewrap still pays off in the long run.

Fernando Pagés Ruiz operates Brighton Construction Co. in Lincoln, Neb. He is also the author of Building an Affordable House: Trade Secrets for High-Value, Low-Cost Construction (The Taunton Press, 2005).

Using Rigid Foam for an Efficient and Dry House

■ BY MARTIN HOLLADAY

Remodelers who open up fiberglass-insulated walls in the middle of the winter are often surprised to see a thin layer of frost on the interior side of the wall sheathing. The frost indicates that warm, humid interior air is leaking through the wall penetrations, leading to condensation on the cold surface of the sheathing.

One way to limit this phenomenon is to keep the sheathing warm by adding a layer of rigid-foam insulation on the exterior side of the sheathing. If there are no cold surfaces in the wall cavities, condensation is unlikely. A layer of exterior foam also makes a house more energy efficient by increasing insulating performance, reducing thermal bridging, and minimizing air leakage.

All three types of rigid-foam insulation—expanded polystyrene (EPS), extruded polystyrene (XPS), and polyisocyanurate—are suitable for use on the exterior of walls and roofs, though they do not perform equally. EPS is the most vapor permeable of the three types; at R-4, it also has the lowest R-value per inch. Foil-faced polyiso is the least vapor permeable and has the highest R-value per inch, at R-6.5. XPS (R-5 per in.) and the denser types of EPS can extend below grade, but polyiso absorbs water and therefore should not be installed in contact with soil.

Every wall needs a water-resistive barrier such as asphalt felt or housewrap. It's also possible to use rigid foam as a barrier, as long as foam seams are sealed with a suitable tape or installed with Z-flashing. Regardless of your choice of barrier, all penetrations, including windows and doors, need to be flashed properly; these flashings need to be integrated with the barrier using adequate overlaps or durable tapes.

Increase Insulation and Prevent Condensation

The benefits of adding a layer of rigid-foam insulation to the exterior of walls and roofs are twofold. First, the foam will increase thermal performance by adding R-value and minimizing thermal bridging. Second, the foam will keep the sheathing warm, so moisture passing through the wall or roof will find no cold surfaces for condensation to occur. For this reason, the roof does not need to be vented. That's why exterior roof foam makes a lot of sense on difficult-to-vent hipped roofs or on roofs with multiple dormers.

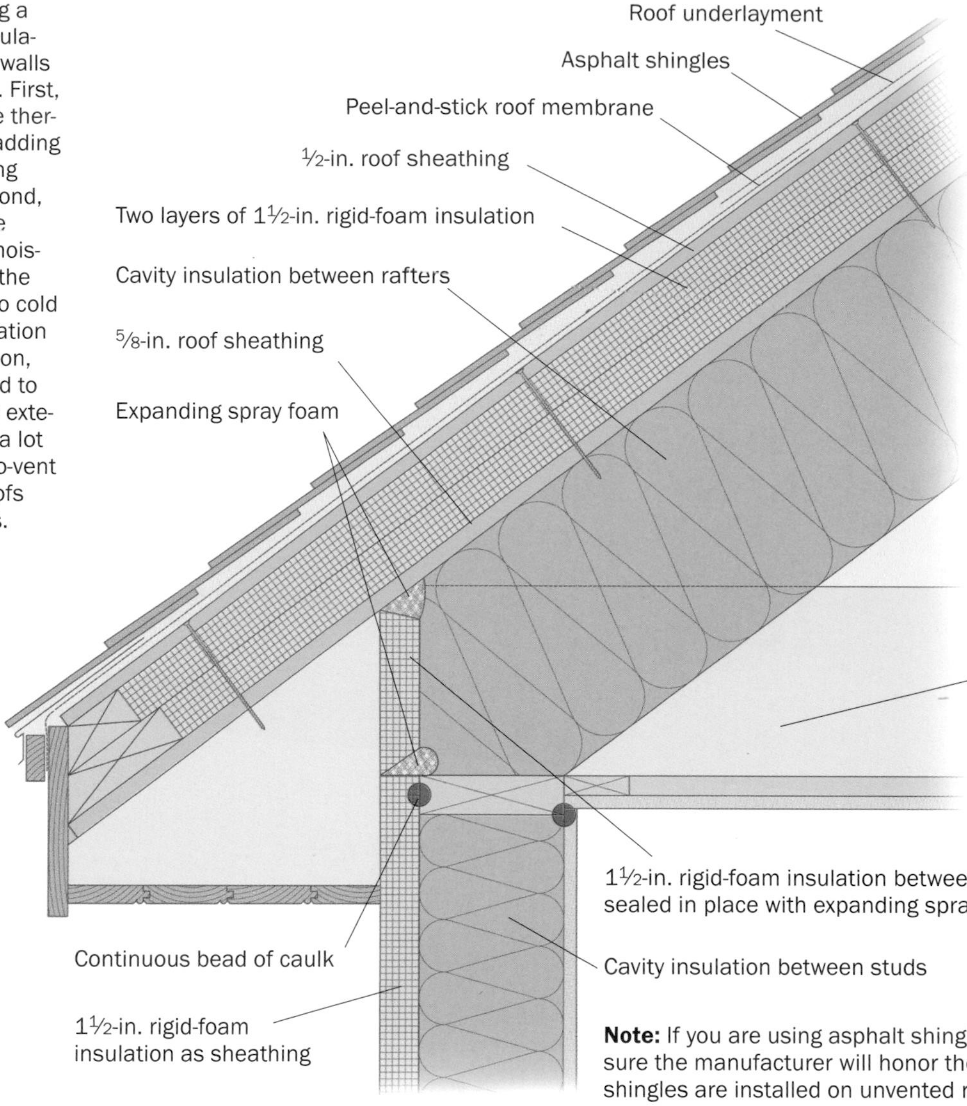

Roof underlayment

Asphalt shingles

Peel-and-stick roof membrane

½-in. roof sheathing

Two layers of 1½-in. rigid-foam insulation

Cavity insulation between rafters

⅝-in. roof sheathing

Expanding spray foam

Ceiling joist

1½-in. rigid-foam insulation between rafters and sealed in place with expanding spray foam

Cavity insulation between studs

Continuous bead of caulk

1½-in. rigid-foam insulation as sheathing

Note: If you are using asphalt shingles, make sure the manufacturer will honor the warranty if shingles are installed on unvented roofs.

Exterior Foam Is a Good Option

Adding exterior foam to walls works well for new construction. As long as you meet local wind and earthquake codes, it's usually possible to build a foam-sheathed wall without structural oriented strand board (OSB) or plywood sheathing. Foam-sheathed walls are braced using one of four methods:

• Diagonal 1×4 let-in braces.

• Diagonal T-profile steel strapping, such as Simpson TWB.

• Inset shear panels.

• A few strategically placed pieces of OSB (they are usually installed at corners).

Of course, you should check with an engineer and your local building official before finalizing your wall-bracing plan.

Exterior foam sheathing is often installed on existing homes as an energy-saving retrofit when new roofing or siding is need-ed. You can install rigid foam on the inside of a wall as well, but adding exterior foam increases the R-value of a wall or roof with-out eating up interior living space.

Installed on the roof, exterior foam makes the living space below more comfortable and reduces the likelihood of ice dams.

The illustration on the facing page shows two layers of OSB or plywood roof sheath-ing: a lower layer conventionally nailed to the rafters and an upper layer installed as a nailing surface for the roofing material on top of the rigid foam. The type of fasteners used and the way they need to be spaced for the top layer of sheathing depend on the pitch of the roof and roof loads, particularly wind and snow loads. It's fairly easy to find screws with a pullout-resistance rating ex-ceeding 400 lb., even when they are secured just to plywood or OSB sheathing. The fas-tener rating increases if the screws are driven into the rafters. (Fastener sources include Wind-lock® and FastenMaster®, which man-ufactures HeadLok® and OlyLog® screws.)

Most foam-sheathed walls include a rain-screen gap between the foam and the siding. After the foam is tacked in place temporarily with a few nails, it is secured in place with vertical 1×3 or 1×4 strapping that is screwed through the foam to the underlying studs. Some siding types, including cedar shingles, may require a drainage mat, kerfed horizon-tal furring, or an OSB or plywood nailer over the foam.

Does Exterior Foam Create a Wrong-Side Vapor Barrier?

Some builders worry that exterior foam sheathing is a "wrong-side vapor barrier" that can trap moisture in walls. In new construction without interior polyethylene vapor barriers, the worry is baseless. As long as the foam sheathing is thick enough, it will reduce the chance that moisture will accumulate in a wall. By warming the wall cavity, exterior foam eliminates cold surfaces where moisture can condense. Here are the minimum R-values for exterior foam for 2×6 walls:

- R-15 in climate zones 7 and 8
- R-11.25 in climate zone 6
- R-7.5 in climate zone 5
- R-3.75 in climate zone 4

When exterior rigid foam is used as an energy-saving detail in warmer climates, condensation is not a concern, so no mini-mum R-values apply.

Since exterior foam reduces a wall's abil-ity to dry to the exterior, foam-sheathed walls should be able to dry to the interior. That means that foam-sheathed walls should never include interior polyethylene or vinyl wallpaper. Painted drywall has a high enough permeance to allow any incidental moisture that enters a wall cavity in the win-ter to evaporate through the drywall during the summer.

If you are considering installing exterior foam on a house with interior 6-mil poly-ethylene, proceed with caution. If water ever enters a wall with foam sheathing and inte-rior poly, the wall has a very limited ability to dry. This raises the stakes, and water-management details must be impeccable.

After all the siding has been removed, inspect the existing wall sheathing for stains or moisture damage. If you find either, you'll need to diagnose the cause and implement remedies. If the existing sheathing is clean, dry, and sound, it's safe to install exterior wall foam, as long as the new siding is installed with a rain-screen gap and meticu-lous flashing.

Martin Holladay is a contributing editor to Fine Homebuilding.

Basement Insulation Retrofits

■ BY DANIEL S. MORRISON

Finished basements are a great way to add living space to a house without adding on. You often can add almost as much living space as the main floor offers. Before thinking about flooring choices and paint colors, though, think about the basics. Moisture, insulation, and air infiltration must be tackled before any finish materials are installed. In new construction, these issues are addressed from the outside before the basement is backfilled. Retrofits mean that you have to work from the inside. In either case, it is important to consider the climate before work begins.

Start with Water Management

Because basements are mostly buried in the ground, they are sometimes wet, are usually damp, and are seldom dry. Rarely do old houses have perimeter-drainage systems, insulation, or capillary breaks. When converting a basement to living space, the basement must manage moisture better than it did before the insulating and air-sealing, because

R-VALUE MINIMUMS BY CODE AND CLIMATE ZONE
Climate zones 6, 7: R-15
Climate zones 4, 5: R-10
Climate zone 2, 3: R-5

a tighter basement is less able to dry out when it becomes wet.

You can use grading to manage bulk groundwater on the outside, but foundations also have to disrupt capillarity. Water in the soil can and will wick up to the roof framing if you let it. Capillary breaks such as brush-on damp-proofing, sill sealer, and rigid insulation block this process.

Air-Sealing Saves Energy and Stops Moisture

The connection between concrete foundations and wood framing is almost always

Insulation Amount Depends on Location

The International Residential Code (IRC) specifies particular R-values for each climate zone; how you get there is up to you. For very cold climates, you may need to add extra thick rigid insulation or fill the stud cavities. Don't, however, treat a below-grade wall like a regular wall. Expect bulk-water problems, and choose insulation that can handle it. Never include a plastic vapor barrier when insulating a basement wall, because it will trap moisture.

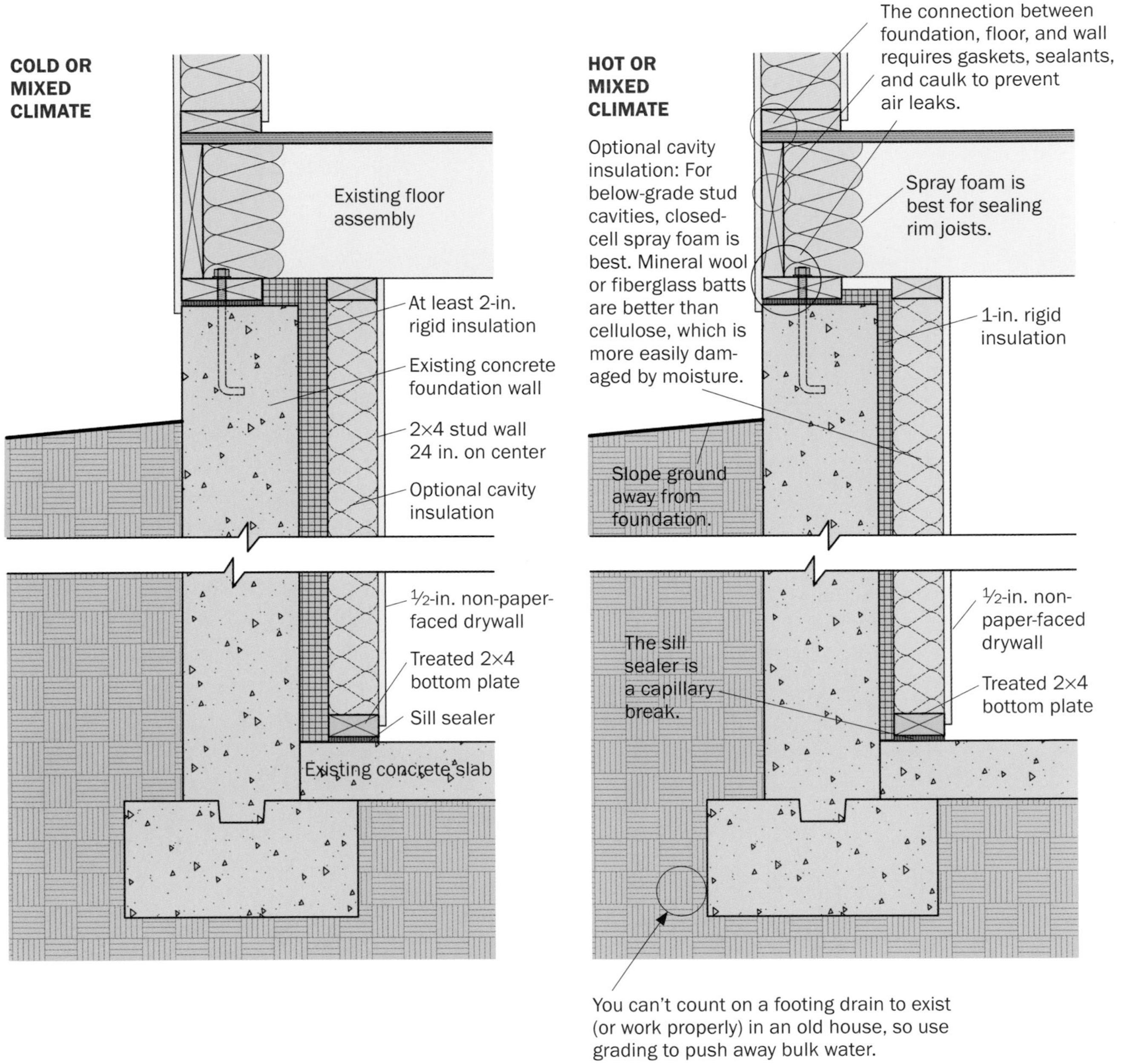

COLD OR MIXED CLIMATE

Existing floor assembly

At least 2-in. rigid insulation

Existing concrete foundation wall

2×4 stud wall 24 in. on center

Optional cavity insulation

½-in. non-paper-faced drywall

Treated 2×4 bottom plate

Sill sealer

Existing concrete slab

HOT OR MIXED CLIMATE

The connection between foundation, floor, and wall requires gaskets, sealants, and caulk to prevent air leaks.

Optional cavity insulation: For below-grade stud cavities, closed-cell spray foam is best. Mineral wool or fiberglass batts are better than cellulose, which is more easily damaged by moisture.

Spray foam is best for sealing rim joists.

1-in. rigid insulation

Slope ground away from foundation.

The sill sealer is a capillary break.

½-in. non-paper-faced drywall

Treated 2×4 bottom plate

You can't count on a footing drain to exist (or work properly) in an old house, so use grading to push away bulk water.

leaky because wood is often warped and concrete is rarely flat. Air leaks waste energy and cause moisture problems. Most basement air leaks occur between the top of the concrete wall and the bottom of the subfloor, where there are many joints and connections. The easiest way to seal and insulate the rim-joist area is with spray foam, but blocks of rigid foam sealed in place can work well, too.

Which Rigid Insulation Should I Use?

Expanded polystyrene

The least-expensive choice, EPS is manufactured in different densities. EPS (typically white in color) is not as strong as XPS, and it's susceptible to crumbling at the edges. EPS is the most vapor-permeable type of rigid foam.

R-value: About 4 per in.

Perm rating: 2.0 to 5.8 for 1 in., depending on density

Extruded polystyrene

Because of its high strength and low permeance, XPS (often blue or pink in color) is the most commonly used type of rigid foam for basement walls.

R-value: About 5.0 per in.

Perm rating: 0.4 to 1.6 for 1 in., depending on density

Polyisocyanurate

Polyiso has a higher R-value per inch than EPS or XPS. Many building officials allow foil-faced polyiso to be installed in basements without any protective drywall, making polyiso the preferred foam for basements without stud walls.

R-value: Up to 6.5 per in.

Perm rating: 0.03 for 1 in. (with foil facing)

Mineral wool

Although many energy experts advise against using fibrous materials to insulate basement walls, some builders may want to consider using mineral-wool batts because they are less susceptible to water damage. Manufacturers include Thermafiber® and Roxul®.

R-value: 3.7 per in.

Perm rating: Hasn't been tested, but highly permeable

Insulation: More Is Better

Rigid-foam insulation in a basement eliminates condensation by keeping the interior surface of the foundation warm. How much insulation you need depends on your climate zone, though energy-conscious builders strive to exceed code minimums. While it's possible to meet code minimums with rigid foam alone, you also can use a combination of rigid foam and cavity insulation.

Daniel S. Morrison is managing editor of GreenBuildingAdvisor.com.

Weatherstripping

■ BY MATTHEW TEAGUE

Over time, houses settle, doors sag, and weatherstripping wears out, creating small cracks around windows and doors. These leaks can account for 20% to 40% of a home's heat loss. As warm air escapes in winter (and cool air in summer), the good money you've paid for heating (or air-conditioning) disappears, too.

Various contractors can bring in high-tech detectors to determine where your house is losing heat, but doing a close inspection on your own reveals more trouble spots than you might imagine. Adding or replacing weatherstripping around windows and doors as well as sealing door bottoms are the obvious remedies to start with.

Many types of weatherstripping are available at your local home center or hardware store. You can install several products easily without specialized tools; others are more difficult to install but can give you much longer service. This survey covers the range of weatherstripping products you're likely to find at a local home center and provides you with the information you need to weigh cost, life expectancy, insulating efficiency, and installation effort.

Rigid Jamb

This type of weatherstripping consists of a metal or vinyl flange attached to a tubular section of either hollow vinyl or rubber. Tubular sections on higher-quality versions are filled with silicone or foam, which provides better insulation and allows the weatherstripping to hold its shape over time.

The flange is nailed, stapled, or screwed to the jamb, and the tubular section compresses to seal the openings. This product can be installed on either doors or windows: Simply close the window or door, butt the tubular section against it, and attach the flange to the jamb. Choose rigid-jamb styles that are adjustable; they usually have elongated holes for fasteners. Don't paint the tubular sections because that reduces their flexibility and efficiency.

Durability:
Good
Cost:
50¢/ft. to about $2/ft.

Durability:
Nail-on V-strips: good
Adhesive V-strips: good
Cost: $1/ft. to $2/ft.

Bronze

Vinyl

V-Strips

Sold in rolls, this flexible V-shaped weather-stripping compresses to seal gaps inside the tracks on windows and doors. V-strips come in bronze, vinyl, stainless steel, copper, and aluminum. One advantage of V-strips is that they disappear into the tracks of windows and doors. Adhesive-backed V-strips are the easiest to install.

Metal V-strips hold up better than the vinyl versions but are trickier to install. The ends of mating pieces must be cut (using tin snips) for a tight fit, and driving brads every 3 in. amounts to a lot of hammering. (Use a nailset for the last taps on the brads.) To prevent the leaves from overlapping at the corners, trim the leaves at an angle. Metal V-strips are quite durable; as they age and compress, run a putty knife, nailset, or screwdriver down the inside of the crease to extend their life.

One caveat: If doors and windows already fit tightly, adding springy V-strips in the tracks will make them harder to open and close. On both windows and doors, you need to trim away parts of the weather-stripping to accommodate locks and pulley mechanisms.

Durability: Poor
Cost: About 13¢/ft.

Nail-on felt weatherseal

Felt

Felt weatherstripping can be purchased in rolls of various thicknesses, widths, and colors. It comes in either pressure-sensitive or nail-on versions; some are adhered to a flexible vinyl or metal backing. The increased rigidity of the metal (or, to a lesser extent, vinyl) improves felt's efficiency.

Wool felt is the most durable. However, because felt can snag on splinters or catch between sliding parts, it tends to wear out quickly on operable windows and doors. In areas prone to moisture, avoid using felt altogether. Although it's easy to install (and was the standard 50 years ago), felt is relatively inefficient compared to other weatherstripping products now on the market.

Pressure-Sensitive, Adhesive-Backed Tapes

These inexpensive tapes come in several varieties: nonporous, closed-cell foam; open-cell foam silicone; and various rubbers, including a product called EPDM (ethylene propylene diene monomer). It's worth spending a few extra cents per foot to buy the more-efficient closed-cell foam or higher-quality silicones. Any of these styles can be purchased in various thicknesses and lengths.

Although installation is easy—little more than peel-and-stick—be sure to clean surfaces using a mild detergent prior to setting the tape in place. In areas that see little use, such as inoperable windows, expect the tape to last roughly three years. On frequently opened windows, you'll need to replace it in as little as a year. Securing the tape with tacks or staples helps to extend its longevity. As a general rule, apply this type of weatherstripping only on parts of windows that are not opened, such as around the upper sash.

Durability: Poor
Cost: Vinyl foam: about 20¢/ft.
X-Treme Rubber: about 30¢/ft.
Rubber foam: about 30¢/ft.
EPDM rubber: about 80¢/ft.
Silicone: about $1.15/ft.

Silicone

Rubber

EPDM

Foam

Window and Door Options

OPTIONS FOR A DOUBLE-HUNG WINDOW

Because window sashes slide in the jamb and past one another, not every type of weatherstripping is appropriate for all parts of a window. The window below is labeled with compatible weatherstripping and where it should be applied.

TOP OF UPPER SASH

V-strips (inside track)

Tapes (inside track)

Rigid jamb (against sash)

Kerf-in (against sash)

WHERE SASH MEETS SASH

V-strips (in the channel on top sash's lower rail)

Rigid jamb, if the top is inoperable (underside of lower sash)

SIDES OF UPPER SASH

Rigid jamb (against sash)

Kerf-in (against sash)

SIDES OF LOWER SASH

Rigid jamb (against sash)

Kerf-in (against sash)

BOTTOM OF LOWER SASH

Tapes (underside of sash)

Rigid jamb (against sash)

Kerf-in (against sash)

Felt (underside of sash)

OPTIONS FOR AN EXTERIOR DOOR

The swinging motion of a door allows you a greater choice of weatherstripping. In most cases, though, you must pay attention to how it should be applied. Some types of weatherstripping attach to the door jamb, and others to the doorstop.

LOCK SIDE OF DOOR

V-strips (attach to jamb; notch to fit around latch plate)

Felt (against doorstop; place separate lengths on each side of latch plate)

Tapes (abut doorstop)

Rigid jamb (attaches to inside face of doorstop)

Kerf-in (against doorstop)

BOTTOM OF DOOR

Vinyl, metal, or wood thresholds

Door seals, sweeps, or shoes; attachment varies by style

TOP OF DOOR

V-strips (attach to jamb)

Felt (against doorstop)

Tapes (attach to doorstop)

Rigid jamb (attaches to jamb and abuts doorstop)

Kerf-in (against doorstop)

HINGE SIDE OF DOOR

V-strips (attach to jamb)

Felt (applied to jamb)

Tapes (applied to jamb)

Kerf-in (against doorstop)

Sources

Accurate Metal Weatherstrip Co. Inc.
www.accurateweatherstrip.com

Duck® Products
www.duckbrand.com

Frost King®
www.frostking.com

M-D® Building Products
www.mdteam.com

Pemko Manufacturing®
www.pemko.com

Randy Surley Manufacturing Company
www.randysurleymfg.com

Resource Conservation Technology Inc.
www.conservationtechnology.com

Available at tool-rental outlets, this laminate trimmer has a 45-degree angled base that slides between the window jamb and stop to cut an angled groove for silicone-bead and other kerf-in weatherstripping.

Cut the groove toward the corners. Plunge the kerfing tool into the seam between the window jamb and the stop that holds the sash, and move it slowly toward the top and bottom corners of the jamb. A vacuum hose sucks up stray sawdust. Silicone-bead and other kerf-in weatherstripping is easy to install. Just cut the corners at a 45-degree angle, and press the flat fin into the kerf.

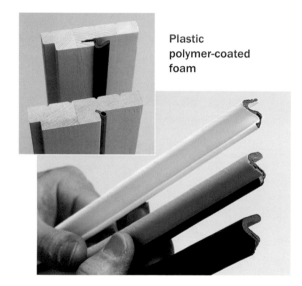

Plastic polymer-coated foam

Silicone bead

Durability: Silicone: excellent
Plastic polymer and foam: good
Cost: Plastic polymer: about 18¢/ft.
Foam: about 38¢/ft.
Silicone: 35¢/ft. to $1.10/ft.

Kerf-In

A kerf is a blade-width notch cut into a door or window jamb with a saw or router. New doors often come with kerf-in weatherstripping in place. Although silicone might last up to 50 years, plastic and foam kerf-in weatherstripping might need replacement sooner. Simply pull out the old weatherstripping and snap the new, self-locking product into place.

Although it's possible to install kerf-in weatherstripping on old windows not originally designed for it, you need to rent a corner-grooving tool (see the photos above left and on p. 87) to create the kerf. If you're tool savvy, these router-like machines are easy to use. Expect to pay about $70 per day for the rental.

Interlocking Metal

Interlocking metal weatherstripping is an efficient way to seal air leaks around doors. It comes with two different pieces; one attaches to the door, and the other to the jamb and the threshold. When closed, the two pieces interlock to form a seal. This type of weatherstripping is the most difficult to install, a job best left to pros. If your doors already have interlocking metal weatherstripping, keep it working smoothly by straightening any bends or dents that prevent the two pieces from fitting together.

Door Thresholds

Because windows often slide in channels on the jamb while doors simply close against the jamb, a typical door is more susceptible to air leaks than a typical window. The top and sides of a door can be weatherstripped using many of the products seen on these pages. The bottom of a door, however, offers a different challenge.

To prevent air leaks properly, the threshold (on the floor) and the shoe or sweep (on the door) work together to create a seal. On exterior doors covered by overhangs or porches, you can install a shoe and a threshold. Doors exposed to the elements,

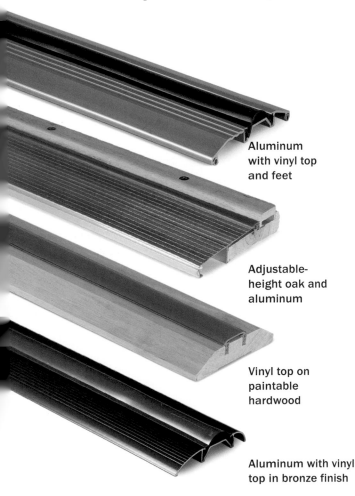

Aluminum with vinyl top and feet

Adjustable-height oak and aluminum

Vinyl top on paintable hardwood

Aluminum with vinyl top in bronze finish

Durability: Excellent
Cost: $3.85/ft. to $7/ft.

Interlocking Metal

HINGE SIDE

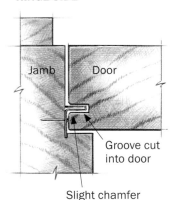

Jamb   Door

Groove cut into door

Slight chamfer

Durability: Excellent
Cost: $1.50/ft. to $3/ft.

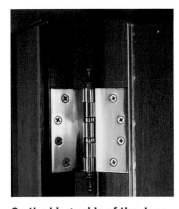

On the hinge side of the door, a bronze strip nailed to the jamb slips into a groove cut in the door.

LATCH SIDE AND TOP

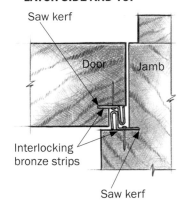

Saw kerf

Door   Jamb

Interlocking bronze strips

Saw kerf

On the head and latch sides, bronze strips let into saw kerfs and nailed on both the door and the jamb interlock.

DOOR BOTTOM

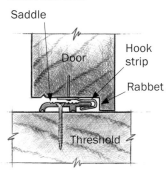

Saddle

Door

Hook strip

Rabbet

Threshold

At the door bottom, a bronze hook strip on the door engages the saddle screwed to the sill.

however, should be outfitted with a threshold designed to shed water away from the house. If an existing wooden threshold shows signs of water damage, simply replacing it will only postpone a larger problem.

Door Sweeps

Installing a door sweep is the final step in sealing air leaks under a door. Sweeps come in various styles, one of which simply attaches to the outside of a door. Metal, vinyl, or wood versions connected to either felt or foam all can be cut to length with a hacksaw, backsaw, or tin snips, and most simply screw to the bottom of a door. When trimming the sweep, cut it about ⅛ in. shy of the overall door width. Some versions are nailed instead of screwed into place. If possible, opt for a version that screws into place through elongated holes because they allow for easy adjustment.

Other sweep styles actually wrap the bottom of the door and rely on a rubber or foam gasket along the door's bottom edge to seal tight against the threshold. Again, look for a model with elongated screw holes that enable you to adjust the sweep. You might have to remove the door to mount the sweep.

Automatic door sweeps are a fairly recent invention, and they come in handy if the door opens over irregular stone or carpeted floors, where a regular sweep would drag or bind. With automatic door sweeps, a vinyl flap drops down to seal leaks when the door is shut, but retracts when the door is open. If it sounds like hoodoo, it's not: A stop button attached to the jamb lifts and closes the flap.

Matthew Teague is a furniture maker and journalist in Nashville, Tenn.

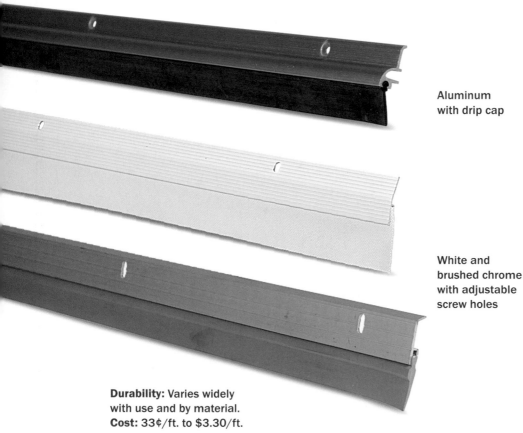

Aluminum with drip cap

White and brushed chrome with adjustable screw holes

Durability: Varies widely with use and by material.
Cost: 33¢/ft. to $3.30/ft.

A Buyer's Guide to Windows

■ BY SEAN GROOM

When you roll up to a house for the first time, you can't help but notice the windows. Their size, style, and placement determine if they're appropriate to the architectural style and, to some degree, if the house will be a pleasure to be in.

For most people, that's as much thought as they give to windows. And that's too bad, because picking the right windows can lower heating and/or cooling costs, improve comfort inside the house, and improve indoor-air quality by dramatically limiting condensation.

To buy the best-performing windows for your house, though, you need to know a bit about how they work and what they need to do.

A Window Has Four Basic Jobs

The first thing a window has to do is control heat gain and loss. Technically, these temperature changes take place through conduction, convection, and radiation. As a practical matter, these temperature changes affect your comfort. If you're sitting next to a window, you'll experience conduction and convection when the glass acts as a cold radiator in the winter; and you'll experience radiation on a sunny day when you feel like an ant trapped under a magnifying glass.

Second, a window must control solar-heat gain. I say *control* because heat gain isn't always bad. If you live in a heating climate—generally speaking, anywhere north of Oklahoma with the exception of California—you should take advantage of the free heat windows can provide.

Third, windows need to regulate airflow. They should be airtight when closed and also offer fresh air when you want it.

Finally, windows provide natural light and frame views both near and far.

Frame Materials Dictate Performance, Maintenance, and Cost

Aluminum Aluminum frames are strong, durable, inexpensive, and require little maintenance. Aluminum is highly conductive, however, leading to heat loss. To achieve even modest insulating levels, the frame and sashes must be carefully engineered with thermal breaks. Even then, they are best in mild desert climates or on impact-resistant windows in hurricane zones.

Aluminum

Wood

Clad

Vinyl

Fiberglass

Wood The only choice for some traditionalists, wood offers a pick of colors (and it can be changed later on). Wood frames are moderately priced and have good insulating value and structural strength, but they're not low maintenance; they require periodic cleaning and painting, which adds to their overall cost.

Clad Windows with aluminum-, vinyl-, or fiberglass-clad wood frames are the most expensive. A clad unit offers the low-maintenance durability of aluminum, vinyl, or fiberglass on the outside and the thermal resistance and appeal of wood on the inside. Well-engineered aluminum clad-ding should strengthen the window. Custom colors for aluminum cladding can match any paint chip at an additional cost.

Vinyl Vinyl frames are formed of extruded PVC. Multiple chambers in the frames and sashes add rigidity. These chambers also act as insulation in the same way as the airspace between glass panes; some manufacturers fill the chambers with foam insulation to improve the frame's insulating ability. Vinyl is available in only a few colors, generally white and some variation on almond. Darker colors absorb too much heat, causing vinyl to deform and degrade. It's typically the least expensive window.

Fiberglass The best you can get if you want to maximize a frame's insulating ability, fiberglass is the least conductive material, and the frame can be insulated with foam. More expensive than aluminum, vinyl, or wood, fiberglass requires little maintenance and is durable and extremely strong. It can be extruded in low-profile frames and sashes in several colors and is paintable. Another advantage is that as the temperature changes, fiberglass expands and contracts at a rate almost identical to the glass. This helps to prevent seals along the glass from failing.

Composite Composite windows, like composite decking, are made of wood fibers (sawdust) mixed with vinyl resins. Up to 40 percent of the window content is recycled. Most, if not all, composite windows are sold as replacements by the Renewal By Andersen® division of Andersen® Windows. The material's tradename is Fibrex®. It looks a lot like wood, will not rot, requires little maintenance, and can be stained on the inside.

What Makes a Good Frame?

When most people choose windows, they begin by considering the frame material. They might be predisposed to traditional wood or low-maintenance vinyl. However, according to Nils Petermann at the Efficient Windows Collaborative, the most important factor to consider is the frame's durability. This is where I'd like to refer you to an independent organization that provides unbiased durability ratings for window frames. Unfortunately, there isn't one.

You can make educated guesses about durability based on the frame material. But whether it's wood, vinyl, fiberglass, aluminum, clad, or composite, a well-constructed window lasts longer and performs better than a poorly constructed one regardless of the relative benefits of its frame material.

The best way to get a sense of window quality is to read all the product literature you can get your hands on and to look at actual windows—a lot of them. Go to the big-box store and the local building supply, and open and close the windows on display, paying attention to how the corners are joined, how well the sashes seal, and how rigid the unit is.

On vinyl windows, look for continuous thermally welded corners. Examine the corner cutaway displays of aluminum windows for a continuous thermal break in both frame and sash. On a clad window, the cladding should have well-sealed corners and gaskets to prevent water from getting behind the cladding. Aluminum is an excellent heat conductor, so be sure that aluminum cladding doesn't contact conditioned interior air at any point.

Another way to sift through the options is to talk to reputable builders and architects in your area. Ask what windows they use and how long they have been using them. They won't stick with windows that make their clients unhappy.

Thirty years ago, when single-pane windows were the rule rather than the exception, companies looking to improve window performance focused their research on insulating glass. It was the lowest-hanging fruit. They've done such a good job that the R-value of insulated glass is good enough to make the window frame the weak link in the thermal chain. That's one reason why manufacturers list performance data for relatively large windows, say, 4 ft. by 5 ft. (When you're comparing windows, make sure the performance data are for windows of the same size.) Windows with large areas of glass yield better performance numbers because the frame is a smaller percentage of the window area. Savvy window designers understand this and tweak their windows accordingly for optimal performance. By using strong materials that permit low-profile sills, sashes, and jambs, they minimize the size of

Window Anatomy

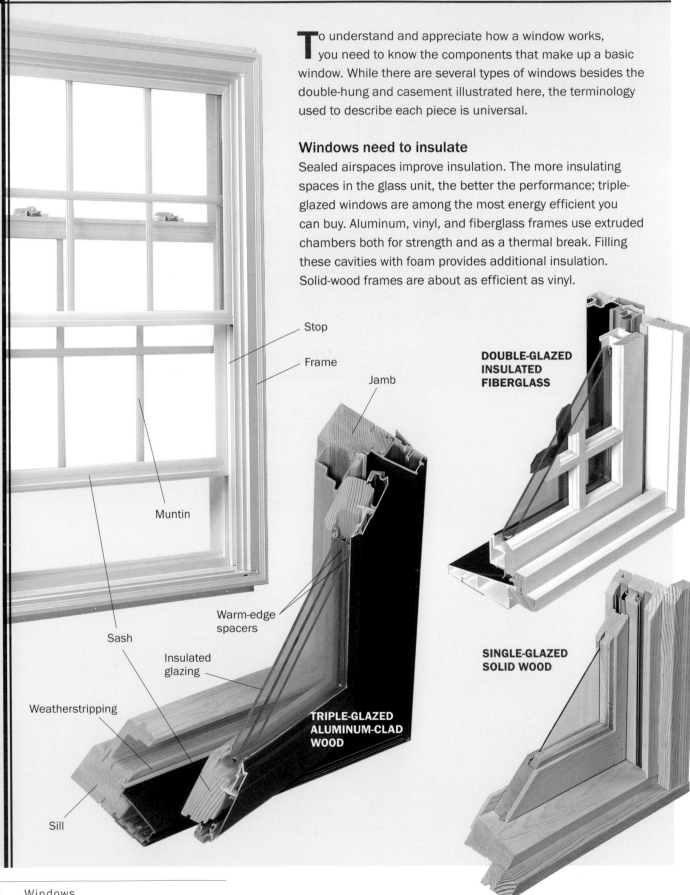

To understand and appreciate how a window works, you need to know the components that make up a basic window. While there are several types of windows besides the double-hung and casement illustrated here, the terminology used to describe each piece is universal.

Windows need to insulate

Sealed airspaces improve insulation. The more insulating spaces in the glass unit, the better the performance; triple-glazed windows are among the most energy efficient you can buy. Aluminum, vinyl, and fiberglass frames use extruded chambers both for strength and as a thermal break. Filling these cavities with foam provides additional insulation. Solid-wood frames are about as efficient as vinyl.

Stop

Frame

Jamb

Muntin

DOUBLE-GLAZED INSULATED FIBERGLASS

Warm-edge spacers

Sash

Insulated glazing

Weatherstripping

TRIPLE-GLAZED ALUMINUM-CLAD WOOD

SINGLE-GLAZED SOLID WOOD

Sill

Window DNA: The NFRC Label by the Numbers

U-FACTOR
A measure of the insulating value. U-factor is the nonsolar heat flow through all parts of the window (glass, frame, and sash). A lower number means better insulation and greater performance.

VISIBLE TRANSMITTANCE (VT)
A measure of the amount of visible light that passes through the window. Values range from 0 to 1 (a higher number equals more light). However, most ratings are between 0.3 and 0.8 because they take into account the light blocked by the frame. Choose windows with higher VT to maximize daylight and views.

SOLAR HEAT GAIN COEFFICIENT (SHGC)
The percentage of the sun's solar heat that passes through the window. Higher numbers mean more passive solar-heating potential.

AIR LEAKAGE (AL)
A measure of the amount of air passing through the window assembly; a source of heat gain and loss. This optional rating is expressed in cubic feet per minute through a square foot of window. Look for ratings under 0.3; lower is better.

CONDENSATION RESISTANCE
A relative scale from 0 to 100 based on the window's properties. It predicts the likelihood of condensation, with higher numbers indicating less condensation.

World's Best Window Co.
Millennium 2000+
Vinyl-Clad Wood Frame
Double Glazing • Argon Fill • Low E
Product Type: **Vertical Slider**

ENERGY PERFORMANCE RATINGS

U-Factor (U.S./I-P)	Solar Heat Gain Coefficient
0.35	**0.32**

ADDITIONAL PERFORMANCE RATINGS

Visible Transmittance	Air Leakage (U.S./I-P)
0.51	**0.2**

Condensation Resistance	
51	

Manufacturer stipulates that these ratings conform to applicable NFRC procedures for determining whole product performance. NFRC ratings are determined for a fixed set of environmental conditions and a specific product size. Consult manufacturer's literature for other product performance information.
www.nfrc.org

---

the conductive frame while being sure to incorporate materials that reduce air leakage.

Frame material can also influence how long a window stays airtight. Like most building materials, windows expand and contract with changes in temperature and humidity. When you see a window with moisture between panes, it's likely that movement between the glass and the sash broke the insulating seal. By choosing stable materials, you can reduce stress on the seal and increase the window's longevity. Fiberglass expands at the rate of glass, while aluminum and vinyl expand respectively 3 times and 7 times more than glass. Wood moves in response to humidity changes rather than temperature.

Insulated Glass Reduces Heat Loss

Manufacturers typically refer to glass as *glazing*. Using glazing as a noun is a bit pretentious, like referring to a window as a *fenestration*, but it does give the sense that glass assemblies in today's windows are a far cry from the single-pane windows installed in the 1970s.

Those single-pane windows have been abandoned in most heating climates because glass is a horrible insulator. A standard window today relies on an insulated glass unit (sometimes called an IG). This unit is a sealed sandwich of two or three pieces of glass with an airspace between the panes. IG units are manufactured by a few glass companies that supply the hundreds of window manufacturers in North America.

The airspace between glass panes, usually ½ in. to ⅔ in. thick, serves as insulation by reducing the transfer of heat through conduction. A single clear pane has a U-factor of 1.04, but a sealed double-pane unit has a U-factor of 0.5 (see "What's a U-Factor?" above). Adding a third pane improves the U-factor to 0.3.

Replacing the air with gas improves the insulating value of the window. Manufacturers use argon or krypton gases because they're inert—chemically stable and nonreactive—and because they reduce heat loss, as they are less conductive than air. Argon and krypton also reduce convective losses because the gases are heavier than air, reducing gas movement within the insulating space.

Krypton performs slightly better than argon, but its bigger advantage is that the optimal spacing between krypton-filled panes is narrower than what's required for argon. That means less stress on the sashes, particularly in triple-pane windows.

Spacers Are Potential Weak Points

Spacers between glass panes perform three functions: They maintain a uniform separation between pieces of glass, they provide a good adhesive surface for the glass, and they create an airtight seal for the insulating cavity.

Although you should choose windows based on their overall performance ratings, the spacer, while small, substantially impacts a window's U-factor and condensation resistance.

The spacer's job is complicated by the fact that it's in contact with both the inside and outside surfaces of the window, forming a bridge between indoor and outdoor environments. Because the spacer is more conductive than the air or gas fill, it changes the temperature of a 2½-in.-wide band around the edge of the glass. As a consequence, the window's overall U-factor is affected. In smaller windows, the 2½-in. temperature band is a larger percentage of the window and has a greater effect on the window's U-factor. While spacers can be considered the Achilles' heel of all windows, a casement window performs slightly better than a double-hung of the same size because the former has less spacer area. Likewise, the thermal performance of true divided-lite windows made up of multiple IG units suffers because of all the spacer area in the window. (Simulated divided lites can also affect U-factor if the grille creates a thermal bridge between the panes.)

Spacers are made of aluminum, steel, fiberglass, foam, and thermoplastics, often in some combination. Foam spacers have the lowest U-factor, while aluminum has the highest. Today, quality windows use "warm-edge" spacers. (It's worth noting that warm-edge means only that it's less conductive than aluminum.) A good warm-edge spacer raises the interior surface temperature of the glass along the perimeter of the window. This is especially important at the window's bottom edge, which is most subject to condensation. At 0°F outside, a good spacer increases the temperature at the bottom of the inside glass pane by 6°F to 8°F. As a result, a more comfortable relative-humidity level indoors is possible during the winter without window condensation.

Coatings Improve Performance

Energy-efficient windows were developed during the previous energy crisis. When Jimmy Carter was installing solar panels on the White House and making conservation a priority, the Department of Energy's Lawrence Berkeley National Laboratory was charged with finding ways to conserve energy. Windows were among their targets. The insulating windows of that era allowed an inordinate amount of heat to escape. The lab's scientists concluded that by using existing technologies to deposit a virtually invisible metal or metal-oxide coating on the glass, insulating windows could be dramatically more efficient. This coating is transparent to visible light, but blocks long- and short-wave radiation by reflecting it. Known as a low-e (for low-emissivity) coating, it's common today even on low-cost windows.

Depending on the nature of this thin coating and which window surface it is applied to, the coating can reflect heat back into the room to conserve it or filter sunlight to keep heat out. Using a coating on two different glass panes can fine-tune the amount of heat that's retained in each direction.

The measure of the amount of the sun's heat a window lets through is the solar heat gain coefficient. SHGC in shorthand, it ranges from 0 to 1, where 1 is uninterrupted heat gain. A clear-glass, two-pane insulated window has an SHGC between 0.56 and 0.68, depending on the frame material and construction. The size of the air gap, which is influenced by frame design, and the amount of light blocked by the frame and grille affect the SHGC.

The Role of Low-E

1. Reflects short-wave radiation to reduce heat gain.

2. Filters UV-rays that cause fading.

3. Tinted coatings, not low-e, temper visible light.

4. Reflects long-wave radiation to reduce heat loss.

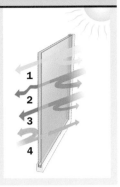

A double-pane IG with two low-e coatings can achieve an SHGC of 0.33 (glass-only value). As the SHGC is minimized, the U-factor declines, which has implications for selecting windows in climates with heating and cooling seasons.

Choosing Energy-Saving Windows

REGIONAL: A GOOD APPROACH

If you're interested in efficient windows, the starting point is an Energy Star rating. The greatest chunk of energy savings comes from good insulating properties. Energy Star performance prescriptions dictate that the colder the climate, the lower the U-factor you'll want. In southern climates, where air-conditioning dominates energy consumption, Energy Star ratings shift focus to a lower SHGC to reduce the impact of the sun.

The Department of Energy divides the United States into four climate regions (see the map on p. 98). Under the Energy Star program, each region is assigned threshold U-factor and SHGC ratings for a qualifying window (see the chart on p. 98). A double-hung vinyl window that's Energy Star qualified in all four zones might start at around $14 per sq. ft., with a clad frame starting at around $28 per sq. ft.

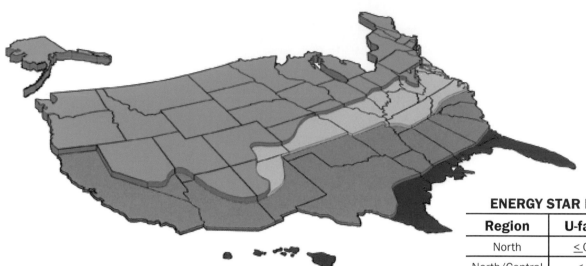

ENERGY STAR REQUIREMENTS

Region	U-factor	SHGC
North	≤ 0.35	Any
North/Central	≤ 0.4	≤ 0.55
South/Central	≤ 0.4	≤ 0.4
South	≤ 0.65	≤ 0.4

≤ *less than or equal to*

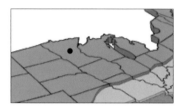

DULUTH, MINN.
Insulated fiberglass frame,
double pane with three films
U-factor = 0.09 (R-11)
SHGC = 0.26
Price = $280/sq. ft.

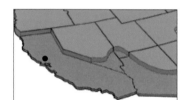

SAN FRANCISCO, CALIF.
Insulated vinyl frame, double
pane with one film
U-factor = 0.27 (R-3.8)
SHGC = 0.47
Price = $50/sq. ft.

LOCAL: A BETTER APPROACH

In the United States, the performance characteristics on an NFRC label (see the sidebar on p. 95) provide a moment-in-time snapshot of performance, but don't relate anything about the long-term energy consequences and peak load demands of window choices.

To get a better-performing window than the Energy Star minimum, you need to take energy costs into account. A quick-and-dirty tool from the Efficient Windows Collaborative (www.efficientwindows.org/selection .cfm) compares the energy costs for a range of windows with different performance characteristics. The cost figures are generated using RESFEN software (see "Site Specific: The Best Approach" on p. 100) and are based on a benchmark house.

Their modeling recommends low U-factor, high-SHGC windows in the north region, the north/central zone, and the upper half of the south/central area; and low U-factor, low-SHGC windows in the southern reaches of the south/central area and in the south region.

The most energy-efficient windows in all locations, except San Francisco and Flagstaff, Ariz., are at least triple-glazed with insulated vinyl or fiberglass frames. These windows are hard to find and expensive. The nice thing about the collaborative's website is that it shows how much annual energy expenditures rise if you opt for a readily

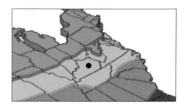

LOUISVILLE, KY.
Insulated fiberglass frame,
triple pane
U-factor = 0.23 (R-4.3)
SHGC = 0.39
Price = $80/sq. ft.

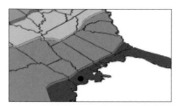

NEW ORLEANS, LA.
Clad-wood frame, double pane
U-factor = 0.3 (R-3.3)
SHGC = 0.21
Price = $52/sq. ft.

available double-glazed window with two low-e coatings and an uninsulated vinyl or clad-wood frame. Exceeding Energy Star minimums saves money over the life of the window. (Examples shown are options exceeding Energy Star thresholds. Consult the collaborative's website or RESFEN for energy performance for your location. Prices are approximate window cost.)

Critics of Energy Star argue that in heating climates, the emphasis on insulating-value performance to the exclusion of solar heat gain misses an opportunity. By omitting an SHGC requirement in the north region, window companies can market a single low U-factor, low-SHGC glass package that meets Energy Star requirements in all regions. An Energy Star label on low U-factor, low-SHGC windows in cold northern regions of the United States means homeowners who think they are buying energy-efficient windows are actually paying more in heating costs and adding more carbon emissions to the atmosphere than if they had purchased windows that accounted for passive solar-heating opportunities. (For some sites, a very low U-factor, such as the Duluth, Minn., example, is the best option.) The Department of Energy is reportedly reevaluating the standard.

While insulating properties may not seem as important in the South, where Energy Star thresholds are fairly high, a low U-factor helps to keep indoor temperatures cool. This reduces peak cooling loads and saves money in two ways: It reduces energy consumption

in peak demand periods with higher rates, and by reducing peak loads saves on mechanical costs with a smaller air-conditioning system.

Window glass isn't the only or even the best way to block summer sun. Deciduous trees on the south, east, and west sides of a house work very well. Another strategy is the use of overhangs and shading devices.

If you need to rely on window glass to control solar gain in the South, you'll need low-SHGC, or spectrally selective, windows. They reflect short- and long-wave infrared radiation to filter out 40% to 70% of incoming heat. Sometimes known as low-e2 or low-e3, the second- and third-generation low-emissivity coatings on these windows not only reduce solar gain, but also filter more than 99% of the UV-light that causes color fading.

Generally, you want a window to block solar gain but let in visible light. The window's light-to-solar-gain ratio (VT/SHGC) provides a gauge of its relative efficiency in transmitting light while blocking heat gain. The higher the number, the more light transmitted without adding excessive amounts of heat. In a cooling-dominated climate, a ratio above 1.0 is better because light transmittance is higher than heat gain.

If glare is a problem, windows tinted bronze, green, or blue limit visible light and are spectrally selective with a low SHGC. However, because they absorb infrared radiation rather than reflect it, tinted windows radiate heat.

CANADIANS HAVE IT EASY

Windows sold in Canada have an energy rating (E.R.) that makes it easy to evaluate the trade-offs in heating-dominated climates. By weighing the amount of solar-heat gain against interior-heat loss through the window and heat loss through air leakage, the E.R. indicates whether a window is a net source of energy (positive E.R. value), energy neutral (E.R. equals 0), or a net loss of energy (negative E.R. value). If you live in a north or north/central zone in the United States or Canada and you're buying a window from a Canadian manufacturer, simply choose the highest E.R. possible.

SITE SPECIFIC: THE BEST APPROACH

Engineers and efficient-house designers use complex modeling software to evaluate the effect of window options on energy consumption. Rather than buying the same window for an entire house (as you would using Energy Star guidelines or the Efficient Windows Cooperative website), they tune the windows to optimize glass performance for each orientation.

The average homeowner or contractor can model the energy performance of a house and compare the effects of different windows with RESFEN, a free software package from the Department of Energy's Lawrence Berkeley National Laboratory (http://windows.lbl.gov/software/resfen/resfen.html). Unfortunately, to get the most out of the program, you'll have to slog through the manual.

Generally, in heating climates, south-facing windows have a high SHGC (greater than 0.5), and east- and west-facing windows have a low SHGC (less than 0.3) to prevent solar gain in the summer.

Until recently, common wisdom was that the SHGC on north-facing windows should match east- and west-facing windows, but software modeling has shown that high-SHGC north-facing windows don't lose any energy.

Films Create Super Windows

Another way to control the flow of heat through a window is with suspended films. These films come in two varieties: high solar gain and low solar gain.

Because these films (similar to mylar) are so lightweight and thin, as many as three films can be suspended between two glass panes. The additional insulating spaces increase the insulating ability of the window, replicating the performance of three-, four-, or five-pane windows without the weight. Serious Windows® uses this approach to create high-performance windows with both high and low solar-gain properties. The company's premium fixed window has an insulating value of R-11.1 (U-factor 0.09), nearly rivaling many wall insulations. The operable version of the window is R-7.1 (U-factor 0.14). Considering that the average insulating window is the equivalent of R-1 to R-3, Serious Windows live up to their name.

Let the Light Shine In

Solar gain and insulating values aren't the only ways that windows save energy and keep you comfortable. Windows also control the view and the amount of natural light.

Daylighting, or window-placement strategies to maximize natural light, save money by reducing the need for electric lighting. Although placement is a design issue, window styles and glass properties affect the amount of light infiltration. The visible transmittance (VT) rating on the National Fenestration Rating Council's label (p. 95) allows you to compare the amount of light that passes through windows, taking into account the light blocked by frames and grilles.

Impact-Resistant Glass Offers Protection

Although they don't affect a window's energy performance, a few options can make you safer.

Tempered glass, for example, can be specified for windows located where someone could potentially fall into one. Many of these locations are covered by code and include windows within 18 in. of the floor, next to doors, in showers or bath areas, and along decks, patios, and walkways.

If you live in a coastal area—particularly along the Atlantic and Gulf coasts, where building codes demand protection during hurricanes—or in a tornado-prone area, you can specify impact-resistant glass. Using the same technology as car windshields, a plastic sheet is laminated between two pieces of glass so that the window maintains its integrity after the glass is broken.

Window frames can also be reinforced to withstand impact. Available in three different strengths (impact zones 2, 3, and 4), the toughest windows in impact zone 4 must withstand strikes from at least two 8-ft.-long 2×4s traveling at 50 ft. per second, followed by 9,000 cycles of negative and positive pressure simulating hurricane-force winds.

Windows That Keep the World at Bay

Manufacturers also offer variations of pebbled, frosted, and wavy glass that add privacy to bathrooms, bedrooms, and other sensitive spaces.

If you live near a busy road, near train tracks, or under a flight path, acoustic windows can take the edge off loud or constant noise. Even if they don't readily advertise the fact, many window companies sell sound-attenuating windows. Residential "quiet" windows are likely to be rated with a sound transmission coefficient (STC). A typical double-pane window has an STC of 25 to 27. Every increase of 10 in the STC cuts the amount of sound transmitted by half. Companies such as Milgard®, Atrium®, Marvin, and Serious Windows have windows in the 40 to 47 STC range.

Self-Cleaning Windows Reduce Maintenance Demands

For those of you who say, "I don't do windows," technology has finally caught up with your sentiment. Several big glass companies market coated glass that resists the buildup of dirt. Product names include Neat® Glass by Cardinal, Activ™ by Pilkington®, and PPG's SunClean®.

By making the glass smoother and hydrophilic, rainwater collects in sheets on the surface and slides off the glass quickly, cleaning the window. Some windows include a titanium-dioxide layer that reacts with UV-light to help organic materials decompose, so dirt washes away more easily.

Window Styles

DOUBLE-HUNG

Traditional window composed of two sashes that slide vertically. A single-hung window looks identical, but the top sash is fixed.

Pros: Available with a wide variety of grille patterns to match different architectural styles. Sashes usually tilt in for easy cleaning of the exterior.

Cons: Sashes rely on draftier sliding-style weatherstripping. The bottom edge of the upper sash is exposed to outdoor temperatures on two faces, increasing surface area for thermal bridging. Two sashes increase spacer area, increasing U-factor. Less than half the window area can be open for ventilation.

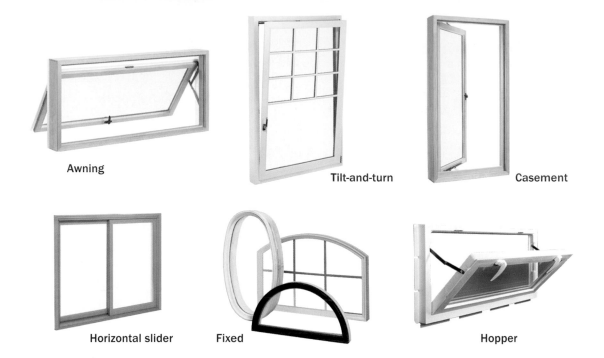

Awning

Tilt-and-turn

Casement

Horizontal slider

Fixed

Hopper

AWNING

Top-hinged window that usually opens outward with a crank.

Pros: Good-sealing compression-style weatherstripping. Single glass unit and recessed sash improve U-factor. Provides ventilation while it's raining. Often used above and/or below large fixed windows for ventilation and additional daylight.

Cons: Screen on inside of window. Open window can present a hazard if installed along a walkway, deck, patio, or porch.

TILT-AND-TURN

Dual-action window that can swing in like a door or tilt from the bottom like a hopper window for ventilation.

Pros: Ventilation options. Secure multipoint locking. Compression weatherstripping. Large egress area and easy cleaning.

Cons: Shades and drapes can interfere with operation.

CASEMENT

Side-hinged window that usually opens outward with a crank. In-swing versions are available.

Pros: Compression-style weatherstripping. Single large glass unit and recessed sash im-

prove U-factor. Largest ventilation area of any window style. Opening can be oriented to "scoop" prevailing breeze.

Cons: Screen on inside of window. Hinge design might not allow outside of window to be cleaned from inside. Open window can present a hazard if installed along a walkway, deck, patio, or porch.

HORIZONTAL SLIDER

The two sashes slide past one another on tracks like a sliding patio door.

Pros: Can be easier to open than other sliding styles, especially when placed over a counter.

Cons: Sliding weatherstripping and greater sash area lower U-factor and airtightness ratings.

FIXED

An inoperative window available in shapes that match operable windows, or as accent windows such as half-rounds to create Palladian windows and octagons.

Pros: Improved airtightness. Can be made in nonstandard, custom shapes.

Cons: Doesn't satisfy egress requirements.

HOPPER

Tilt-in bottom-hinged window.

Pros: Compression-style weatherstripping. Single glass unit and recessed sash improve U-factor.

Cons: Hazardous if installed at head height or lower.

Choosing Replacement Windows

You have three choices for replacing existing windows: a sash-only replacement; an insert-style frame and sash replacement window; or a new-construction window.

If the existing frames have water damage, the only choice is a new-construction window (see the photos on p. 92).

If you're looking to improve comfort or energy performance, replacing the sashes or using a frame insert can help. They're a good choice on older homes where you want to preserve period trim, but from an energy and comfort standpoint, they're not the best option.

Replacement windows that leave the existing frame in place don't stop air leakage. If you've ever pulled out an old window, then you've seen fiberglass insulation stuffed between the window and the rough opening. Typically, the insulation is dirty. It wasn't dirty when it was put there; dirt was filtered out of the air moving through and around the window frame.

Another negative is that insert-style frame and sash replacement windows reduce the glass area because the unit fits inside the existing frame. You might be willing to live with diminished views, but are you willing to pay for that privilege every year? In a southern climate, the reduced glass area does not affect heating bills, but in northern heating climates, reducing the south-facing glass area gives away a lot of free heat.

An insert-style frame and sash replacement window is generally a bit pricier than a

Insert-style replacement fits inside an existing new-construction window.

new-construction window. Installation costs are lower, however, because it leaves the existing trim in place and doesn't require any siding removal.

Regardless of the type you choose, replacement windows are expensive. If you're trying to save on energy expenses, new windows shouldn't be considered until you have improved the insulation and the air-tightness of the rest of the building envelope.

Former Fine Homebuilding *editor Sean Groom is a freelance writer in Bloomfield, Conn.*

Sash-only replacement

Sources

There are hundreds of window manufacturers, the majority of them local companies. A sample of large national and smaller specialty manufacturers is listed here. Visit **www.efficientwin dows.org** for a more comprehensive list.

Accurate Dorwin
www.accuratedorwin.com

Andersen
www.andersenwindows.com

Integrity®
www.integritywindows.com

Jeld-Wen®
www.jeld-wen.com

Loewen®
www.loewen.com

Marvin
www.marvin.com

Milgard
www.milgard.com

Pella
www.pella.com

Quantum
www.quantumwindows.com

Serious Windows
www.seriouswindows.com

Thermotech
www.thermotechfiberglass.com

Weather Shield®
www.weathershield.com

Do Europeans Really Make the Best Windows?

■ BY MARTIN HOLLADAY

A good window seals out cold, windy weather and admits as much light as possible into a house's interior. While those functions seem rather obvious, some claim a new class of window can perform these duties better than any window made in the United States.

Only a handful of window manufacturers in the United States and Canada sell high-performance windows suitable for cold-climate homes. Sensing an opportunity, manufacturers from Germany and Austria have eagerly filled the market niche by introducing a host of high-performance units to American builders.

Defining High Performance

The two most important measures of a window's performance are its U-factor and its solar heat-gain coefficient (SHGC), numbers that can be found on a new window's National Fenestration Rating Council (NFRC) label.

A window's U-factor is the inverse of its R-value; the lower the U-factor, the better the window is at resisting heat flow. A low U-factor is desirable in all climates. While the best double-glazed windows have a U-factor of about 0.27, triple-glazed windows have U-factors as low as 0.17.

Closed   **Tilt**   **Turn**

Efficient Wood Windows from Across the Pond

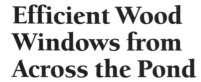

Optiwin® windows, which exemplify Passive House® certified European windows, are manufactured by Müller Schreinerei in Lautenbach, Germany. The company produces two cold-climate windows, the Three-Wood (Drei-Holz) window and the Two-Wood (Zwei-Holz), pictured on the facing page.

Like all European tilt-turn windows, Optiwin windows open inward. This feature allows the windows to be installed in a recessed location so that foam sheathing (a common feature on superinsulated walls) can be extended to cover the exterior of the window frames. This installation detail—sometimes referred to as "overinsulating the exterior of the window frames"—improves the windows' overall thermal performance.

SHGC is a measure of how much solar heat is admitted through a window. In general, windows with a high SHGC help to heat a house (a desirable feature during the winter), while windows with a low SHGC help to prevent a house from overheating (a desirable feature during the summer). Cold-climate houses need windows with a high SHGC (at least 0.39), especially on the south elevation. On the other hand, hot-climate houses need windows with a low SHGC (0.30 or lower), especially on the west elevation. Cold-climate builders should look for windows with a low U-factor and a high SHGC. The higher a window's visible-light transmittance (VT), the better. VT indicates the amount of visible light that enters a window.

Many high-performance European windows meet stringent standards established by the Passivhaus Institut in Darmstadt, Germany. To be certified, a Passive House window needs a European U-factor no greater than 0.80 $W/m^2 \cdot K°$ (see "It's Difficult to Compare U-Factors," on p. 106).

In central Europe, such low-U-factor windows maintain an interior pane temperature of 17°C (62.6°F) or more on the coldest day of the year. The Passive House U-factor requirement can be achieved only by windows with insulated frames and triple glazing with two low-e coatings and warm-edge spacers.

U.S. distributors now sell Passive House windows from several European manufacturers, including Internorm® and Silber in Austria, and Henzmann, Optiwin, Pazen ENERsign, and Unilux UltraTherm in Germany.

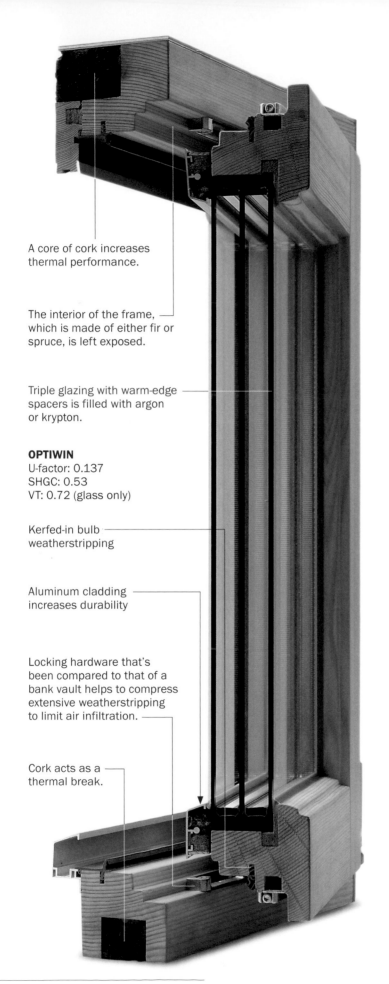

A core of cork increases thermal performance.

The interior of the frame, which is made of either fir or spruce, is left exposed.

Triple glazing with warm-edge spacers is filled with argon or krypton.

OPTIWIN
U-factor: 0.137
SHGC: 0.53
VT: 0.72 (glass only)

Kerfed-in bulb weatherstripping

Aluminum cladding increases durability

Locking hardware that's been compared to that of a bank vault helps to compress extensive weatherstripping to limit air infiltration.

Cork acts as a thermal break.

It's Difficult to Compare U-Factors

The U-factors reported by European window manufacturers—whether given in European units (W/m²•K°) or North American units (Btu/ft²•F°)—are difficult to compare with U-factors reported by North American manufacturers. European and North American laboratories use different protocols to test window U-factors, and most glazing experts agree that European U-factors would look worse if the windows were tested according to NFRC requirements.

U.S. distributors of European windows don't follow a consistent method for reporting U-factors. Some use European metric units, while others report North American U-factors or even R-values. Although the NFRC requires U-factors and SHGC to be based on the performance of the whole window, including the frame, many European manufacturers report U-factor and SHGC numbers that measure the performance of the glazing alone.

There is a straightforward conversion factor for converting a European U-factor in $W/m^2 \cdot K°$ to a North American U-factor in $Btu/ft^2 \cdot F°$: Simply divide by 5.678. Unfortunately, while this method converts the units, it doesn't account for the fact that the European protocol tests windows of a different size from the size used in North American testing, or for the fact that European windows are tested at different temperatures than required for North American tests.

An American Standard

To appreciate the performance of the windows featured here, it's helpful to look closely at a typical window made by an American manufacturer. The argon-filled, double-paned window made by Marvin (above) is an example of a unit suitable for houses built to code minimums.

The European Difference

For the most part, the glass in European Passive House windows is quite similar to the glass used in the best Canadian windows: argon- or krypton-filled triple glazing with two low-e coatings and warm-edge spacers. That's why many energy experts report that the thermal performance of the best European windows is about the same as that of fiberglass-framed, triple-glazed Canadian windows. Katrin Klingenberg, founder of the

MARVIN ULTIMATE PUSH-OUT CASEMENT
U-factor: 0.28
SHGC: 0.25
VT: 0.42
Cost: $670

Passive House Institute US, gives a bottom-line analysis: "Our experience has been that the overall performance of the fiberglass-framed Canadian and U.S. windows is almost as good as the German Passive House windows if you look at the overall systems design [using Passive House Planning Package software]."

However, European window manufacturers continue to push the performance envelope, and glazing manufacturers are always striving to improve their products. The latest versions of low-U triple glazing from Europe may have a higher SHGC than comparable low-U triple glazing available in North America. According to some window experts, European manufacturers are already selling windows with better insulated frames and glazing with a slightly lower U-factor than any frames or glazing available from North American manufacturers.

Typical European Passive House windows have composite frames, often including a wood lamination on the interior, a core of foam or cork to act as a thermal break, and a weather-resistant exterior cladding of aluminum or rot-resistant wood.

Although the wide frames on European windows reduce the windows' thermal performance—especially their potential for solar heat gain—compared to narrow-framed

THERMOTECH FIBERGLASS
U-factor: 0.19
SHGC: 0.42
VT: 0.44

Fiberglass frames don't expand and contract like vinyl, which leads to longer-lasting windows.

SERIOUS WINDOWS
U-factor: 0.13
SHGC: 0.20
VT: 0.30

Heat Mirror glazing is high performance, but comes with skepticism.

North American fiberglass windows, the thermal breaks incorporated in European frames are usually more effective than those used by North American manufacturers.

North American Products Rely on Narrow Frames and Synthetic Materials

Although European triple-glazed windows are well built and attractive, they cost far more than North American windows with similar performance specs. (For an operable triple-glazed casement window measuring 8 sq. ft., you can expect to pay between $400 and $520 for an Inline, Fibertec, or Thermotech® window. A Serious window with Heat Mirror™ glazing will have a lower VT rating, but it will cost about the same—$400 to $560, depending on the glazing chosen.) Windows from Europe also have a long lead time—anywhere from 10 to 12 weeks.

Unlike almost all U.S. manufacturers, Canadian manufacturers of fiberglass windows offer full-thickness (1⅜ in.) triple-glazing. Even when U.S. manufacturers offer triple glazing, it's usually thin (1 in. or ⅞ in.), low-performance glazing. While Canadian window manufacturers offer both low-solar-gain and high-solar-gain triple glazing, it's difficult to buy high-solar-gain triple glazing from a U.S. manufacturer.

Canadian fiberglass windows have other attributes that make them more attractive than European offerings. Canadian windows have narrower frames than European windows. Because frames have a lower R-value than a superinsulated wall, narrower frames mean better thermal performance overall. Also, narrow-framed windows allow more light and more solar heat gain than wide-framed windows.

When looking for high-performance windows made domestically, you'll come across the following materials.

PULTRUDED FIBERGLASS FRAMES

The pultruded fiberglass used for the best Canadian window frames is similar to the fiberglass used to make stepladders, only denser and smoother. Even when left unpainted, pultruded fiberglass is extremely durable and weather resistant. Because it has a coefficient of thermal expansion that closely matches that of glass, it's a much more suitable material for window frames than vinyl.

HEAT MIRROR GLAZING

Heat Mirror glazing has only two panes of glass; the performance of the glazing is improved by one or more stretched plastic films suspended between the two panes. The plastic films create two or three separate air spaces between the inner and outer panes of glass, mimicking the performance of triple or quadruple glazing but with less weight.

The best-known manufacturer of Heat Mirror windows is Serious Materials. Serious offers windows with lower U-factors than any triple-glazed window. Its best-performing operable window (a 1125 series casement or awning window with three plastic films) has a whole-window U-factor of 0.13. The low-U-factor glazing comes with a downside, however: a very low SHGC (0.20) and a very low visible transmittance (0.30). In other words, the windows don't let in much light or heat. European window manufacturers (and most Passive House builders in the United States) have been reluctant to use Heat Mirror windows due to lingering skepticism about the long-term durability of the plastic films and an unwillingness to accept lower SHGC and VT ratings.

VINYL FRAMES WITH TRIPLE GLAZING

Builders experiencing triple-glazing sticker shock may want to consider a lower-cost option: vinyl windows. Paradigm Windows of Portland, Maine, offers casement windows with foam-injected frames. Paradigm's best performing krypton-filled triple-glazed casement windows have a whole-window U-factor as low as 0.17. Unfortunately, these

PARADIGM WINDOWS
U-factor: 0.22
SHGC: 0.23
VT: 0.38

Triple-glazed windows are a must on high-performance homes, and vinyl frames help to reduce cost.

windows also have a low SHGC (0.23). Like almost all U.S. window manufacturers, Paradigm Windows doesn't yet offer high-solar-gain triple-glazed products.

High-Performance Windows Don't Make Sense in All Homes

The high cost of triple-glazed windows is hard to justify unless you're building a superinsulated house in a cold climate. But once your wall specs reach the R-40 level, triple-glazed windows start to make sense. A triple-glazed Optiwin tilt-turn window will cost at least $880, while a window from Bieber® will cost almost twice as much. Fortunately, Canadian windows with comparable performance specs cost roughly half the price of an Optiwin window.

Because of their positive latching hardware, casement, awning, and tilt-turn windows always outperform single- or double-hung windows.

Martin Holladay is a contributing editor to Fine Homebuilding.

Sources

NORTH AMERICAN

Accurate Dorwin:
www.accuratedorwin.com

Duxton:
www.duxtonwindows.com

Fibertec:
www.fibertec.com

Inline:
www.inlinefiberglass.com

Paradigm:
www.paradigmwindows.com

Serious Windows:
www.seriouswindows.com

Thermotech:
www.thermotechfiberglass.com

EUROPEAN

Bieber:
www.bieberusa.com

Heinzmann:
www.europeanwindows.com

Internorm:
www.internorm.com

Optiwin:
www.optiwin-usa.com

Pazen ENERsign:
www.quantumbuilder.com/pazen

Silber:
www.silberfenster.com

Unilux Ultratherm:
www.unilux.de

Installing Replacement Windows

■ BY MIKE GUERTIN

Windows wear out before a house does. Sometimes the need for replacement windows is obvious, such as when you encounter poorly functioning single-pane sashes with weights. But even windows with insulated glass become difficult to operate, suffer from damaged seals, or show signs of deterioration.

The good news is that replacement windows eliminate these problems, offering improved appearance and easier operation, along with greater levels of energy efficiency. Window replacement could save you 5% to 15% off your heating and cooling bills, but how much you'll save depends on where you live (the potential is much higher in cold climates) and how inefficient your existing windows are.

In some cases, air sealing and better insulation elsewhere in your house (see "Home Remedies for Energy Nosebleeds," pp. 12–19) offer more bang for your energy buck. The best way to tell is with a home-energy audit, which will identify the biggest deficiencies in your home's energy envelope (see "Every House Needs an Energy Audit," pp. 4–11).

If you find that your windows are costing you energy dollars, you can go one of two ways: Hire a full-service installer to measure, order, and install new windows for you; or buy and install them yourself. Replacement windows are easy to order and quick to install, and you can save money if you tackle this project yourself.

Evaluate Existing Windows

The installation shown here took place in a modest Cape that still had its original single-glazed, sash-weighted windows—a perfect candidate for replacement windows. I chose frame-and-sash replacement windows (also known as pocket windows) because the existing window jambs, sills, and trim were solid, and the siding was in good condition. Had the window frames been rotted or the siding in need of replacement, I would have had to install new-construction windows using the old rough openings. The budget didn't allow for the extra labor to tackle full

Accurate measurements, thorough caulking, and proper installation will maximize your savings.

window replacement, which would have required the siding to be stripped back, and the interior and exterior trim to be removed and then reinstalled or replaced.

Finally, I didn't want to disturb the homeowners. Pocket windows are quick to install and create little mess inside or out. On average, working alone, I can install one in less than 30 minutes.

Choosing the Right Windows

As a contractor, I order windows directly from more than a dozen manufacturers. Some are national, others regional, and a couple make their windows locally near where I work. National and regional manufacturers generally don't sell directly to

Once I've checked to make sure the window I ordered fits in the opening, I lay down a drop cloth to catch paint chips and debris. Stripping out old window sashes is easy, but I still work carefully because the windows can be fragile and the glass can break easily. I'd rather spend extra time in preparation than on cleanup.

Measure thrice to avoid ordering twice

- Use the shortest of three horizontal measurements (See the drawing at near right).
- Use the shortest of three vertical measurements.
- Double-check for square by measuring the diagonal.

Watch for lead

If your home was built before 1978, the old windows may have been painted with lead paint. Either have a professional test done to determine if lead paint is present (and the extent of it), or presume lead paint is present and follow lead-safe work practices. You can find out more from your local health department or the U.S. Environmental Protection Agency (www.epa.gov/lead).

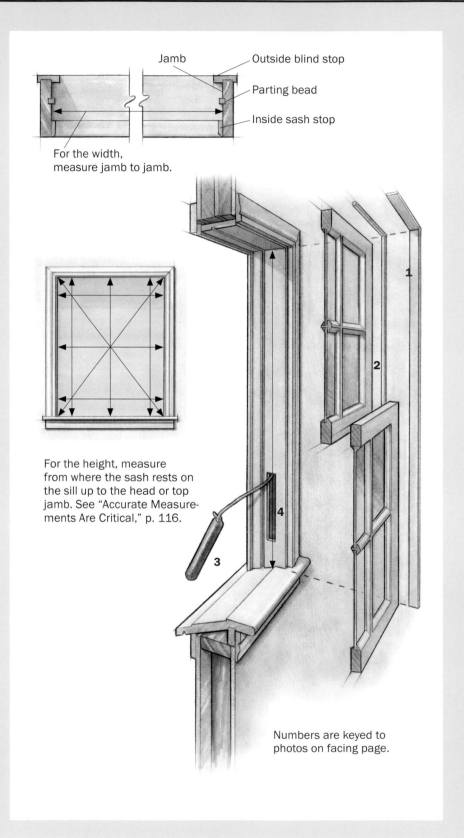

Jamb · Outside blind stop · Parting bead · Inside sash stop

For the width, measure jamb to jamb.

For the height, measure from where the sash rests on the sill up to the head or top jamb. See "Accurate Measurements Are Critical," p. 116.

Numbers are keyed to photos on facing page.

1. Remove sash stops. Cut the paint at the jamb joint with a utility knife; then drive a stiff paint scraper into the joint to pry off the stops. Be careful not to damage anything because the sash stops will be reused.

2. Carefully remove the sashes. Swing the inside sash out of the window opening, and cut the counterweight cords to free the sash. Remove the small parting bead between the sashes, and take out the outer sash the same way.

3. Remove the weights. Open the counterweight doors to remove the weights and cords; then unscrew the pulleys and remove them. Some installation guides suggest hammering the old pulleys into the jamb, but I disagree. The pulley holes make good view spots when installing insulation.

4. Insulate the cavity. Use an old parting bead to slide strips of batt insulation into the cavity. Don't overstuff the cavity, or you'll reduce the insulation's R-value. Replace the counterweight doors, and scrape loose paint from the jamb and stops. Prime any bare wood on the jamb and sill to protect it from rot.

Install the New Window with Expanders, Shims, and Screws

Different manufacturers have different details for securing and weather-sealing their windows. However, they all have a sill expander of some type at the top and bottom, and rely on screws to secure the frame to the jamb.

1. Install the bottom sill expander. Use a Speed Square® to make a level reference line so that you can measure how much the sill slopes. Then use a utility knife to cut the bottom sill expander to fit snugly against the sill. Tap the expander into the window frame with the butt of a hammer handle.

2. Install the head expander. If the replacement window doesn't overlap the head stop, you need to add the head expander that fits over the top of the window and fill the airspace with low-expanding foam or fiberglass insulation.

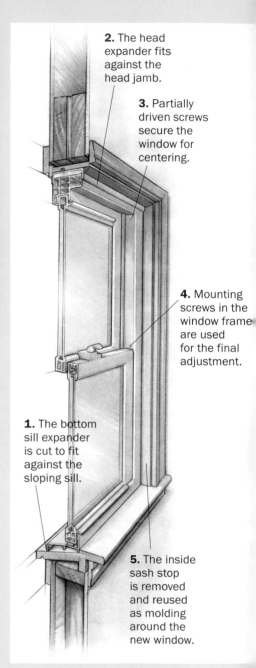

2. The head expander fits against the head jamb.

3. Partially driven screws secure the window for centering.

4. Mounting screws in the window frame are used for the final adjustment.

1. The bottom sill expander is cut to fit against the sloping sill.

5. The inside sash stop is removed and reused as molding around the new window.

homeowners, but many local fabricators have a retail store on site that will sell you windows at a small premium over whole-sale prices.

You can also buy replacement windows at a home center. If your house is 50 years old or less, you can find fairly good-quality windows in standard sizes to fit the existing openings.

I advise shopping around, but be sure you're comparing equal products and services. Some companies' standard features are options that cost more from other fabricators. Frame thickness and extrusion designs

3. Insert and center the window. Drive two mounting screws partway through the window frame and into the jambs to keep the window in place. Then use a small pry bar to get the frame centered, level, and plumb.

4. Secure the window. Insert shims between the window and the jamb as backing for mounting screws. Drive mounting screws in all the pilot holes. Sometimes these holes are concealed by sash stops or balance guards that can be slid out of the way or removed.

5. Replace the sash stops. The payoff for removing the old stops carefully is that they can be reused to finish the new window. Before installing the stops, I fill gaps between the window and the jamb with low-expanding foam, part of the weathersealing process (see the sidebar on p. 116).

can differ. Bargain windows might have lower-quality frames that require more time to shim and brace adequately for proper operation.

If I have a choice, I use high-quality vinyl windows made locally. Although they might not be a popular name brand, the warranty is good (20 years) and the price is reasonable. Also, if problems arise, there's someone local to call.

Get Maximum Value with a Good Weatherseal

If I've spent the money, time, and effort to replace a window, I want to get the best performance I possibly can. Proper weathersealing calls for spray foam and caulk.

Foam the gaps. Use low-expanding foam to fill gaps between the old jamb and the new window.

Caulk the stops. Apply exterior caulk to the blind stop before installing the swindow; then caulk all the exterior trim joints.

Accurate Measurements Are Critical

I always take measurements myself, and if the sales rep comes out to help, I check that person's work. The last thing I want is to show up on the morning of a whole-house window replacement and find out that someone else messed up the order.

Most important is checking top, bottom, middle, and diagonally for square. The new window has to be sized for the shortest measurement (see the drawing on p. 112). I use a systematic approach with my own order sheet to note dimensions and location.

Writing measurements on a block of wood just doesn't cut it. One wrong measurement, and you own a perfectly good window that doesn't fit.

Know How the Windows Are Sized

Replacement-window fabricators make units on a ¼-in. basis, a ½-in. basis, or a combination of the two. This guideline forces you to order a unit smaller than anticipated when a dimension falls on a ⅛-in. increment, but undersizing a window is better than having it too tight. Window height is more forgiving than width due to the sill and head

Choose the Right Window

Many manufacturers that make windows for new construction also make replacement windows. In addition to the factors listed below, you'll need to consider cost and warranty details.

Style

Double-hung, single-hung, casement, awning, and other window styles are available.

Glass

The choices include different types of insulated glass, such as glass with heat-reflective coatings and gas-filled glass. You can also order windows with snap-in grilles or true divided lites.

Material

The type of material used in the window determines its price, its durability, and its appearance. Here's a quick tour:

Vinyl

- Usually less expensive than other types
- Durable, low maintenance
- Limited color choice

Wood

- Requires painting
- Compatible with historic houses

Fiberglass

- Stronger than vinyl and just as durable
- Available with wood interior surfaces
- Low maintenance
- Usually more expensive than other types

Aluminum-clad

- Durable exterior, wood interior
- Many colors available
- Aluminum can be painted

Vinyl-clad

- Durable exterior
- Wood or finished interior
- Limited color choice

---

expanders, which is why many fabricators offer ¼-in. width sizing and only ½-in. height sizing. If I have to choose between leaving only ⅛ in. of wiggle room or having ⅝ in. to play with, I'll take the bigger measurement.

Some window fabricators take orders based on opening measurements, and they make the deductions to actual unit size from information you supply. I never order this way because it does not account for out-of-square conditions. Make your own deductions from the measured opening, and order the actual window size (sometimes called tip-to-tip size).

Guarantee a Smooth, Safe Installation

Wherever I start, I move the furniture out of the way for clear access to the window, and I cover the floor with a drop cloth to collect paint chips and debris. I always use a vacuum and a dust brush to clean out the windowsill and to clean up the floor when I'm done working.

Mike Guertin (www.mikeguertin.com) is a builder, remodeling contractor, and writer in East Greenwich, R.I.

Is Your Heating System an Energy Beast?

■ BY DAVE YATES

The economy is down, fuel costs are up, and chances are that your heating budget is already busted. You need to do something—but what? Only a few of us are ready to invest in geothermal or solar. The rest of us need to find the answer in the heating system we already have.

For 70% of U.S. households, that system consists of a furnace that forces hot air through ducts; for 17%, it's a heat pump; and for 11%, it's a boiler that heats with water or steam radiators. The remaining 2% of homes use wood, coal, geothermal, solar, or other heating methods. When it comes to fuel, 58% of us use gas (either natural or propane), about 35% use electricity, and almost 7% use fuel oil.

Your home might not have the most efficient heating system available, but there's good news: You can tune up your current system so that it performs better, keeps you more comfortable, and doesn't put as big of a dent in your wallet. The following can help. Although the topics might seem simple, they're useful in diagnosing deficiencies. In fact, I usually end up fielding a lot of these questions from homeowners based on their observations of how their heating system is or isn't working. Once you know where your system is falling down, it's possible to boost it (and its efficiency) back up.

Q&A

Q: I hear a whistling noise around the blower compartment of my furnace. What is causing the noise? Should I be concerned?

A: You're hearing air leakage. All air handlers (any device with a blower, including furnaces, heat pumps, and central air) have two ducts: one for supply, the other for return. I often find considerable air leakage at both connection points. If the blower is located in an unconditioned location (attic, crawlspace, or basement), it is bleeding out heat, or Btu, on the supply side while pulling in unconditioned air that must be warmed (or cooled and dehumidified) on the return side. This energy loss can add 10% or more to your heating and cooling bills.

You can fix these leaks by sealing the connection with sealant and/or top-grade mastic tape rated to withstand the area's exposure. While you're at it, check the air handler's access door, another frequent

source of air leaks. Because the access door must be opened to service the equipment, you want to use only tape or magnetic strips to seal gaps. Other spots to seal include filter slots and openings for wiring. Last but not least, the accessible ductwork should be examined for leaks. Seal them with high-quality tape, mastic, or sealant that's compatible with the duct material and with exposure to surrounding air temperatures.

Q: Streaks of dirt are visible around the ceiling registers in our house. What's causing them?

A: Those streaks are tiny particles of soot blasted across the ceiling by air leaking from around a register that isn't connected properly. Think of your ceiling as the inner layer of a sandwich. If you had X-ray vision, you'd see the duct boot resting on the attic side of the ceiling with the register below, sandwiching the ceiling between them. If the boot isn't firmly attached, you're heating (or cooling) your attic—typically unconditioned space—which means your energy dollars are being lost to the great outdoors. The same goes for floor registers. In either case, the cure is the same: Remove the register, use a sealant to close the gaps between the boot and the ceiling (or floor), and add foam weatherstripping between the ceiling (or floor) and the register to prevent air leakage.

Furnace Basics

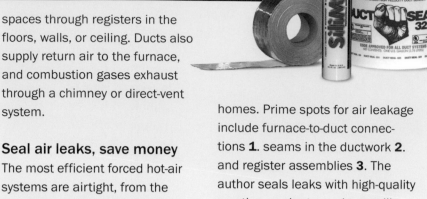

Furnaces use natural gas, propane, oil, or electricity, and are fired when a remote thermostat detects that the temperature in a room has fallen below a preset level. Once in operation, the burner fires in a combustion chamber and warms a heat exchanger (electric furnaces have coils much like a toaster). A blower pushes air over the heat exchanger, or coils, and hot air flows through a series of ducts and enters a home's living spaces through registers in the floors, walls, or ceiling. Ducts also supply return air to the furnace, and combustion gases exhaust through a chimney or direct-vent system.

Seal air leaks, save money

The most efficient forced hot-air systems are airtight, from the furnace to the registers. Those systems, however, are few and far between, especially in older homes. Prime spots for air leakage include furnace-to-duct connections **1**. seams in the ductwork **2**. and register assemblies **3**. The author seals leaks with high-quality mastics, sealants, and tapes like the Hardcast® products shown above (www.hardcast.com).

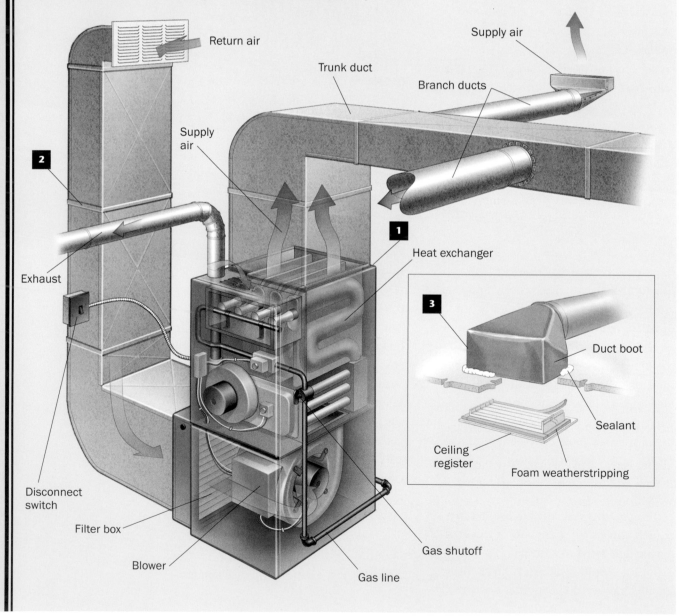

Return air

Supply air

Trunk duct

Branch ducts

Supply air

2

Exhaust

1

Heat exchanger

3

Duct boot

Sealant

Ceiling register

Foam weatherstripping

Disconnect switch

Filter box

Blower

Gas shutoff

Gas line

Q: Our local oil company is offering a $29.95 service special. It seems like a bargain, but does heating equipment need to be serviced every year?

A: Just as people should get an annual physical, all heating equipment should receive an annual checkup to maintain peak performance and to keep the home's occupants safe. Part of the service is a test for proper combustion using an analyzer that provides CO (carbon monoxide), O_2 (excess oxygen), and CO_2 (carbon dioxide) levels, as well as net stack (exhaust) temperature. You should ask for a copy of this test, or combustion analysis.

While the internal surfaces of some gas appliances don't need to be vacuumed (unlike oil units), regular maintenance is particularly important for newer high-efficiency models. Also, in all units, the chimney or venting should be inspected periodically to make sure it's not obstructed. Dirty heat exchangers in oil burners rob efficiency, which results in increased fuel usage. A layer of soot just $1/16$ in. thick reduces operating efficiency by 10%.

That said, it's not physically possible to clean and tune up an oil-burning appliance properly for $29.95. Companies offering prices that low often pay technicians a flat rate for each call they make; the more they fit into a day, the more profitable it is for them—at your expense. I often see those furnaces six to eight years later, when they're malfunctioning. So accept the fact that if it sounds too good to be true, it probably is, and call in a professional technician you can trust at a believable price.

What Should I Expect from a Service Call?

- Preliminary combustion analysis
- Chimney inspection
- Top of boiler removed and combustion chamber cleaned
- Soot vacuumed from all surfaces
- Oil filter replaced
- Oil-burner nozzle replaced
- Reassembly; draft in flue and over burner checked; boiler operation tested
- Final combustion analysis

Q: Our ductwork is located in the attic. There doesn't seem to be as much warm air blowing from the registers as there used to be. Is that my imagination?

A: Ductwork that travels through unconditioned spaces (basements, crawlspaces, garages, and attics) needs to be well insulated. Uninsulated ducts waste gobs of energy and create drafts as chilled air spills out of ceiling registers; it's hard to believe how noticeable this is until you've felt it firsthand. Newer codes require R-8 minimum insulation on ducts, but on older flex and duct-board systems, it can be as low as R-2.5. Before you consider more insulation, however, remember that insulation can hide the real problem: air

Duct board

Insulation helps, too. Once all ducts are air-sealed, use insulation to limit heat loss. Owens Corning makes insulated rigid ducts, insulated flexible duct wrap, and foil-faced insulation that can be used to wrap existing ducts (www.owenscorning.com).

Flexible duct insulation sleeve

Duct wrap

leakage. According to the Department of Energy, you could be losing 40% of the heat through duct leaks. A home-energy audit that includes a duct-pressure test can identify those leaks; sealing them with mastic can result in substantial fuel savings. Once the leaks are sealed, add more insulation around the ducts, either blown-in, loose fill, fiberglass batt, or a duct wrap, as seen above.

Heat-Pump Basics

Air-to-air heat pumps use pressurized Freon® gas to absorb heat from the air outside and transfer it to your home. When the thermostat calls for heating, Freon is pressurized, it condenses, and then it turns to hot liquid. A blower forces air across warm Freon-filled coils and through a system of ducts; warm air is distributed through registers in the floors, walls, and ceiling. At the same time, a fan in the condenser sends cold air outside. You can reverse the cycle for cooling in the summer. (Ground-source heat pumps use a water/glycol mixture to exchange heat energy with the earth.)

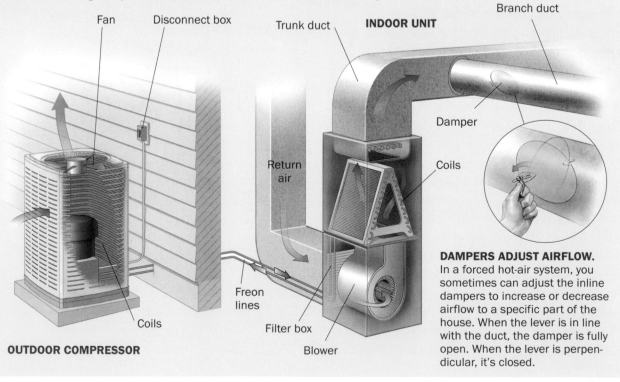

Fan   Disconnect box

Trunk duct   **INDOOR UNIT**   Branch duct

Return air

Damper

Coils

Freon lines

Filter box

Coils

Blower

OUTDOOR COMPRESSOR

DAMPERS ADJUST AIRFLOW. In a forced hot-air system, you sometimes can adjust the inline dampers to increase or decrease airflow to a specific part of the house. When the lever is in line with the duct, the damper is fully open. When the lever is perpendicular, it's closed.

While adjusting airflow this way could improve comfort, it doesn't help the system to perform better. To do that, you need to call in a pro. A good HVAC contractor uses a nationally approved design program to size an entire duct system properly. Ask the contractor to show you how he or she does the design work, and ask questions. The fix can range from a few simple adjustments to installing a mini-split inverter heat pump in the affected areas to ripping out everything and starting over, costing from a couple of hundred dollars to several thousand.

Q: The temperatures upstairs and downstairs are uneven; some rooms are colder or hotter than others. What's causing this problem? Can it be fixed?

A: You're likely describing an out-of-balance duct system. If a forced-air system isn't ducted properly, the flow of supply and return air is unbalanced, resulting, for example, in a ground floor that doesn't stay warm in heating season or a second floor that's not sufficiently cooled in AC season. Sometimes it's due to poor duct design; other times it occurs when air-conditioning is added to a heating system without re-evaluating and possibly resizing the ductwork.

If you have problems with individual rooms and you've made sure all the ducts are connected properly (believe me, I've seen my share of ducts to nowhere), you might be able to adjust the dampers and guide a little more (or less) air to those areas. Dampers are normally located within the first few feet of each branch, or takeoff, and are adjusted by turning an external lever. Generally, when the lever is in line with the duct, the damper is fully open. Airflow also can be regulated somewhat at the register if it's an adjustable model; however, that can create an objectionable noise as air rushes past the louvers.

Q: I hear a lot about tuning up furnaces, but how can I boost the efficiency of my heat pump?

A: Like furnaces and boilers, your heat pump should be serviced annually. Cleaning the coils and changing the filter can increase the heat pump's efficiency by up to 10%. Heat pumps are rated in SEER for cooling efficiency and HSPF or COP for heating efficiency. (See "Say What?" on p. 124.) The higher the numbers, the higher the efficiency and the lower the operating costs.

If your heat pump operates below 13 SEER and 6.5 HSPF (the current minimum standards set by the federal government), you should plan to replace it. When you do, ask for a 410A refrigerant-based system (Carrier® calls it Puron®). The 410A-based systems are a bit more efficient and a bit more expensive, but the R-22 refrigerant currently in use is being phased out. As a result, it's unlikely to be available when new equipment wears out.

With today's fuel costs escalating, you might also want to consider a hybrid heating system, wherein a fossil-fuel furnace is coupled with a high-efficiency heat pump, allowing you to choose whichever system is least expensive to operate at specific times.

These setups often use automatic controls that seamlessly switch from one system to the other based on the internal programming.

Q: I keep hearing about "modulating" technology in furnaces and boilers. What's that?

A: Traditionally, heating equipment operates on one speed: Either it's on, or it's off. The minute a furnace or boiler fires up, it produces the same amount of Btu whether it's trying to raise the temperature of a house 2°F or 20°F, and whether the air outside is -5°F or 50°F. But a number of new, high-efficiency stepped-input ("hi-lo fire") furnaces can operate at two levels: low input or high input, with a lower or higher fan speed.

Because the low-input level can be used when outdoor air temperatures are relatively moderate (roughly 70% of the heating season for many of us), modulating equipment promises fuel savings of 30% or more. When the heat-demand load exceeds the "lo-fire" output, the furnace control steps on the gas to meet demand.

Modulation technology has been limited to boilers—until now. York International's recently released Affinity 33 is the industry's first truly modulating gas furnace that uses outdoor reset, which adjusts the system based on the air temperature outside, to determine how hard it needs to run to meet a home's heat loss (from 35% to 100% in 1% increments). Both the burner and the blower modulate as a team to maximize Btu, and the manufacturer claims 98% thermal efficiency.

A furnace first. The York® Affinity™ 33 is the industry's first modulating gas furnace and boasts 98% efficiency (www.york.com).

Modulation is an almost universal feature found on high-efficiency condensing boilers. Here, too, you'll find products that can achieve 98% thermal efficiency. Virtually all these high-efficiency products use outdoor reset to achieve superior comfort and efficiency.

Q: We're not ready to replace our heating equipment right now. What can we do to improve our comfort and reduce fuel bills?

A: If you've performed the fixes I already mentioned and you're still uncomfortable (or breaking open the piggy bank to meet fuel costs), you might consider fine-tuning your system with an auxiliary appliance. One option is spot-treating one or more rooms with high-efficiency mini-split heat pumps. With efficiencies topping out at 26 SEER and 12 HSPF, these ultraquiet heat pumps give you the option of conditioning just the space you're occupying while letting the rest of the home's mechanical systems hibernate. They're basically self-contained units with supply tubes for refrigerant running through the wall. The best ones use inverter (variable-speed) technology, allowing the units to sip only as much electricity as they need to maintain comfort.

If you have a hot-air system, adding humidification can increase comfort while letting you reduce the temperature by several degrees. You can plug in a freestanding unit or have a pro connect one to your furnace for $600 or more.

High-grade your hydronics. Thermostatic radiator valves fine-tune hydronic heating systems by controlling temperatures in individual rooms. Set the dial to raise the temperature in one room and lower it in another (www.danfoss.com).

If you have a central system that's not zoned, a motorized damper system can deliver heat where you need it most. Multiple dampers can be daisy-chained so that several rooms operate as one zone. One caution: It's important to have a good professional do this work.

If you have a hydronic system, you can fine-tune the zones with thermostatic radiator valves, which can be installed in every room except where the thermostat is located. Once you set the dial, the valves open or close automatically based on the room's temperature. They're a good solution in rooms that are chronically overheated or that are seldom used.

In an uncertain economy, investing in energy—that is, the energy you use in your own home—could be your wisest move. Your ROI (return on investment) begins the second you start using the equipment and can well exceed anything the stock market can yield. You'll add value to your largest investment (your home), you'll be more comfortable, and you'll get to keep more of your hard-earned money.

Q: What separates low-efficiency heating systems from high-efficiency models?

A: One difference is the way the unit is vented. A 78%-efficient furnace (or boiler) vents into a chimney and uses the home's interior air for combustion. New 92%-efficient models are designed for sealed combustion. A direct venting setup draws outdoor combustion air.

A damper with horsepower. Motorized dampers allow for controlled airflow through ducts from remote locations and can create heating zones in a formerly one-zone house (www.aprilaire .com).

Boiler Basics

Boilers heat water with gas, propane, oil, or electricity, and the water heats the home through a hydronic delivery system that can include baseboard fin-and-tube radiators, steam radiators, or in-floor radiant heating. When the thermostat fires the boiler, fuel burns in a combustion chamber, and warm water is pumped through a closed circuit of tubing. (Electric boilers have direct-immersion heating elements.) The water can get as warm as 180°F, depending on the system's design. Because hot water expands, a pressure gauge and a relief valve prevent the system from failing due to excess water pressure. Combustion gases exit the house through a chimney or a direct-vent system.

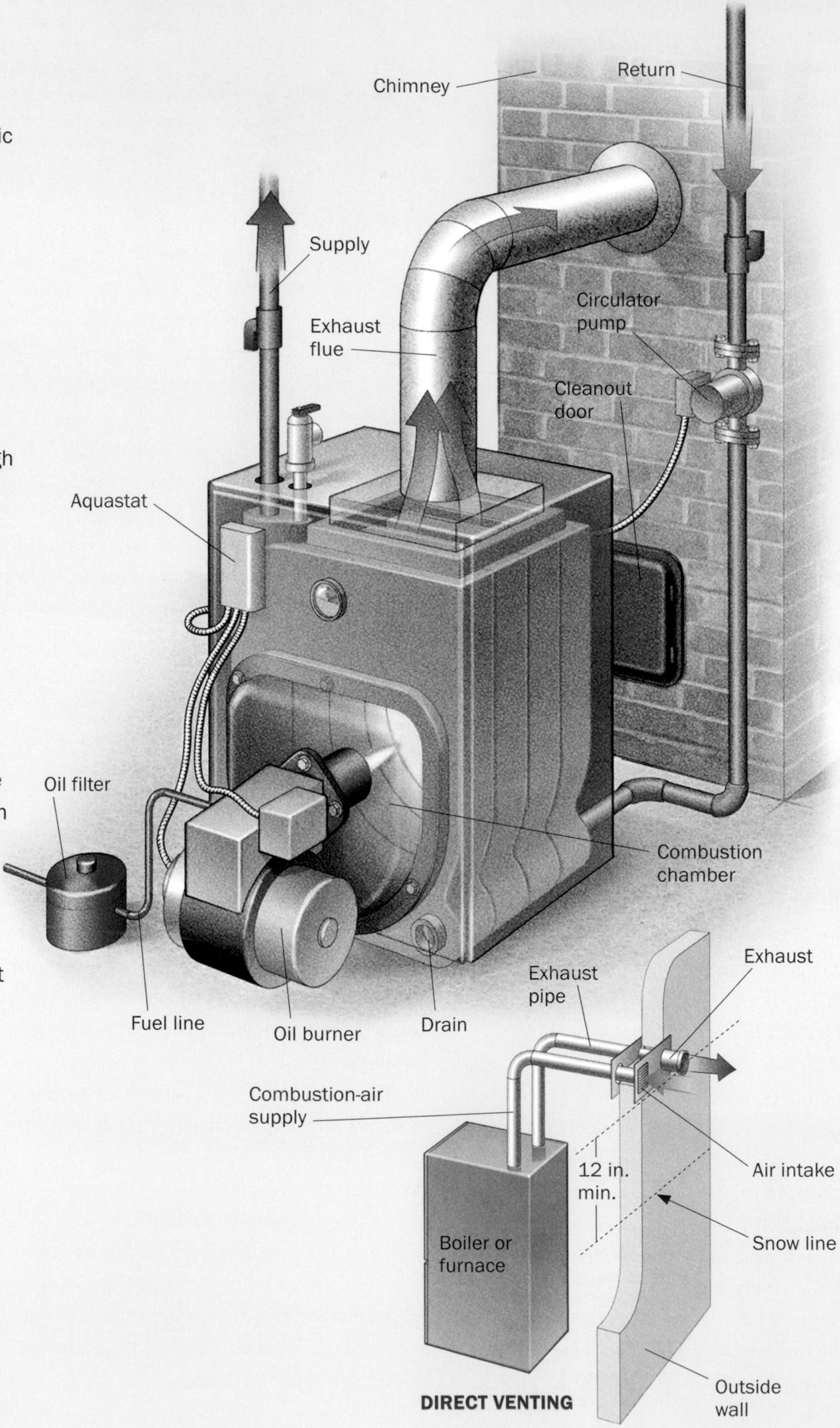

Chimney

Return

Supply

Exhaust flue

Circulator pump

Cleanout door

Aquastat

Oil filter

Combustion chamber

Fuel line

Oil burner

Drain

Exhaust pipe

Exhaust

Combustion-air supply

12 in. min.

Air intake

Snow line

Boiler or furnace

DIRECT VENTING

Outside wall

Chimney-vented heating equipment continuously drafts heated air out of the house and strips away some of the Btu produced when the furnace is operating. There's also a hidden energy cost: air infiltration. Whenever its burner fires, the chimney-vented unit draws in warm room air to support combustion—air that must be replaced by cold outside air drawn through cracks and gaps in the home's shell. Eliminate that draw with a sealed-combustion model, and your fuel bills could fall by 30% or more.

Cost also separates the top performers from the rest. But the difference in price between 78%- and 95%-efficient gas-fired furnaces has narrowed considerably, to about $1,500 for the equipment and installation costs. If your system burns oil, you have fewer choices, and the price gap is wider (about $4,000). But with ever-shifting oil prices, it's easier to justify the extra expenditure.

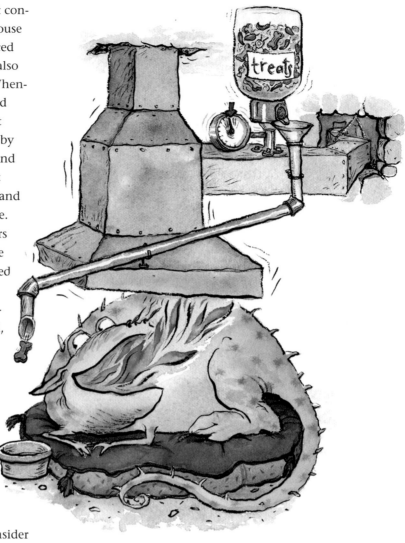

Q: My furnace still works, but my heating bills are sky-high. Should I think about getting a new one?

A: Given today's rapidly escalating fuel prices, you really can't afford not to consider upgrading to a new high-efficiency furnace. Older furnaces were constructed with durability, not efficiency, in mind. Trimming 20% to 70% off your fuel bills is a realistic expectation when you upgrade to high-performance equipment.

Your existing furnace most likely has a 60% to 78% efficiency rating, which was once considered respectable. The current federally mandated minimum efficiency for furnaces is 80%, but there are models—hundreds of them—that operate above 92% and qualify for Energy Star rebates. There are even a few that can achieve 98% efficiency by using a feature called "outdoor reset," which modulates both the blower speed and the burner's fuel input. As you might expect, the better the efficiency, the higher the up-front costs. But with the rise in fuel prices and the anticipated 20- to 30-year life span of a furnace, the increased purchase price pales by comparison to the fuel costs saved over time.

Dave Yates owns and operates F.W. Behler Inc., a mechanical-contracting firm in York, Pa.

Finding the Sweet Spot: Siting a Home for Energy Efficiency

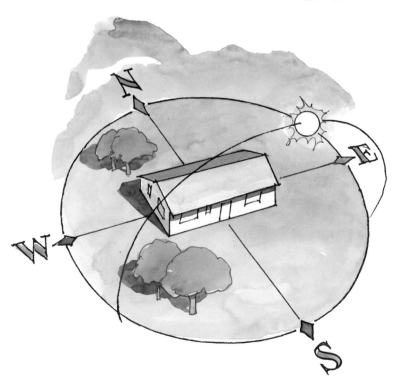

■ BY M. JOE NUMBERS

Architecture professors love a good riddle. Here's one: How do ancient Greek town grids, Anasazi Indian pueblos, and New England saltbox houses differ from most residential construction today? Give up? Each culture understood how to site a house. The ancient Greeks oriented their town grids to receive winter sun and summer shade. The Anasazi Indians located their dwellings beneath cliff overhangs to take advantage of natural shading. Early American settlers oriented and configured their saltbox houses to minimize the cold northern facade and to maximize the warm southern facade.

Regrettably, the siting lore known to our ancestors has practically disappeared because of central-heating and -cooling systems. That's too bad, because a house's energy efficiency, comfort, and marketability are all affected by its siting. A house that's sited to take advantage of the sun, the wind, and the topography costs less to heat and cool, and lets you enjoy indoors and outdoors longer, two strong selling points.

In the site-design classes I used to teach, we divided solar-siting strategies into three categories: orientation, or which way the house faces; location, or where the house sits; and configuration, or how it's shaped. Figuring out the best orientation, location, and configuration requires a little knowledge of local climatic conditions and an analysis of the site and its surroundings. Here, I'll discuss what to look for and where to find the information you need to reap the benefits of a properly sited house.

Long Side Faces South

When siting a house, the most effective strategy you can use is to orient the building with the long side aligned on the east-west axis. This orientation places the long side of the building where it can be reached and heated by the low-angle rays of the winter sun. Conversely, it places the short sides of the building to the east and west to minimize solar gains during the overheated periods of summer.

Your house doesn't have to be exactly on the east-west axis; somewhere within 15 degrees of this axis is fine. What's more important is that the house is oriented toward true south, not magnetic south. Compass needles point to magnetic north, which deviates from true north by as much as 20 degrees. The difference between magnetic north and true north is declination, and it varies across the United States (see the sidebar on pp. 130–131). Information on declination can be found on U.S. Geological Survey topological maps or the NOAA website (http://www.ngdc.noaa.gov/geomag/geomag.shtml).

Once you know your area's declination angle, it's a matter of spinning the dial on a compass. For example, in Boise, Idaho, the declination angle is approximately 14 degrees east. Line up a compass on magnetic north, then rotate the dial until the needle is pointing to 14 degrees east of the north mark on the dial; now the dial markings (not the needle) point to true north.

Lots of related strategies make a true-south orientation more effective. One is to reduce openings (i.e., windows and doors), especially on the north side of the house, because doors and windows conduct more heat than a well-insulated wall. In cold climates, only about 5% to 10% of non-south-facing walls should be openings. In warmer climates, you can get away with slightly more openings as long as the house is well insulated.

On south elevations, increase openings for winter solar gain, but shade them during summer months. Deciduous trees provide summer shading, as do awnings. You can also build overhangs, but they shouldn't be so deep that they block the sun in winter (see the drawing on p. 131).

To figure out the optimal depth for overhangs in your area, use the shade-line-factor formula: The depth of an overhang equals the height from the bottom of a window to its overhang divided by the shade-line factor. This number varies with latitude, so you'll need to know your location's geographic latitude to choose the right shade-line factor. Most maps of the United States and most state maps show latitude.

Another way to make a southern exposure work harder for you is to coordinate the floor plan with the house's orientation. Locate public living spaces, such as the living room, the dining room, the kitchen, and such, to the south side of the house, where they will receive light and warmth throughout the year. Locate private and unoccupied rooms—bedrooms, utility rooms, storage rooms, etc.—to the north, where they will act as insulating buffers for the home's public spaces (see the floor plan on p. 130). These buffer spaces serve as a form of insulation (particularly if they can be closed off

Orient the House to the Sun

Placing the long side of a house along the east-west axis exposes the south elevation to year-round light and warmth. In summer, this orientation minimizes overheating on the short east and west elevations. Grouping private and unoccupied spaces on the north side of the house, where they act as insulators for the south-facing public rooms, maximizes the benefit of southern exposure.

Finding True North

At the bottom margin of U.S. Geological Survey maps, there are three north bearings: magnetic north, true north, and grid north. Magnetic north is compass-needle north, but it's not helpful for solar siting, which calls for true north, indicated by the star. The difference between these bearings is the declination, in this case, 13.5 degrees.

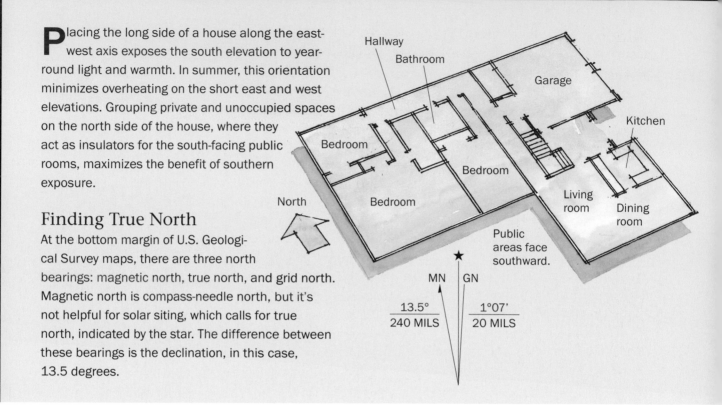

Hallway

Bathroom

Garage

Kitchen

Bedroom

Bedroom

North

Bedroom

Living room

Dining room

Public areas face southward.

MN | GN

13.5° | 1°07'
240 MILS | 20 MILS

from the rest of the house), much like the closed airspace in a thermos keeps the cold air outside from cooling the warm liquid inside.

Hillside Lots Are Cooler, So Plan Accordingly

Donald Trump once said that the three most important considerations when buying real estate are location, location, and location. I doubt that he was referring to the potential for lower heating and cooling costs, but a house's location on a piece of land can make it less expensive to heat and cool.

If you're considering building on a hillside, for example, locate the house according to its most appropriate zone. In cold or temperate climates, it's best to locate a house midway between the ridge and the valley.

There, the house is not exposed to increased wind velocities at the ridge or to subsiding cold air that settles at the valley bottom.

In hot, humid climates—the Gulf Coast states and the Southeast—ridges generally provide the most exposure to year-round cooling breezes. In hot, arid climates such as the Desert Southwest, valley floors tend to collect cold air overnight that helps to cool a house. You can trap this cold air by opening doors and windows at night and by closing them during the day.

Building on a south-facing slope, or aspect, of a landform increases the exposure of the house and surrounding grounds to the low-angle rays of the sun during the winter. In cold and temperate climates especially, you should avoid north-facing aspects whenever possible.

You should also take a good look at the adjacent area to the south of the building

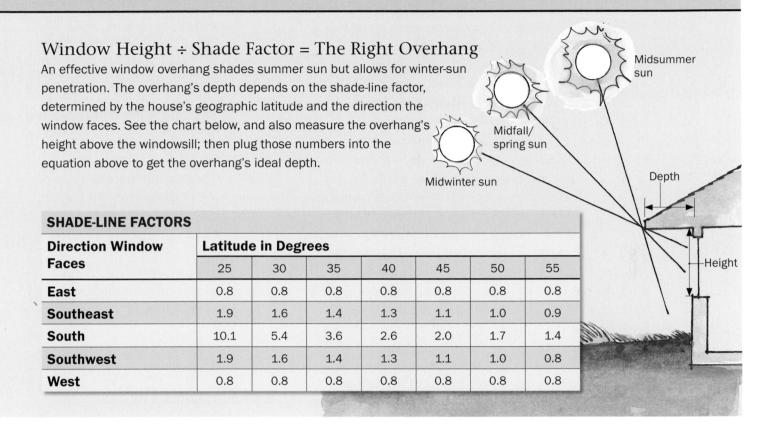

Window Height ÷ Shade Factor = The Right Overhang

An effective window overhang shades summer sun but allows for winter-sun penetration. The overhang's depth depends on the shade-line factor, determined by the house's geographic latitude and the direction the window faces. See the chart below, and also measure the overhang's height above the windowsill; then plug those numbers into the equation above to get the overhang's ideal depth.

Midsummer sun

Midfall/ spring sun

Midwinter sun

Depth

Height

SHADE-LINE FACTORS

Direction Window Faces	Latitude in Degrees						
	25	30	35	40	45	50	55
East	0.8	0.8	0.8	0.8	0.8	0.8	0.8
Southeast	1.9	1.6	1.4	1.3	1.1	1.0	0.9
South	10.1	5.4	3.6	2.6	2.0	1.7	1.4
Southwest	1.9	1.6	1.4	1.3	1.1	1.0	0.8
West	0.8	0.8	0.8	0.8	0.8	0.8	0.8

site. Avoid building on areas that will be shaded during winter by tall buildings, coniferous trees, or landforms (ridges, etc.).

If you're in a cold or temperate climate, where it's best to build midway along the hillside rather than at the ridge or in the valley, you should study the contours of the hillside. Any natural drainages or depressions in the topography are poor choices for a building site (see the drawing on p. 132). A natural drainage or depression channels cold air down the hillside. This cold air collects behind obstructions to its natural flow, so a house should be built away from these cold-air flows. If you simply cannot follow this strategy, use evergreen vegetation or solid fencing to divert cold air around and away from the house.

Whenever possible, recess the north, east, and west sides of the house into the natural slope of the site, or pile soil against the house on these sides. These earth-berming

strategies provide additional, permanent insulation against both winter winds and summer overheating.

Earth-berming strategies require careful detailing to prevent water damage to the structure. They are generally more expensive than typical aboveground construction. When properly done, however, earth berming provides long-term, low-maintenance energy savings.

If you are not familiar with earth-berming strategies but have a site that is suitable, consult an architect or a designer experienced in this type of construction.

Make the Wind Work for You

Generally, summer and winter winds come from different directions. It's usually possible to divert winter winds and to channel summer breezes by carefully locating the house in relation to its surroundings. Check with your local airport, meteorological station, or state energy office to determine the prevailing summer- and winter-wind directions for your area. Also, this data can be obtained from the U.S. Department of Commerce National Climatic Center in Asheville, N.C. (www.ncdc.noaa.gov/oa/climate/climatedata.html).

Study the adjacent topography, trees, and buildings during your initial site inspection. Look for those existing conditions that can block or divert cold winter winds around the building site. Locate the house in these lee-side areas (see the top drawing on p. 134).

In warm or humid climates, place the house in a part of the site that maximizes summer ventilation. For example, the process of evaporation cools summer breezes as they pass over water bodies. These water bodies don't have to be big to have an effect. Locate the house to catch prevailing summertime breezes coming off lakes, ponds, rivers, and even streams.

Conversely, in cool and temperate climates, avoid locations near bodies of water on the lee side of prevailing winter winds. In other words, if winter winds generally blow from the north, avoid sites at the south end of a water body.

Water isn't the only medium that induces cold winter winds. Landforms, vegetation, and buildings all can increase wind velocities because of a phenomenon called the Venturi effect.

The Venturi effect occurs when any moving medium—in this case air—squeezes

Build at an Elevation to Match the Climate

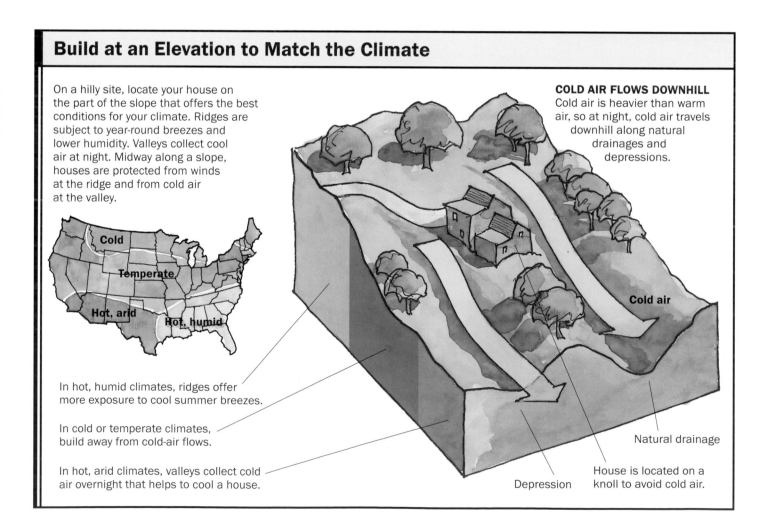

On a hilly site, locate your house on the part of the slope that offers the best conditions for your climate. Ridges are subject to year-round breezes and lower humidity. Valleys collect cool air at night. Midway along a slope, houses are protected from winds at the ridge and from cold air at the valley.

COLD AIR FLOWS DOWNHILL
Cold air is heavier than warm air, so at night, cold air travels downhill along natural drainages and depressions.

Cold
Temperate
Hot, arid
Hot, humid

In hot, humid climates, ridges offer more exposure to cool summer breezes.

In cold or temperate climates, build away from cold-air flows.

In hot, arid climates, valleys collect cold air overnight that helps to cool a house.

Cold air

Natural drainage

House is located on a knoll to avoid cold air.

Depression

through a constricted opening. To maintain a constant volume of air passing through the opening, the wind velocity increases accordingly. That's why it's so windy at the base of tall buildings.

Keep away from topography, adjacent buildings, or vegetation that funnels cold winter winds at increased velocities. If you do have a problem because of the Venturi effect, you can position adjacent outbuildings and evergreen trees and shrubs where they will block winter winds.

Conversely, locate the house (and any new vegetation, fences, or outbuildings) to take advantage of increased wind velocities created by the Venturi effect during summer months (see the bottom drawing on p. 134). Use buildings and vegetation to channel summertime breezes into the house. As a rule, try to orient the house within 30 degrees of perpendicular to prevailing summer winds to maximize their cooling effects.

If solar orientation and siting for wind are at cross-purposes (that is, if optimum solar orientation is perpendicular to optimum siting for wind), then solar orientation should take precedence because it has a greater cumulative effect on the heating and cooling of a house.

House Shape Should Fit the Climate

Are you familiar with the aluminum heat-radiating fins that can be slipped over hot-water pipes in a basement? They're supposed to turn hot-water pipes into heating elements to heat the basement space. The principle behind the fins is that they increase the heated surface area so that more heat escapes from the pipe with the fins than from the bare pipe.

The same principle applies to a house's shape, or configuration. As a house's surface area increases, so does the amount of heat it loses. To hold on to the heat, configure the house so that it is relatively compact. Compact shapes, such as cubes, lose less heat

through the building skin than narrow or elongated shapes.

As a general rule for siting a house in cold regions, the long dimension of the house should be approximately 1.1 to 1.3 times the length of the short side. This proportion yields a high ratio of heated interior space to exterior skin. Remember that the longer side of the house is oriented along the east-west axis.

For temperate climates, the configuration is not as important. There is less environmental stress on the building skin, so the designer has more freedom in terms of building configuration. For this region, a ratio between 1.6:1 and 2.4:1 provides good energy performance.

In hot, arid climates, the environmental stresses are greater, so buildings should be shaped similarly to cold-climate configurations. A ratio somewhere between 1.3:1 and 1.6:1 is the most energy-conserving for hot, arid climates.

In warm or humid climates, elongated shapes with openings on the long sides allow for cross ventilation. Generally, ratios in the range of 1.7:1 to 3.0:1 are preferred. When these elongated plans are oriented with the long side on the east-west axis, summer overheating at the short east and west elevations is avoided.

Try to keep corners on the house to a minimum. Unnecessary corners mean more exterior-wall surface is exposed to wind, which increases heating loads on the house.

Regardless of wind direction and particularly in areas where wind direction changes frequently, a good overall strategy is to use a compact, low-profile house design. Avoid tall facades and roof designs that block or trap wind. For example, a tall, broad gable is less aerodynamic than a hip roof, which allows for smoother airflow around and over the house. Orient the narrowest dimension of the house into prevailing winter winds to minimize wind exposure.

Control Exposure to the Wind

Use plants and outbuildings to direct prevailing summer breezes into the house and to divert prevailing winter winds away from the house. Once you know the direction of prevailing winter winds, choose a site where topography, vegetation, and other buildings offer protection.

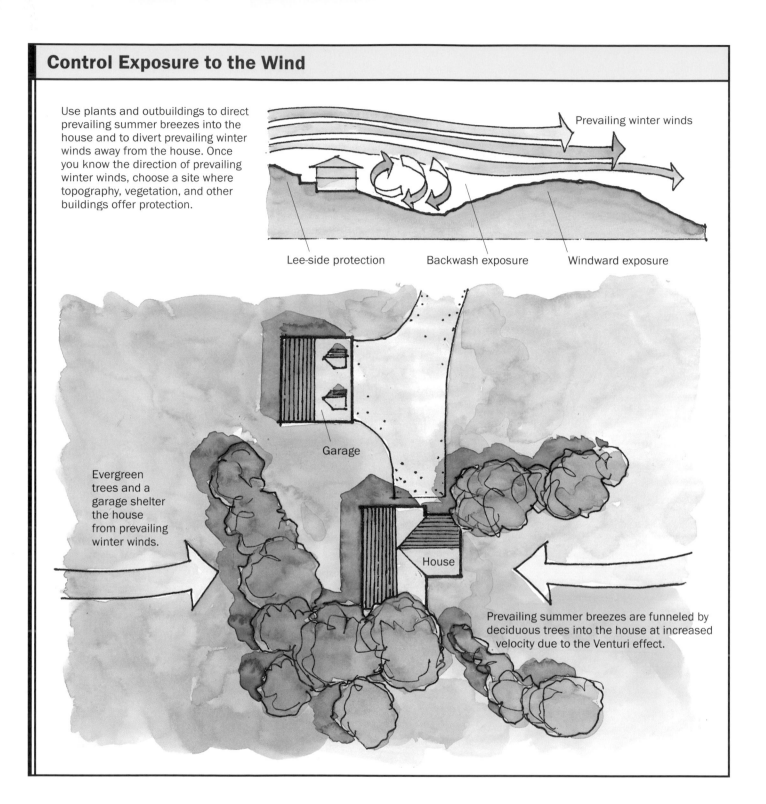

Prevailing winter winds

Lee-side protection

Backwash exposure

Windward exposure

Evergreen trees and a garage shelter the house from prevailing winter winds.

Garage

House

Prevailing summer breezes are funneled by deciduous trees into the house at increased velocity due to the Venturi effect.

Configure the house and its surroundings to funnel or channel cooling summer breezes into windows and screened-door openings. For example, you can orient breezeways and window openings to accept these summer winds. Use roof overhangs to trap incoming breezes and channel them into window openings. On the other hand, locate and configure the house to avoid channeling any cold winter winds into doors and windows.

Learn More about the Principles of Siting a House

For more information on siting principles, additional detailing, and solar-design strategies for houses, as well as the mathematical formulas required to analyze these strategies for their potential energy savings, check out the second edition of *Sun, Wind & Light: Architectural Design Strategies* by G. Z. Brown and Mark DeKay (John Wiley & Sons Inc., 2000).

Although out of print, another good resource available at used-book stores and libraries is *Climatic Building Design: Energy-Efficient Building Principles and Practice* by Donald Watson and Kenneth Labs (McGraw-Hill, 1993). Both books contain a wealth of helpful charts, meteorological data, and examples of solar siting and building design.

M. Joe Numbers is an architect with Gile-Buck & Associates in Boise, Idaho.

Guidelines for Shaping an Energy-Efficient House

A house with a high ratio of interior space to exterior surface costs less to heat and cool. In very cold or very hot areas, then, houses should be more square than rectangular. In temperate areas, shape is not critical, but in humid areas, a long, narrow house allows for cross ventilation.

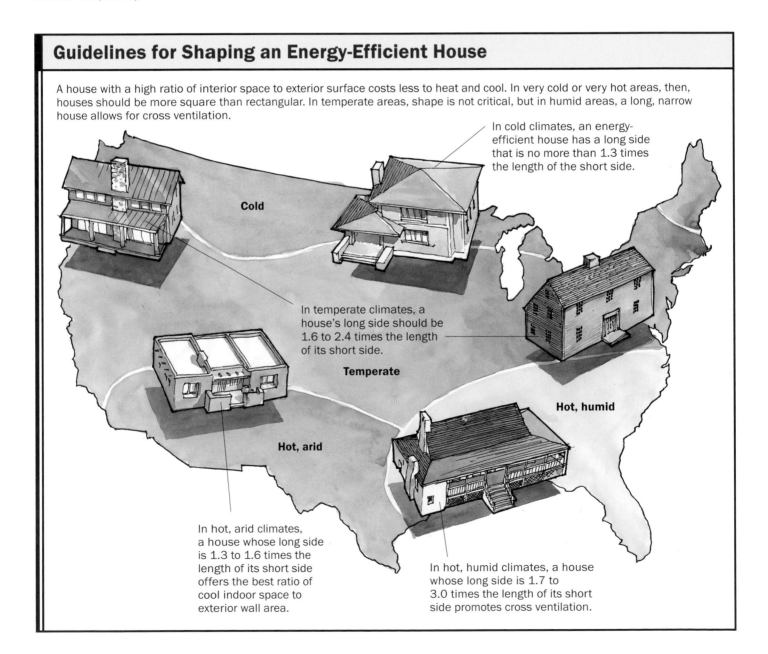

In cold climates, an energy-efficient house has a long side that is no more than 1.3 times the length of the short side.

Cold

In temperate climates, a house's long side should be 1.6 to 2.4 times the length of its short side.

Temperate

Hot, humid

Hot, arid

In hot, arid climates, a house whose long side is 1.3 to 1.6 times the length of its short side offers the best ratio of cool indoor space to exterior wall area.

In hot, humid climates, a house whose long side is 1.7 to 3.0 times the length of its short side promotes cross ventilation.

Cool Design for a Comfortable Home

Passive in practice. The author's house demonstrates passive-cooling strategies that include east-west orientation, overhangs formed both by eaves and a second-floor balcony, and a vertical design that promotes good ventilation.

■ BY SOPHIE PIESSE

I live in North Carolina, and I love the look on people's faces when I tell them that I haven't turned on my first-floor air-conditioning in 10 years. There's always a pause, and then they lift their jaw off the floor and ask me, "Really? How?"

As an architect who designs new homes, renovations, and additions, I encourage my clients to explore options for passive heating and cooling and energy-smart design before we ever look at mechanically assisted options. To make your house truly energy-efficient, you must design it with the goal of using as little energy as possible. It's great when people get excited about adding solar hot-water panels and photovoltaic systems, but before exploring any of that, you should first look at how you can design your new home or alter your existing home to reduce its energy needs. When your house naturally needs less energy, you can use smaller mechanical systems to support it. This saves money both up front and in the long run.

Passive Solar vs. Passive Cooling

When we talk about passive-solar design, we often focus on how it can help to heat your home. Passive-cooling design is really the opposite side of the same coin, using the properties of the sun to promote cooling rather than heating.

Passive-solar design can cut heating bills, but in the South and in many areas of the country, keeping your house cool in the summer is a bigger concern. Here, passive-cooling strategies become more important, and more economical. These simple design elements can save you hundreds of dollars every year in energy bills and also make your house more comfortable to live in.

Passive cooling refers to nonmechanical ways of cooling your home. It focuses on orientation and shading, air movement, thermal mass, and a tight building envelope. All these strategies can be complemented by mechanical means—from air-conditioning to ceiling fans—but these passive elements can also work successfully on their own.

While the potential for saving energy with any design-focused strategy is greatest when you're planning a new house, several of the techniques I describe can be used when renovating or adding to an existing home. You may not be able to pick up your house and face it in another direction, but you can add shade structures and window overhangs, relocate window openings, and mitigate nearby "heat islands" (such as a driveway baking in the midday sun), all of which enhance your home's ability to maintain a comfortable temperature with less mechanical intervention.

So let's take a look at how your house can work with the environment. By designing your home to work with nature instead of against it, you can benefit from lower energy bills, better daylighting, and greater indoor comfort.

1. Face the Sun, and Shade the Glass

The first step to passively cooling your home is to stop the heat before it ever comes in. This is where siting and shading come into play. When designing a new house, you have a great opportunity to take advantage of orientation, but it's also important (and often ignored) when adding to or altering an existing house.

Here in the Northern Hemisphere, a house that faces south is optimal because that is where the sun comes from. Southern orientation makes it easier to control the amount of sunlight that enters the house. Even in the South, designing a house with a long east-west axis (minimal exposure to the east and west, maximum exposure on the north and south) allows you to take the best advantage of the sun. This strategy is associated with passive heating, but passive cooling also benefits from the same type of siting.

When the house faces south, simple overhangs can shade it for the hottest part of the day, generally from 10 a.m. to 2 p.m. The

Degrees of shade. Pergolas can be designed specifically to admit or block sunlight at various times of the day or year, making them an especially versatile type of shade structure.

West is best. Placing a screened porch on the west side of the house minimizes late-afternoon heat gain in the summer and leaves the south side unobstructed so that it can collect as much solar gain in the winter as possible. This porch runs along the entire west side of the house, adding living space and providing cross breezes to the living room and master bedroom through two French doors.

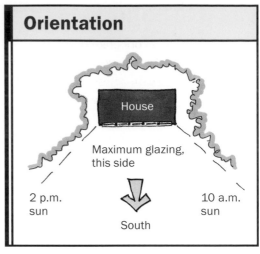

Orientation

Maximum glazing, this side

2 p.m. sun

10 a.m. sun

South

overhangs need to be sized correctly so that they not only block the sun at its hottest, but also allow light and warmth inside when the sun's angle changes in the winter, and in the mornings and evenings. Because this factor is based on the latitude where you live, the proper size of the overhang varies from region to region. The latitude where I live in North Carolina is 35 degrees north. That means the sun rises to 78 degrees above the horizon in summer and 30 degrees in winter. Here, a 2-ft. overhang is optimal because it blocks the hottest summer sun but lets the low winter sun shine inside (see the drawing on the facing page). To determine the optimal overhang where you live, see the chart on p. 131.

In the early morning and at sunset, when the summer sun is much lower in the sky, it's harder to keep heat out of the house, even with overhangs. You can minimize this morning and evening heat gain by minimizing the number of windows on the east and west sides of the house.

Another strategy is to locate shading devices, such as a screened porch, on the east or west sides of the house to provide protection from the low sun. By keeping the porch away from the south side, you're not compromising the daylighting and heat benefits available from the south. Other options for shading include pergolas, screens, and plantings. Pergolas, in particular, are a great option; they not only shade the house but also create an outdoor space to enjoy. Growing vines on pergolas can increase the structure's shading ability. Be sure to select deciduous varieties; they'll provide maximum shade when fully leafed out in summer, but won't block sunlight in winter.

Landscaping complements your house visually and also can help to keep it cool. Plant larger plants and trees to the east and west for shade. Plants absorb heat, lowering the temperature of air moving over them, so air that enters your house after traveling over the garden is actually cooler than the surrounding air. Low bushes and plantings also help by minimizing hard surfaces that absorb heat and radiate it back toward the house. These "heat islands"—driveways, walkways, and patios—work against any passive-cooling measures you might have taken, particularly if your house has windows that are low to the ground and capture the hot air that radiates off these surfaces. Lower roofs on porches or bump-outs, especially those covered with asphalt shingles, radiate heat that can enter the house through windows open above them. In these situations, casement windows are the most effective at guiding cool breezes into the house, and they allow less of the heat radiating off the roof to gain access inside. Avoid awning windows, which channel rising hot air into the house.

Enhancing passive cooling through orientation and siting is easiest when designing a new home. But installation of window overhangs and the use of plantings and attached structures can boost the cooling power of existing homes as well.

BLINDS DON'T REALLY HELP

People often use internal shading, such as blinds, to keep the heat out of their homes. While it's certainly better than letting sunlight stream in unimpeded, it's really not a good strategy if you look at the science. When sunlight shines through the glass in windows, its wavelength lengthens. These longer wavelengths cannot travel back out through the glass, so the heat gets trapped inside. (This is how greenhouses maintain their warm environments.)

When you put up blinds, you block light from getting into the room. However, the heat from the sun's rays has already entered through the glass. Because heat always moves from hot to cold areas, the heated air trapped between the window glass and the blind moves into the cooler areas of the house. Blinds may help a bit, but it's better to invest in exterior shading devices to stop the sun from ever entering the house rather than trying to control it once it's there.

2. Let the House Breathe a Bit

When mechanical systems are sized for a home, they're often designed with the mind-set that the house is never open to the elements. I find this is rarely true; in fact, most of my clients very much want to connect their home's indoor and outdoor spaces. Doesn't it make more sense, then, to

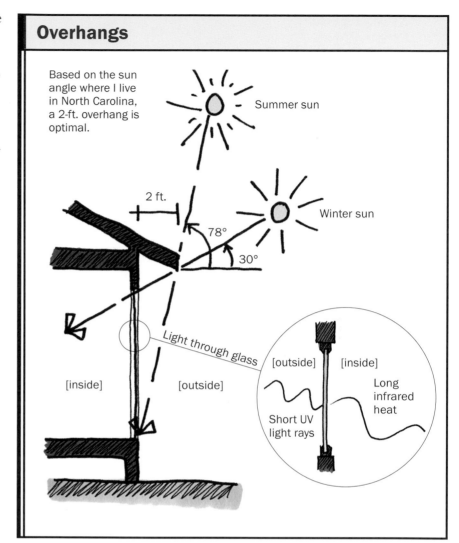

Overhangs

Based on the sun angle where I live in North Carolina, a 2-ft. overhang is optimal.

Summer sun

Winter sun

2 ft.

78°

30°

Light through glass

[inside]

[outside]

[inside]

[outside]

[outside]   [inside]

Short UV light rays

Long infrared heat

design houses to work in partnership with their environment rather than to function with no regard for it?

To understand best what ventilation can do for your home, you need to remember two simple principles: One is that heat always moves from hot areas to cold areas, and the other is that warm air rises.

If you are designing a new house, spend some time on the site, learn where the breezes come from, and use that information when locating the windows on your house. Use casements that swing open to help catch breezes. Having different units open in different directions allows you to take advantage of winds coming from multiple directions.

A studied approach.
Designing this second-floor library as an open balcony permits warm air to rise unimpeded up and out the second-floor windows. Ceiling fans assist the natural airflow.

The simplest form of smart ventilation is cross ventilation. When you open a window in your home, you can let in a slight breeze, but when you then open a window on the opposite side of the room, the strength of that through-breeze increases significantly. If the entry window is small and the window through which the breeze exits is large, it increases in speed. A cool breeze in the evening when the sun is going down absorbs the heat in your house (heat moving from hot to cold); as the air heats up, it rises. So the best way to let hot air out of your house

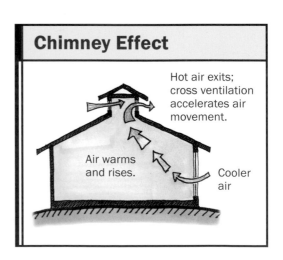

Chimney Effect

Hot air exits; cross ventilation accelerates air movement.

Air warms and rises.

Cooler air

is to have a large opening up high. The greater the distance between the intake and the output, the better.

This air movement is called the chimney effect (see the drawing on the facing page). I use it in my three-story home. When a cool breeze comes at the end of the day, I open the windows downstairs and the French doors on the third floor and wash out the entire house in minutes. The effect is heightened by an open plan, a small footprint, and a staircase in the middle that makes the whole house very much like a chimney.

Vaulted ceilings and high windows in a clerestory or cupola also promote the chimney effect. The sloped ceiling encourages air to move to the top of the cupola, and operable windows on both sides allow cross ventilation.

If you live in a dry climate, you can boost your home's ventilation cooling with water cooling. Dry air moving over water absorbs moisture and subsequently drops in temperature. (This is how evaporative coolers work.) Placing windows near a pond or another water feature lets you capture the cool air as it comes off the water and into the house. You get free air-conditioning along with the soothing bonus of a water view.

Agriboard panel

3. Tighten Up and Insulate the House

As I mentioned in section 2, passive cooling involves being able to control the airflow and heat moving through a house. This means stopping unwanted air infiltration by creating a tight building envelope. You can tighten up the house with good insulation, caulking all penetrations and sealing around windows and doors. Weatherstripping exterior doors and installing double-paned, argon-filled windows with low-e coatings can help as well. Put a tight-fitting damper in the chimney and a properly insulated cover over any attic access. Making your home's envelope tight enables you to let air

in and out when you choose and to close up the house when you want.

If you can, use more insulation than local codes require, and add the sealing package that many insulators offer. Spray-foam insulation provides a high R-value in a small amount of space and can double as an air seal. That's particularly important here in the Southeast, where moisture in the air can lead to mold, poor indoor-air quality, and even structural damage.

If you're building a new house, look into building systems that offer insulation values that are at least double what standard stick-built structures offer. In addition to precast concrete panels and AAC (aerated autoclaved concrete) block, you might consider agriboard panels. Made of compressed wheat straw sandwiched between oriented strand board (OSB), these 8-in.-thick panels offer an R-value of 25.4 versus the R-13 or R-15 of a standard 2×4 fiberglass-filled wall.

4. Control Heat with Mass

With the correct orientation and south-facing windows, your house can have great light and heat in winter—but it also can have the potential for overheating if you don't balance the amount of windows in the house with the amount of mass. Thermal mass comes from materials that absorb heat, such as concrete, tile, brick and concrete

Floor mass. The floor is the easiest place to add thermal mass, which regulates temperatures all year long. This colored concrete floor is covered with a soy-based sealer and runs throughout the first level of the house. During the day, it absorbs excess heat from the south-facing windows, releasing it at night.

block, and water. However, water requires diligence to prevent algae and mold, and it is harder to incorporate into the structure of a house. The easiest mass to build into a house is some form of masonry.

Generally, the more south-facing windows there are, the more mass a house needs to balance the heat gain indoors and keep it cool. When sun shines through the windows, it strikes interior surfaces. Sunlight can either radiate into the air, heating the house, or be absorbed by the material it strikes. If it is absorbed, you get light in the house but not heat. Because heat moves from hot to cold, the mass material will continue to absorb heat as long as it remains colder than the surrounding air.

The right amount of thermal mass draws heat out of the air during the day, and radiates the heat to warm the home in the evening when the air temperature drops, making mechanical heating less necessary. In the morning, when the atmosphere heats up

once more, the cooled mass material starts to absorb the day's heat all over again.

The easiest way to add mass to a house is on the floor. A significant amount is needed: In a typical passive-solar home, the concrete, tile, or brick floor should be 4 in. thick. Tile installed on cementboard on a subfloor is not enough.

Trombe walls are another design option. They are interior masonry walls behind south-facing windows with a narrow airspace between them. When the sun comes in, the heat is trapped in the airspace and then is absorbed by the wall. It acts as a heat sink for the house and can radiate the heat inside.

If you're planning a new house, you also can build mass into the walls. Precast concrete panels or AAC blocks introduce a significant amount of mass. These walls can be finished in a variety of ways; stucco is the simplest and most low-maintenance option, but you can attach siding if you prefer.

On the inside, concrete panels are typically painted, while the AAC can be finished with stucco or drywall. Finished this way, the interiors look like any other house, except for the added aesthetic of deep windowsills.

Thermal mass has an added benefit: Not only does it absorb heat, but it's also cool to the touch, which cools you. You can keep the air temperature of your home several degrees higher in the summer if you're walking on a cool floor. One way heat is transferred is through conduction—the movement of heat from one object to another through direct contact. You touch the floor, and because you are warmer than the floor, the heat in you (the warmer object) moves to the floor (the cooler object). You feel cooler, no mechanical means required.

Massing is the hardest strategy to add to an existing home. If the house was not designed to accommodate a 4-in.-thick masonry or concrete floor, it's not easy to add one. If you are adding to the south side of your house, however, you can consider a slab floor, a masonry wall, or a masonry fireplace.

5. Choose Energy-Efficient Mechanical Help

While I'm a firm advocate for passive cooling, I also believe there is a place for mechanical systems. Used in conjunction with passive-cooling techniques, the effectiveness of both can be enhanced, leading to lower energy use without any compromise in comfort.

That said, if you are going to use both passive and mechanical systems, it's important they work together. When hiring a heating and cooling contractor, choose someone who can size a mechanical system with your passive-cooling elements in mind and who will recommend energy-efficient equipment.

Start small. Strategically placed mechanical devices, such as the fan at the top of the hallway, can enhance passive design.

Mechanical assist. This fan, at the top of the sloped ceiling, can also enhance passive design.

If your climate demands it, one mechanical component you might consider is a dehumidifier. When you rely on natural ventilation to cool your house, you need to be aware that letting in the breeze also means letting in moisture. When the air leaves, the moisture may remain. In these cases, mechanical systems can help to dehumidify the air, preventing mold and damage to your home.

The best way to introduce mechanical cooling to a passive house is to start small. Ceiling fans are a simple way to enhance natural ventilation. If you've installed radiant-floor heating tubes in the floor slab, you can boost its cooling effect by pumping cool water through the pipes in summertime. Although this strategy must be carefully monitored to avoid condensation, it can have the added benefit of preheating your domestic hot water.

That brings us back to mechanical air-conditioning. I like to view the AC as support for the passive systems in the house, rather than the default switch we all reach for the moment the weather outside heats up. For those of us whose climate or personal comfort level demands some air-conditioning, passive cooling can still extend the "shoulder seasons," limiting AC use to a few weeks a year. In the hot, moist Southeast, occasional AC use is particularly beneficial for dehumidification. Like the passive-cooling strategies you choose, the mechanical system you install should be geared to your home, your climate, and your comfort needs.

Sophie Piesse is a LEED-accredited architect in North Carolina.

Central Air-Conditioning: Bigger Isn't Better

■ BY CHRIS GREEN

Sitting in a green-and-white woven lawn chair, fanning away the sweat, my grandmother said, "It's not the heat, it's the humidity." With seven Virginia summers behind me, I suspected that the heat did have something to do with it, but I kept this thought to myself.

It turns out that each of us had it partly right. It was the combination of high heat and humidity that raised us to our exalted level of discomfort on that oppressive summer day.

Seven years later, my parents finally built a house that included central air-conditioning. Although it was better than being without, the air-conditioning system wasn't ideal. The house had cold and hot spots, and my basement bedroom always felt cold and damp.

Unfortunately, these problems weren't limited to my parents' house nor to the 1970s. Problematic air-conditioning systems abound nationwide. According to a recent study, 95% of new air-conditioning installations fail in regard to operating efficiency, with more than 70% of systems improperly sized or installed.

The top three reasons for poor air-conditioner performance are improper sizing (1.5 to 2 times too large is common); improper installation (incorrect refrigerant levels and airflow); and poorly designed and installed duct systems. Because air-conditioning systems integrate refrigeration, air distribution, and electronics, there are lots of opportunities for mistakes.

Air Conditioners Move Heat Outside

Heat naturally moves from a higher energy level (warm) to a lower energy level (cool). You could say that heat, like water, flows

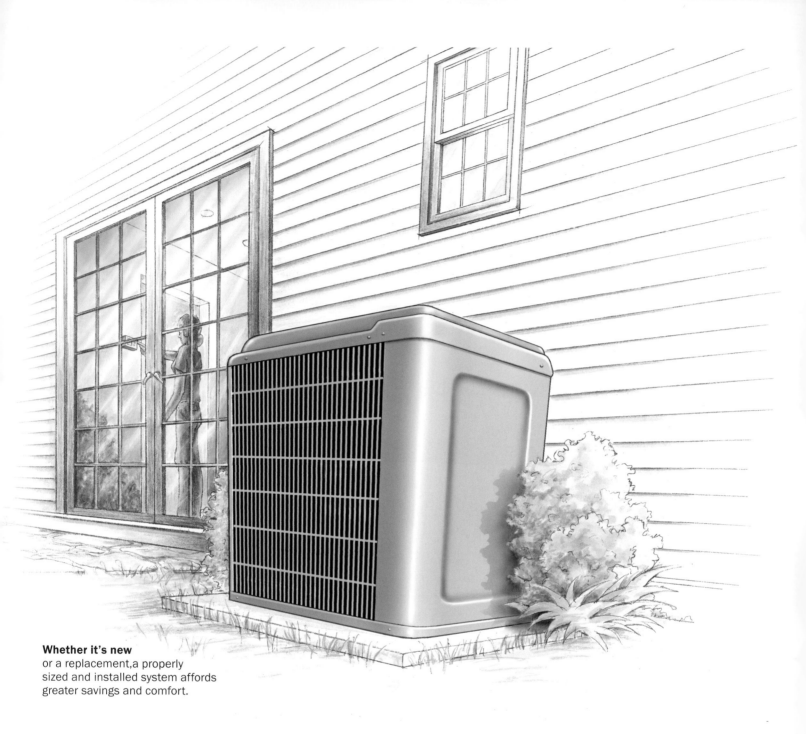

Whether it's new
or a replacement, a properly
sized and installed system affords
greater savings and comfort.

downhill. Without help, heat that accu-
mulates within a home will not leave on
its own unless the heat sources (the sun,
people, appliances, etc.) are removed. Help
comes in the form of air-conditioning,
which uses refrigeration combined with ventilation essentially to push heat uphill, or
move it outside, where it's even warmer.

Residential air-conditioning systems are
made up of an indoor and an outdoor unit
connected by a pair of pipes that circu-

late refrigerant in a loop. By manipulating
pressure and temperature, the indoor unit
absorbs heat by blowing warm indoor air
over a cold coil. The heat is released to the
outdoor unit, which houses a compressor
(which compresses refrigerant and itself
generates heat) and a condenser coil and fan
(which dissipates the heat to the outside).

In addition to cooling, air conditioners
serve another important function: They
dehumidify the air. In the same way that

How It Works

Residential air conditioners are split systems—an indoor and an outdoor unit—that remove heat from the house and release it outdoors. A pair of pipes, which circulate refrigerant, form a loop and connect the units. Cold air is produced when compressed refrigerant is forced through a tiny valve or **metering device (1)** and expands into the **evaporator coil (2)**, similar to the cold spray an aerosol can produces as the compressed liquid passes through the valve. This causes the refrigerant's pressure and temperature to drop quickly, cooling the coil. As warm air passes over the evaporator, it is cooled and dehumidified. Moisture condenses on the evaporator's fins and drains away. After absorbing heat from the home's interior, the refrigerant is pumped to the outdoor unit, where it passes through the **compressor (3)** and is sent to the **condenser (4)** to lose some of its heat.

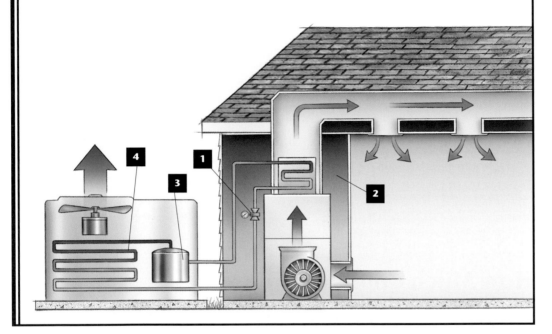

moisture condenses on the side of a cold soda can sitting outside on a hot day, air conditioners wring moisture from warm, humid air as it is forced across the indoor unit's cold evaporator coil. Once past the evaporator, cool dehumidified air is delivered to the rest of the house—unless there's a problem.

Oversize Units Dehumidify Poorly and Waste Money

Approximately two-thirds of all residential air conditioners are too large. According to Bruce Harley, an HVAC consultant with Conservation Services Group in Westborough, Mass., these oversize units "will cool your house, but they're not necessarily designed to run efficiently." The first problem is that they dehumidify poorly. Oversize units satisfy the temperature at the thermostat so quickly that only a little moisture has time to condense on the evaporator coil. This phenomenon is known as short cycling, and it's more of a problem in humid climates. If cycles are very short, moisture on the coil can evaporate back into the house before it drains away.

Second, air-conditioning units are least efficient when they start up. It can take 15 minutes to reach operating efficiency, so oversize units run more short cycles, and more of their time is spent running in the least efficient part of the cycle. As a result, they use more energy, and costs to operate them run 20% to 30% higher than for properly sized systems. Finally, at an installed

Reducing Your Cooling Needs

Air conditioners consume about two-thirds of electricity use during peak summer periods. Save money by making energy-efficient improvements before installing a new air-conditioning system.

- A tight, well-insulated building reduces cooling needs by keeping warm, humid air outside.

- Buy high-performance, low-e, argon-filled windows to reduce solar gain, which accounts for up to 70% of the cooling load on air-conditioning systems.

- Wide overhangs, trees, or vegetation is helpful. East-west glass is more of a problem than south-facing glass in summer.

- Use radiant barriers on the underside of uninsulated roof rafters if the HVAC equipment is in the attic; otherwise, just insulate the attic. In addition, insulate the ductwork.

- Install smart thermostats that turn off the air-conditioning when it's not needed and then bring the house to the right temperature before you arrive home.

cost of around $1,000 per ton, oversize systems cost more. Why pay for 5 tons if 2½ will do the job?

How Much Cooling Do You Need?

Smaller systems use less energy and remove more moisture because they run long enough to reach peak efficiency. So what's the right size for an air-conditioning system? It depends.

The standard method for calculating the proper size for a residential central air-conditioning system is found in ACCA's (Air Conditioning Contractors of America) *Manual J—Residential Load Calculation* by Hank Rutkowski, P. E. It's a methodical approach to arrive at room-by-room cooling loads for sizing ducts and whole-house systems. The room-by-room totals are important because you can't design a duct system properly without this calculation.

Manual J takes into account and averages solar-heat gains, which don't peak in all rooms at the same time. It also includes the house's orientation to the sun and shading, which greatly affect the cooling load as well

as the insulation values of walls, ceilings, and floors. Window types, locations, and specifications as well as internal-heat gains (people, lighting, and appliances) also are figured in.

The right-size system is not a rule-of-thumb amount derived from the square footage of a house. In her book *Air-Conditioning America* (Johns Hopkins University Press, 1998), Gail Cooper writes that air-conditioning engineers 100 years ago called sizing by the rule-of-thumb method "futile and foolish." According to the folks that I've talked to, that remains true today.

Contractors Sell Large Systems because They Fear Complaints

In defense of the people selling and installing large air-conditioning systems, they do so for a reason. Profit plays a part, sure: If you install a bigger system, you make more money. More important, though, contractors fear complaints about their systems' inability to maintain set temperatures in extremely hot conditions. Using a rule-of-thumb measurement or some other method, the contractor sizes the system larger. If 3 tons is good, 4 is better, right? Besides, "Maybe *Manual J* sizing isn't quite big enough," a contractor might say, or "Here, it gets hotter than that."

A recent study, however, puts these fears to rest. Proctor Engineering Group (PEG), Electric Power Research Institute, Nevada Power, and Arizona Public Service tested a typical house with outdoor temperatures of up to 116°F (3°F above the mean extreme). The actual cooling required was less than *Manual J* predicted in all but three of the 1,316 hours that the house was monitored.

It's not necessary to oversize beyond *Manual J*, which has a built-in oversizing margin. On the first page of the introduction, *Manual J* states that "slightly undersized cooling equipment—by a margin of 10% or less—may actually provide more comfort at a lower cost."

Most Air-Conditioning Systems Are Installed Improperly

Another major reason for poorly performing air-conditioning systems is faulty installation: incorrect refrigerant levels, low airflow, and poorly designed and installed duct systems. In one study of 55,000 air-conditioning systems by PEG, refrigerant levels were wrong 62% of the time; in another study, the figure was 68%.

Condenser units arrive from the factory with the proper amount of refrigerant for a given length of piping—usually 15 ft. or 25 ft.—to connect the indoor and outdoor units. Refrigerant levels often are wrong because line length in the field can vary, and technicians frequently don't make adjustments according to the manufacturer's recommendations.

What difference does it make if refrigerant levels are wrong? According to Armin Rudd of Building Science Corporation, if

You Just Want to Be Comfortable

Most of us don't want to worry about our air conditioners. They aren't high on our priority list. We expect air conditioners simply to make our homes comfortable, summer after summer. But what is comfortable?

Feeling comfortable isn't about temperature only. It's about a favorable blend of temperature and humidity. And of course, what's just right for one person might not be right for another, so comfortable becomes a range.

That comfort zone is somewhere between 68°F and 78°F with relative humidities ranging from about 25% to 65%. To remain in the comfort zone as temperatures go up, relative humidity must go down (see the drawing below).

Even though most of us can sense changes in temperature of 1°F to 2°F, we are less sensitive to humidity. Levels between 25% and 65% feel about right. According to ASHRAE (American Society of Heating, Refrigerating and Air-Conditioning Engineers), less than 25% relative humidity can lead to dry nose, throat, eyes, and skin. Greater than 70% can lead to mold, corrosion, and decay. High relative humidities in carpet and fabric can lead to dust-mite infestation and mildew (mildew is mold growing on fabric).

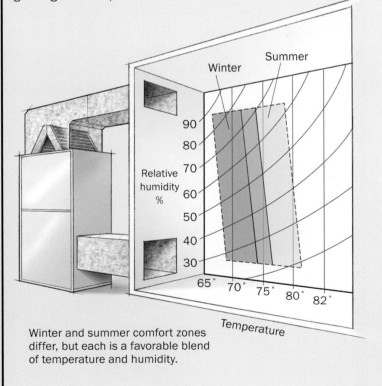

Winter and summer comfort zones differ, but each is a favorable blend of temperature and humidity.

How Do You Find a Good Installer?

Because 70% of all central air-conditioning systems are installed improperly (according to a California new-home construction study), you could be paying anywhere from 25% to 50% too much in air-conditioning bills. Choose your air-conditioning installer carefully, or pay the difference in higher energy and maintenance costs.

One measure of a technician's expertise is whether he or she has completed a training program. All the major manufacturers offer training on installing their systems. In addition, several national certification programs are available through NATE (National Association of Training Excellence®; www.natex .org) and CheckMe! (through Proctor Engineering Group; www. proctoreng.com).

CheckMe! is available in California, much of the Northeast (in some places under the Cool Smart name), and several other states. Technicians who complete their program perform diagnostic tests on each system and call in their results to a CheckMe! staff person to receive immediate feedback on the health of the system. Afterward, PEG sends a certificate of completion to the homeowner.

Local electric utilities are another source for installer-certification programs similar to NATE or CheckMe! Rebates or incentives might be available for high-efficiency equipment.

In addition to asking about certified training, here are some other questions to ask installers:
- Do they use *Manual J* for sizing air-conditioning systems?
- Are they using proper design temperatures for your area?
- Will they verify that the indoor unit's evaporator coil and the outdoor unit's condenser coil match and that the system has the proper amount of refrigerant?

- Do they seal the ducts and test the system for leaks to a level of 10% or less?
- Do they test airflow at the evaporator coil?
- Can they provide references?

they are a little low, up to 20%, there's some loss of cooling. More than that, and there's an unacceptable loss of cooling along with frosting of the evaporator coil and, eventually, complete loss of cooling. If refrigerant levels are too high, the story is similar: loss of cooling with possible damage to the compressor.

The speed and the volume of air moving through air-conditioning systems were incorrect (usually too low) in about 72% of units tested in the PEG study. This was due partly to mismatched indoor and outdoor units, which occurs more often on retrofits than on new installations because only the exterior compressor/condenser unit typically is replaced. Also, airflow at the evaporator coil often is low because it usually isn't tested, so no one actually knows what it is.

Fan speeds at the evaporator coil should be around 400 cfm (cu. ft. per minute) per ton of cooling capacity. Slightly lower fan speeds improve dehumidification. In dry climates, fan speed should be increased.

Tied to airflow and directly affecting it are duct design and installation. Ducts are the least expensive part of the system and frequently are given short shrift. A properly designed duct system begins with determining the cooling load for each room (not based on the square footage), which can vary greatly. Duct runs need to be as short as possible; they need to be insulated; and when possible, they should be installed within conditioned space. Ducts also should be sealed. Leaky ducts waste energy and in the right conditions might draw dust, spores, or combustion gas from a gas appliance back into the house.

Adequate return air also is important to minimize air-pressure imbalances that can affect cooling. The placement of registers in the room and the quality of the grilles greatly affect the duct system's ability to throw air across the room and to mix the air properly.

Chris Green is a carpenter and cabinetmaker in New Milford, Conn.

Low-Energy Lighting, High-Energy Design

■ BY RANDALL WHITEHEAD

Talk about energy-efficient lighting these days, and there are two technologies that are sure to dominate the discussion: fluorescents (usually compact fluorescents) and light-emitting diodes, or LEDs. As a lighting designer in California—where energy regulations are the strictest in the nation—I have a lot of these conversations. And I can tell you that rather than getting turned on by these newer, watt-saving technologies, most people are immediately turned off.

Why? Because most people have already had a lifetime of bad experiences with flickering, buzzing fluorescents and know little about LEDs, except that they've become ubiquitous as strings of the latest must-have holiday lights.

It's not that these new light sources aren't as good—or better—than the incandescent bulbs they're designed to replace. But here is a classic example of trying to fit a square peg in a round hole (or in lighting terms, a pin connector into a screw-in socket). We keep expecting these new lighting technologies to act (and cost) the same as the old ones. The problem is that they don't.

A prime example is the typical screw-in compact fluorescent lamps ("lamp" is the industry term for "bulb") offered at big-box stores. Technology-wise, they are the worst examples of what's currently available. But marketers wanted to provide a CFL at roughly the same price as an incandescent lamp. What you end up with is a cheaply made bulb that can buzz, produce an off-color light, and is not dimmable. So what happens? CFLs in particular, and energy-efficient lighting in general, gets a bum rap. The fact is that many manufacturers (see "Bulb Sources," p. 154) are making efficient lamps that perform well. Yes, they do cost more up front, but in the long run, they offer greater energy savings and let you be earth friendly and design savvy at the same time.

Evocative and efficient. In the author's living room, a collection of photographs is uplit with LED festoon lamps from Phantom™ Lighting. Ambient light is provided by recessed fixtures from Lucifer® Lighting that are outfitted with LED MR16s from Focus Lighting®.

It's my job to practice what I preach. My house is filled to the brim with energy-efficient light sources. In fact, the only two incandescent lamps I own are in my refrigerator and oven. Other than that, it is all high-efficacy all the time. Is it warm and inviting? Absolutely. You don't have to change every lamp in your house, as I did. Start slowly. Maybe put A-lamp shaped CCFLs (cold-cathode compact fluorescent lights) in your exterior lanterns and CFLs in the basement and the attic. Try using daylight-colored CFLs in your closets for better color matching for articles of clothing. Every little bit helps—but it helps the most when each of these different light sources is used to its best advantage.

Layering: Shining New Light on the Old Rules

While new ways of producing light offer lots of design possibilities, it still makes sense to stick with the tried-and-true basics of light layering that designers have long relied on to produce attractive, well-lit spaces. Light layering incorporates four specific types of lighting to create a well-lit environment: task, accent, decorative, and most important, ambient light. The rule here is that more than one light source is needed to illuminate a room properly. The challenge when working with new, energy-efficient types of lighting is that you have to go beyond light layering and understand how these new sources create light in order to use them correctly.

For example, CFLs, CCFLs, and ESLs (see "Low-Energy Lighting: The Latest Bulb Technologies" on the facing page) are omnidirectional sources of light. This means they throw light out evenly in all directions, which is what a standard household "A" lamp (like our old incandescent) does. That makes all of these types good sources of ambient and decorative lighting, and occasionally task lighting; but they are ineffective as accent lights.

LEDs, by contrast, are unidirectional, meaning that their light is projected out in one direction. As a result, they can provide a very good source of accent lighting and task lighting, and occasionally ambient light if used correctly or if designed in a luminaire (fixture) that compensates for their unidirectional tendencies.

In addition to the differences in how they project light, these new light sources differ in the color (temperature) of light they produce. Other characteristics, such as resistance to temperature change, ability to dim, and available wattages, also can influence your decision on what type of bulb to use where.

Once you know the properties of these earth-friendly light sources, you can begin to include them more confidently to produce each of the layers of light that combine to produce a well-lit room.

Low-Energy Lighting: The Latest Bulb Technologies

COMPACT FLUORESCENT LAMPS

An aversion to fluorescents is understandable because they have been so awful for so long. They didn't dim easily; they buzzed and gave off weird colors. And sadly, the push to offer CFLs at a price point close to that of a standard incandescent household bulb has given fluorescents a bad name all over again. The color of these cheap CFLs is poor, they burn out prematurely, and they aren't dimmable. There are much better products on the market. Be prepared to pay more, but they will be worth it. Top-of-the-line screw-in CFLs by manufacturers like MaxLite™ and Earthtronics® (see "Bulb Sources," on p. 154) offer an energy-efficient, dimmable (down to 30%) light source that can be controlled by a standard incandescent dimmer.

A new category of CFL is the GU-24, characterized by a proprietary lamp and socket assembly that cannot be replaced with a standard screw-in incandescent lamp

ESL: The Next Bright Idea in Low-Energy Lighting

You may not have heard of ESL technology, but it's the newest kid on the lighting block. It looks like an incandescent lamp, and it dims like an incandescent lamp—but it's not. ESL (electron stimulated luminescence) lighting technology uses accelerated electrons to stimulate phosphors to create light. But unlike fluorescents, ESLs contain no mercury, turn on instantly, and promise full-range dimming. They also don't require the heavy heat dissipation designs of LEDs. The color of the light is warm—very close to that of incandescent. Developed by Seattle-based VU1® Corporation (www.VU1 .com), they began shipping R30 reflector lamps, commonly used in recessed fixtures, in late 2010. Other lamp styles are expected to follow.

(although MaxLite makes a screw-in adapter that allows a typical lamp to accept a GU-24 socket). The GU-24 lamps meet California's Title 24, which requires that 50% of the wattage in kitchens must come from hardwired high-efficacy sources and 100% of the wattage in the bath must come from high-efficacy sources, unless controlled by a switched motion sensor.

For savvy people everywhere, lighting manufacturers are now offering decorative fixtures in modern and traditional styles that have hardwired fluorescent sources. Many use the new GU-24 socket and lamp technology, which is no bigger than a standard household bulb and socket assembly. They

CFL

Bulb Sources

1000BULBS.COM®:
Specialty lamps online;
www.1000bulbs.com

Earthtronics:
Dimmable CFLs
and CCFLs;
www.earthbulb.com

**Philips Color
Kinetics:**
LED MR16 lamps and
color-changing LEDs;
www.colorkinetics.com

Cree Lighting:
Recessed LED lights,
including retrofit trims;
www.creelighting.com

Edge Lighting:
LED strip lights;
www.edgelighting.com

LiteTronics®:
Cold cathode fluores-
cent lamps (CCFLs);
www.litetronics.com

MaxLite:
GU-24 lamps and sock-
ets, and screw-in CFLs;
www.maxlite.com

Phantom Lighting:
LED shelf & display
lights; www.phantom
lighting.com

**Progress Lighting
(Everlume™ Series):**
Recessed LED lights,
including retrofit trims;
www.progresslighting
.com

**Tresco
International®:**
Fluorescent , LED,
and xenon puck lights;
www.trescointerna
tional.com

can be installed where there is an existing incandescent fixture and can be dimmed with the existing incandescent dimmer. No special wiring or dimmer is needed.

COLD CATHODE FLUORESCENT LAMPS

CCFLs are a newer generation of fluorescent lamps. They can look just like regular household bulbs, globe lamps, or flame-tip lamps. They cost more than an incandescent, about $12 each, but save an average of $33 in energy costs over their lifetime. An 8w CCFL produces 40w worth of illumination and lasts 25,000 hours, compared to an incandescent with an average rated lamp life of 750 hours. What makes them better than regular CFLS is their wide variety of color temperatures and that they can dim down

CCFL

a full 90% (CFLs can't dim that much). Their swirls are thinner, and they're more widely available than CFLs in low wattages. They are still a bit hard to find; they must be special-ordered through lighting specialty stores or bought online.

LIGHT-EMITTING DIODES

In use since the 1960s, LEDs were used as colored indicator lights. About three years ago, manufacturers came up with an LED source with the same color qualities of incandescent light and daylight. These new LEDs use considerably less electricity than standard incandescent sources and last much longer—30,000 to 50,000 hours, while emitting no ultraviolet radiation. Even better, they contain no mercury, as do fluores-

LED

cents. Companies like Cree Lighting® and Progress Lighting® offer both screw-in and hardwired LED kits as retrofits for existing housings, as well as IC-rated, airtight housings for new construction.

High-Energy Design: Creating a Well-Lit Room with Four Types of Lighting

TASK LIGHTING: BOTH LEDs AND FLUORESCENTS ARE UP TO THE JOB

Task lighting is the lighting by which you do work, including undercabinet lighting in a kitchen, closet lighting, and reading lamps. The optimum task light provides shadow-free light and is located between your head and the worksurface.

Depending on the type of fixtures being used, both fluorescents and LEDs can provide effective task lighting. Fluorescent puck lights, such as those by Tresco International (www.trescointernational.com), offer shadow-free illumination along worksurfaces such as kitchen counters. Because much of today's architecture is open plan (where one room flows into the other), choose a light with a color temperature of 2,700 K so that the color is complementary to light sources in other rooms.

For task lighting in closets and laundry rooms, consider using 5,000 K lamps from LEDs or CFLs for excellent color matching. Although some people dislike the lag time associated with CFLs, I like to use them in closets. In fact, I don't need a sudden punch of light in the morning. I also appreciate the color rendering—very important when matching clothes—that's possible with a combination of CFLs and LEDs.

Those energy-eating xenon and halogen festoon lamps used in undercabinet task lights and shelf lights come in LED versions; those offered by companies such as Phantom Lighting (www.phantomlighting.com)

Closet coordinated. A strip of 5,000 K LED festoon lights above the clothing shows their true colors under daylight conditions (top) compared to incandescent lighting (bottom).

are dimmable. Other options for undercabinet task lights include LED puck lights from Lucifer Lighting (www.luciferlighting.com) and LED strip lights by Edge Lighting (www.edgelighting.com).

One caution when using LEDs as task lights: because they are point sources of illumination, they tend to create multiple shadows, which can be distracting. Hiding LED sources behind a diffusion material eliminates this problem.

ACCENT LIGHTING:
THE SPOTLIGHT GOES TO LEDs

Accent lighting is used to highlight specific objects, adding depth and dimension to an environment. Recessed adjustable fixtures, track lights, portable uplights, and directional landscape lights all fall into this category. Accent lighting can be very dramatic, but when overused can make the objects you own appear more important than friends

and family. This unfortunate result is often referred to as the "museum effect."

LEDs work well as accent lighting for several reasons: They provide directional light, they produce no UV (ultraviolet) rays that can harm fine artwork or textiles, and, unlike incandescents, the color temperature doesn't alter when they are dimmed. Fluorescent light sources are usually too broad in their beam spreads to be effective as accent lights. An exception to this rule would be the illumination of a wall mural or a large hanging tapestry. In these cases, I recommend adding a UV-filter to the light fixture to reduce possible degradation of the art.

DECORATIVE LIGHTING:
CCFLs SHOW OFF JUST ENOUGH

Decorative lighting also could be called architectural bling. Its purpose is simple: to look pretty and to add visual sparkle to a space. Chandeliers and candlestick-type wall

The right accent. Here, this niche is illuminated with a single LED MR16 housed inside a square-trimmed recessed low-voltage fixture from Lucifer Lighting. The absence of UV light will help to preserve the integrity of the photograph.

Just enough light. Because they can be obtained in flame-tip styles and lower wattages than typical CFLs, CCFLs are often more suitable (and less overpowering) in decorative fixtures with multiple bulbs, such as this breakfast-room chandelier.

sconces fall into this category. Decorative lighting should not be relied on to provide primary light for a room. If it's too bright, it can be overpowering. These fixtures were originally designed around incandescent light sources, particularly those of a low-enough wattage so as not to be overpowering. The best replacement, then, among the newer light sources would be CCFLs, because they can have a color temperature similar to that of a dimmed incandescent lamp. I particularly like the MicroBrite™ A19 by LiteTronics, which has a very warm color temperature of 2,250 K and, being a CCFL, dims down a full 90%. LEDs would have to be the worst choice for decorative lighting because they do not provide an even, overall glow.

AMBIENT LIGHTING: FLUORESCENTS HAVE A SLIGHT EDGE

Ambient lighting is the gentle light that fills the volume of an interior with a warm glow. Because it is indirect light, it not only provides overall illumination, but it also softens the shadows on people's faces, helping them to look more relaxed and youthful. I refer to it as architectural Botox. The best ambient light comes from illumination that is bounced off the ceiling. Opaque wall sconces, torchieres, pendant-hung indirect fixtures, and cove lighting can be used to create ambient light (see "Green—and Unseen," below). Translucent fixtures can sometimes serve double-duty as both ambient and decorative light. Both LEDs and fluorescents can provide excellent ambient light.

Green—and Unseen

When I show my clients a typical CFL—the type shaped like swirly soft ice cream—they immediately hate it. It doesn't matter if the light it produces has a beautiful color, if it operates quietly, or if it's dimmable. They just have a visceral, negative reaction because they can see that the source

Layers of efficiency. All four basic layers of light combine in this open-plan living room/kitchen. The Flotation pendant fixtures by Ingo Maurer® are fitted with dimmable CFLs, providing both decorative and ambient light. Reading lamps flanking the sofa provide task light, and the square aperture recessed lights add ambient light.

of light is fluorescent. I've learned to apply a technique I call stealth lighting. Stealth lighting simply means hiding the bulb behind a diffusion material such as a shade, an architectural detail, or a lens. If they can't see that it's a fluorescent source, most people assume the light is incandescent and find it perfectly acceptable.

When selecting a decorative fixture—for example, a pendant light—find a bowl-shaped one that hides the bulbs; in the case of a drum-shaped fixture, look for one with a lensed (translucent) bottom. The CCFLs that are now on the market are available in shapes that are closer to traditional "A" lamps and flame-tipped bulbs that are easily accepted as incandescent without any disguise.

Another good way to create energy-efficient ambient light for a space is to install the light source within an architectural

High on efficacy. Ambient light for this kitchen comes from linear fluorescent lighting mounted on top of the kitchen cabinets. The lighting over the counters comes from warm-colored fluorescent puck lights, made by Tresco International.

Stealth lighting. Energy-efficient light sources can be unobtrusive: The Lightspann pendant fixtures in this living room conceal dimmable CFLs. Art and tabletops are lit by Juno® track fixtures using LED MR16s, and LED strips by Edge Lighting mounted on top of the trusses provide ambient light.

Sources for Energy-Efficient Decorative Fixtures

The Basic Source®:
Faux and real alabaster pendants with fluorescent lamp options; www.thebasicsource.com

Birch & Willow:
Light fixtures made of natural materials with fluorescent lamp options; www.birchandwillow.com

Boyd Lighting:
High-fashion fixtures with fluorescent lamp options; www.boydlighting.com

Dave Meeker Art:
Pendants, wall sconces, and portable fixtures made of plastic straws, using CFLs; www.davemeekerart.com

Elica®:
Pendants with integrated fans; www.elica.com

Hans Duus Blacksmith:
Traditional and transitional fixtures

with LED and GU-24 options; www.hansduusblacksmith.com

JH Lighting:
Traditional and transitional alabaster fixtures with hardwired CFL options; www.jhlighting.com

Juno Lighting:
Recessed, track, undercabinet, and decorative lighting; www.junolightinggroup.com

Kalco®:
Decorative lighting, much of which is available in hardwired fluorescent versions using GU-24 technology; www.kalco.com

Lightspann:
Sculptural fixtures with GU-24 lamp options; www.lightspann.com

Schmitt Design:
Bamboo pendants with GU-24 lamp options; www.schmittdesign.com

detail that runs the perimeter of the room or on top of cabinetry that does not go all the way to the ceiling. Here, a dimmable linear fluorescent source can do an excellent job, as well as some of the newer LED strip lights now available. In these cases, the light is bounced off the ceiling, so you want to make sure that the actual light source is completely hidden from view and that the paint on the ceiling is a flat or matte finish. A gloss, semigloss, or eggshell finish reflects an image of the light source onto the ceiling and ruins the effect.

Randall Whitehead is a San Francisco–based lighting designer.

The Bright Future of Lighting

■ BY SEAN GROOM

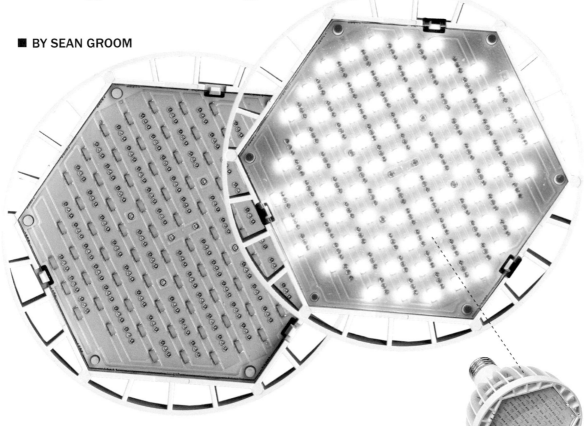

Small, powerful, and efficient. Now that they produce white light appropriate for residential settings, LEDs grouped together in a bulb pack enough punch that this 8w LED from Nexxus™ can replace a 75w PAR30 incandescent bulb.

Although still a relatively small slice of the incandescent-dominated lighting market, energy-efficient compact fluorescents (CFLs) and light-emitting diodes (LEDs) have gained traction over the past few years, thanks to green-building programs and some progressive local energy codes. They're about to get a real boost.

The Energy Independence and Security Act (EISA) of 2007 soon will limit the number of watts a bulb can consume for a given number of lumens, a measure of light output. The legislation takes effect Jan. 1, 2012, when the luminary equivalent of today's 100w incan-

Continuous task lighting.
The unique tubes and connectors of Feelux®'s Slimline allow end-to-end installation, eliminating shadows and dark spots between fixtures in undercabinet and cove lighting.

Replacement bulbs for every application. Often part of the fixture, fluorescent lights need a ballast to operate. These replacement bulbs from Philips, however, have onboard electronic ballasts, which means they can be screwed into existing fixtures for more efficient ambient and decorative lighting. CFLs with pin bases are for fluorescent-only fixtures required by some energy codes.

descent bulb will be allowed to consume only 72w. (Lower-wattage bulbs also will be affected.)

In other words, incandescent lightbulbs need to become about 28% more efficient to survive. Some industry insiders think they will, but CFLs and LEDs already meet the new requirements. Consequently, the most likely scenario is that incandescent bulbs will be replaced either by CFLs or LEDs, depending on the application.

Compact Fluorescents Come of Age

CFLs were introduced in the early 1990s, but they weren't ready for prime time. Early CFLs produced harsh blue light, hummed, and flickered, making a poor first impres-

sion. Today's CFLs, however, produce light in the 2,700 K range, mimicking the warm, amber-hued light of incandescent bulbs (see the sidebar on the facing page). Also, the old magnetic ballasts have been replaced with quiet electronic ballasts that don't flicker.

CFLs are dramatically more efficient than incandescent lightbulbs, using between 50% and 80% less energy, and they last for about 10,000 hours, nearly 10 times longer than incandescents. They also cost dramatically more. However, replacing one 50¢, 75w incandescent bulb with a $3.50, 19w CFL saves 563kwh of electricity over the life of the bulb. That comes to about $75 in savings, depending on the cost of electricity where you live.

On the downside, a typical CFL contains somewhere between 4 mg and 5 mg of mercury. Critics of CFLs highlight the health and environmental hazards of mercury, and special precautions should be taken if the bulbs break in your house. Proponents argue that the mercury in a CFL is far less than the amount of mercury emissions that would be released from a coal-fired power plant if you were using an incandescent bulb. Regardless, when a CFL burns out, it must be recycled so that the mercury doesn't end up polluting the environment. Some retailers of CFLs, including Ikea® and The Home Depot®, offer CFL recycling. To find other recycling locations, visit www.epa.gov.

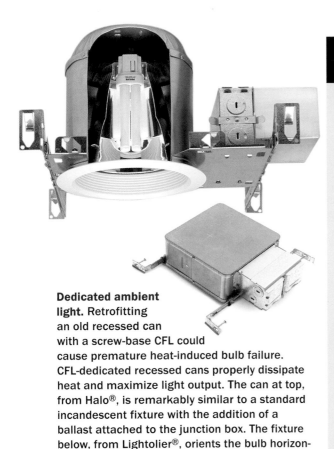

Dedicated ambient light. Retrofitting an old recessed can with a screw-base CFL could cause premature heat-induced bulb failure. CFL-dedicated recessed cans properly dissipate heat and maximize light output. The can at top, from Halo®, is remarkably similar to a standard incandescent fixture with the addition of a ballast attached to the junction box. The fixture below, from Lightolier®, orients the bulb horizontally and needs just 3½ in. of clearance.

Light-Emitting Diodes Are the Future

LEDs are a Silicon Valley technology, manufactured in a clean room, just like a computer chip. Electrical current runs through the 1-sq.-mm chip, exciting the electrons and creating light. A small bulblike cover focuses the light. LEDs can't actually produce white light; white light must be created either by combining colors or by using a phosphor coating inside the bulb.

The lighting industry is betting heavily on forging ahead with significant advances in white-light LED technology in the next few years. Many of today's LEDs, however, already perform well when used in the appropriate location.

Manufacturers describe LEDs as cool-operating lamps. While it's true that the lit end of an LED is cool to the touch, the semiconductors do produce heat. And just as computer chips require cooling to perform

The Color of Good Light

No matter what type of fixture or bulb you're using, you need to understand light temperature to light your home effectively. There is a spectrum of white light from "warm," which has a yellow-gold hue, to "cool," which has a bluish cast. The hue of the light is described by correlated color temperature (CCT) and is measured in degrees kelvin, as shown on the scale on the right. Lower numbers are associated with warmer light and higher temperatures with cooler light. For example, an incandescent bulb commonly used in homes has a temperature of about 2,700 K, while the daylight fluorescents commonly used in office buildings are about 4,100 K.

Along with most finishes in our homes, people look best under warmer light—2,700 K to 3,000 K. Although cooler light looks harsh on wood, it can be complementary to white and stainless-steel finishes, which are common in homes with modern designs.

A second measure of light quality is color-rendering index (CRI). When you compare the same color under different light sources, you might notice a color shift. CRI is an attempt to quantify this shift by describing— on a scale of 0 to 100—how well a light source renders color. Good CFLs have a CRI above 80.

If you're in the market for LED lighting, you'll have to see the light for yourself to make an educated purchase. LED standards for CCT or CRI have been voluntary, and some manufacturers' ratings might be called generous.

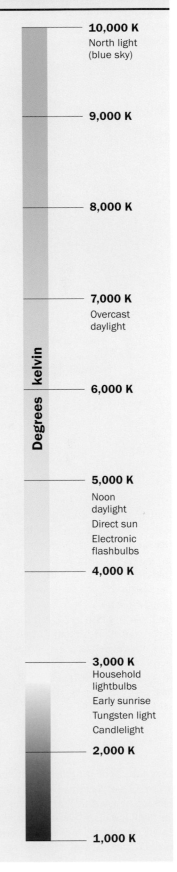

Degrees kelvin

- **10,000 K** North light (blue sky)
- **9,000 K**
- **8,000 K**
- **7,000 K** Overcast daylight
- **6,000 K**
- **5,000 K** Noon daylight / Direct sun / Electronic flashbulbs
- **4,000 K**
- **3,000 K** Household lightbulbs / Early sunrise / Tungsten light / Candlelight
- **2,000 K**
- **1,000 K**

Out-of-sight task light. Under cabinets is a natural place to use LEDs because their small size keeps them out of sight and because they're cool to the touch. Also, unlike fluorescents, they don't interfere with radio or TV reception. Lights are available in a range of styles. Select only the amount of light you need so that glare off the counter isn't an issue. The fixture to the left from Kichler® is one example.

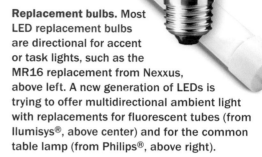

Replacement bulbs. Most LED replacement bulbs are directional for accent or task lights, such as the MR16 replacement from Nexxus, above left. A new generation of LEDs is trying to offer multidirectional ambient light with replacements for fluorescent tubes (from Ilumisys®, above center) and for the common table lamp (from Philips®, above right).

Excellent accent lighting. Small disks (from Kichler, above left) and night-lights (from Kichler, above right) provide the low light levels needed for highlighting artwork or providing safe nighttime navigation. Easily concealed, they work in enclosed cabinets without heat buildup and use very little energy to illuminate.

properly, LEDs need thermal management. The heat sink, usually a number of large aluminum fins located near the base of the lamp, is a critical component of an LED.

LEDs are already more efficient than incandescent bulbs, producing approximately 60 to 70 lumens per watt, and manufacturers expect efficiency to surpass that of CFLs soon. Their 50,000-hour average life span translates into 34 years when used four hours a day. There are other advantages to LEDs' solid-state engineering as well: They are immune to vibration, and their performance improves in cold temperatures, making them ideal for outdoor applications.

Cost is currently the biggest drawback to LEDs. A screw-in LED replacement for a recessed light costs about $120, but remember that LEDs are the lighting equivalent of a computer chip: Just as Intel® founder Gordon Moore predicted that chip capacity would double every two years (Moore's Law), Haitz's Law (named for scientist Roland Haitz) states that every decade, LED prices will fall by a factor of 10 while performance will increase by a factor of 20.

Still, a word of caution is appropriate. There are some well-engineered LED bulbs and fixtures on the market, but with so many manufacturers jumping on the bandwagon, there are plenty of LEDs with harsh light and poor switching and dimming response. It's a good idea to evaluate these products carefully before purchasing.

Match the Light to the Job

Both CFLs and LEDs are available with screw-in bases as replacement bulbs for existing fixtures, but if you are building a new home or remodeling, you might consider fixtures dedicated to one technology or the other. Dedicated fixtures can lengthen the lifespan of the bulb and maximize its strengths. Both CFLs and LEDs play a role in providing ambient, accent, task, and decorative lighting, the four layers that create a well-lit room. But CFLs and LEDs aren't necessarily interchangeable. That's largely because CFLs are a multidirectional light source and LEDs are a point source.

Because they are multidirectional and produce large amounts of diffuse light, CFLs work well for ambient, task, and decorative lighting (photos pp. 160–161). They can be used nearly everywhere that incandescent bulbs are used, particularly in table lamps and in shielded sconces, where the fabric or glass adds color to the light. In the bathroom, when they're used behind opaque glass, CFLs do a great job of lighting your face. In kitchens, in laundry rooms, and in offices, CFLs produce bright-enough ambient light to illuminate worksurfaces.

CFLs are not appropriate everywhere, however. Locations where lights are switched on and off quickly—say an entry hall or a coat closet—are not ideal because CFLs need time to attain their full brightness and because short-cycle switching reduces the bulbs' lifespan. Also, if you're using a CFL bulb in an outdoor fixture, make sure that it's labeled for outside use, which means that the ballast will work in cold temperatures.

Efficacy at a Glance

One measure of lighting efficiency is efficacy. Efficacy is expressed as lumens per watt (lm/w)—the amount of light produced for each unit of electricity consumed. Incandescent lights have efficacies between 10 and 20 lm/w, and fluorescents range from 60 to 100 lm/w. LED products tested recently by the U.S. Department of Energy's Solid-State Lighting program were in the 70 to 80 lm/w range. However, LEDs are expected to surpass fluorescents soon and exceed 150 lm/w by 2015. The chart below shows representative examples.

COMPARING RECESSED FIXTURES

	Incandescent	CFL	LED
Watts	65	15	12
Lumens	52	675	730
Efficacy (lm/w)	10	45	60

Task and Accent Lighting Require Focused Light

LEDs produce a focused beam of light. Although their relatively small output means they can't throw light as far as some incandescents, there are plenty of circumstances where they work well as task lights. And they're ideal for accent lights because they don't produce UV-light that damages paintings and fabrics. Because LEDs are small and easily produced as pucks or strip lighting, they are ideal for undercabinet illumination or as accent lights hidden in coves or inside cabinets, where small size and low heat output are important.

Glare can be a concern with bright LED fixtures, especially recessed lights. San Francisco Bay Area lighting designer Eric

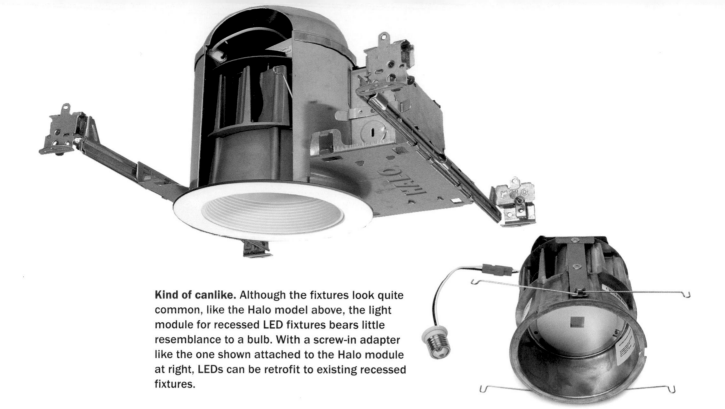

Kind of canlike. Although the fixtures look quite common, like the Halo model above, the light module for recessed LED fixtures bears little resemblance to a bulb. With a screw-in adapter like the one shown attached to the Halo module at right, LEDs can be retrofit to existing recessed fixtures.

Johnson recommends using a diffuser with recessed cans or, at the very least, recessing the bulb as deep into the fixture as possible.

Lightolier®'s Calculite™ is a lensed fixture that uses a diffuser to create white light. Instead of coating the LED bulbs with phosphor, the phosphor is applied to the diffuser.

Under the first approach, variations in the amount of phosphor coating on each diode affect the overall color of the light. When you have multiple downlights in a room, this can result in variations in the light from the different fixtures. It's easier to apply an even, consistent phosphor coating to a glass diffuser, improving the consistency and the color of the light. Placing the reflector above the phosphor layer results in more light output than other methods and less glare, according to the manufacturer.

A unique feature of LEDs is that a single fixture with different types of diodes can create multiple temperatures and colors of light, opening new design possibilities for accent lighting.

One last thing: Both CFLs and LEDs can be tricky to dim. The ballasts and drivers, respectively, must be compatible with the dimmers, and the light may cut out before dimming down all the way. This information is usually indicated on the product.

Sean Groom is a contributing editor to Fine Homebuilding. *He lives outside Hartford, Conn.*

Sources

The companies listed here had products that impressed us at LightFair®, the annual lighting-industry trade show. Visit **www.americanlightingassoc.com** for a comprehensive list of lighting manufacturers.

American Fluorescent:
www.americanfluorescent.com

Cooper Lighting (Halo):
www.cooperlighting.com

Cree:
www.cree.com

Feelux:
www.feelux.com

Ilumisys:
www.ilumisys.com

Journée Lighting®:
www.journeelighting.com

Kichler:
www.kichler.com

Lightolier:
www.lightolier.com

MaxLite:
www.maxlite.com

Nexxus:
www.nexxuslighting.com

OSRAM® Sylvania®:
www.sylvania.com

Philips:
www.philips.com

The Energy–Smart Kitchen

■ BY ALEX WILSON

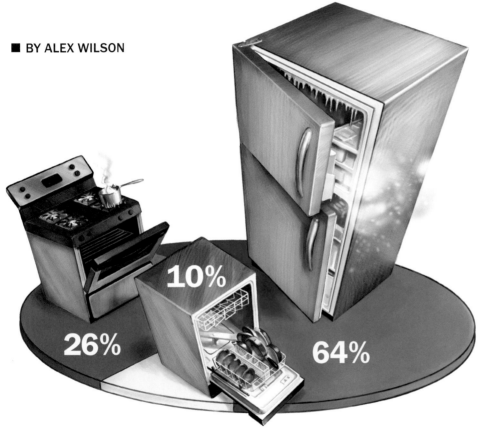

10%

26%

64%

When it comes to electricity consumption, the kitchen is the hungriest room in the house. Kitchen appliances—including refrigerators, freezers, ranges, and dishwashers—account for nearly 27% of household electricity use. Collectively, that's more than 300 billion kilowatt hours (kwh) per year in the United States, or roughly the electricity output of 90 average-size coal-fired power plants.

Not all appliances are equally voracious, however. Refrigerators and freezers account for nearly two-thirds of kitchen energy use, with ranges, ovens, and cooktops accounting for a little over one-quarter, and dishwashers the rest. Add in the heating, air-conditioning, hot water, and lighting used in a kitchen, and this room is clearly the energy hog of most houses. Putting your kitchen on an energy diet might be one of the best things you can do to save money and resources. Like most diets, it all comes down to making informed choices.

Where does the energy go? Kitchen appliances on average account for more than a quarter of household electricity use, and the appliances we use to keep food cold—refrigerators and stand-alone freezers—together are the biggest consumers. Ovens, coffeemakers, and cooktops, as a group, are the second-hungriest appliances in the kitchen, followed by dishwashers.

Two Tools to Measure Energy Efficiency

The blue Energy Star label and the yellow EnergyGuide sticker help consumers identify energy-efficient appliances. Energy Star labeling denotes compliance with guidelines set by the U.S. Environmental Protection Agency and the U.S. Department of Energy. Appliances rated by the program include dishwashers, refrigerators, and freezers (but not cooking appliances). Although Energy Star compliance indicates an energy-efficient appliance, some models exceed the requirements more than others (see www.energystar.gov). Unlike the voluntary Energy Star program, the EnergyGuide label is required by the Federal Trade Commission on all fridges, freezers, and dishwashers (but not on cooking appliances). The label shows the model's capacity, its estimated annual energy consumption and operating costs, and a scale that compares its efficiency to that of similar models. The EnergyGuide label helps in comparison shopping but does not indicate Energy Star compliance.

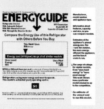

Refrigerators Are the Top Energy Guzzlers

In a typical American home, the refrigerator accounts for about 15% of total electricity use. Assuming heat and hot water are not electric, that makes the refrigerator a home's single largest electricity consumer. This is the case even though refrigerators have improved dramatically since the mid-1970s; today's models use about a third as much power as those from 30 years ago.

Refrigerators: Style and Use Determine Efficiency

WHAT TO AVOID

- **Through-the-door ice and water dispensers.** Both the lost insulation and the additional cooling coils in a through-the-door ice and water dispenser increase electricity consumption.

Frugal features. The most popular features with consumers—such as automatic defrosting and through-the-door ice and water dispensers—are not always the most energy efficient. Still, Maytag®'s Ice$_2$O® refrigerator meets Energy Star requirements and is equipped with two potentially energy-saving features: an alarm that alerts homeowners to a refrigerator door left ajar and a vacation mode that saves energy by limiting automatic defrosting when the fridge isn't opened for several days.

- **Automatic ice makers.** Ice makers consume energy, though exactly how much is difficult to determine.

WHAT TO LOOK FOR

- **The Energy Star label.** The U.S. Environmental Protection Agency confers its Energy Star label on models that are at least 20% more energy efficient than the federal minimum. Shopping for this label is an easy way to be sure the refrigerator you choose is not an energy waster.

- **Freezers on top or bottom.** Side-by-side refrigerators use more energy.

- **Manual defrost cycles.** The most energy-efficient refrigerators and freezers have manual defrost, although they can be hard to find, particularly among high-end models.

- **Door alarms.** Some manufacturers offer an alarm that will sound if the fridge door is left open—helping to save energy and to prevent food spoilage.

MAINTAINING HIGH PERFORMANCE

- **Place fridges away from heat sources**—especially a range or oven, but also a dishwasher. Radiant heat from these appliances warms the surface of the fridge, requiring more energy to keep the inside cool. If the refrigerator must be adjacent to a heat source, provide space for air circulation.

- **Clean the coils, at least annually.** Dust and dirt buildup on refrigerator/freezer coils reduces the heat-exchange efficiency and makes the compressor work harder. Most refrigerators now have coils that can be accessed from the front, eliminating the need to pull the unit away from the wall.

- **Turn off the condensation-control feature.** Essentially, these are heating elements under the protective shell that consume energy in two ways: by using electricity to warm the outer shell and by increasing the difference in temperature across the unit's insulation. Models with

---

Innovations to Watch For

VACUUM-PANEL INSULATION

Thermos bottles keep coffee hot because most of the air molecules in the double wall have been removed, keeping conductive heat transfer very low. The same idea has been incorporated into flat vacuum panels. Back in the mid-1990s, Whirlpool® produced high-efficiency refrigerators that used inch-thick vacuum panels made by Owens-Corning, which had center-of-panel insulating values of R-75. The technology hasn't completely caught on, but it's currently used by KitchenAid®, a Whirlpool brand. Silica-aerogel insulation is another material that could find its way into refrigerators; it insulates better than the polyurethane foam used in most models.

VARIABLE-SPEED COMPRESSORS

Compressors account for 83% of a refrigerator's energy use, so an efficient compressor means an efficient refrigerator. Variable-speed compressors save energy by operating at low speed during low-usage periods (such as overnight) and then running faster during periods of high usage. Still mostly limited to European brands and professional-style built-ins, variable-speed compressors are used in some GE® Profile™ and Monogram® products, as well as Whirlpool's high-end built-in lines. Other manufacturers may soon follow suit.

---

this feature usually have a switch to turn it off; do so, unless condensation becomes a problem.

- **Keep the freezer full.** Frozen food serves as a thermal stabilizer that reduces the amount of on-off cycling. If you don't have a lot of frozen food, freeze containers of water (use plastic, and allow for expansion as the water freezes) to take up the extra space. When you need ice for a cooler, you can use these frozen containers.

- **Don't keep an extra fridge in the garage.** When you buy a new refrigerator, avoid the costly mistake of keeping the old one as a backup.

Cooking Options Pit Efficiency against Cost

More efficient cooking saves energy and money directly, of course, but by keeping waste heat out of the kitchen, it also saves on air-conditioning. Although this impact might not be huge in a typical home, it can make a difference. As a rule, electric cooking appliances are more efficient than gas-fueled ones. But the relative price of natural gas versus electricity often makes natural-gas-fueled appliances a more economical choice. Gas cooktops also afford better heat control than their electric counterparts.

Because their functions are so different, it's important to consider cooktops and ovens separately, even though they might be combined in a stand-alone kitchen range.

Gas Ovens Draw Electricity, Too

With ovens, rapid heat-up and cooldown aren't as important as with cooktops, making electric ovens more competitive with gas, even for serious cooks. In fact, it is not uncommon for high-end ranges to have a gas cooktop and an electric oven. Again, electric models are more efficient: Electric ovens are 1.8 to 3.5 times as efficient as gas ovens, according to U.S. Department of Energy (DOE) data. Cost efficiency, however, largely depends on which type of fuel costs the least in your area.

Most gas ovens also use a lot of electricity while operating. In nearly all gas ovens today, when the gas burner is operating, an electric glow-bar igniter (sometimes called a "gas oven igniter") is on, drawing about 375w. (Interestingly, at a recent International Builders' Show, not one kitchen-appliance salesperson who was asked seemed aware of this fact.) Found in all self-cleaning models, the glow bar ignites the gas when the oven is turned on and reignites it as it cycles off

and on during the cooking or self-cleaning process. Those 375w (or even as much as 500w in some ovens) are a significant amount of electricity. If low electricity use is a priority in your home, consider a model without a glow bar, such as ranges made by the Peerless-Premier Appliance Co. (www.premierrange.com), which operate with a pilot or a spark ignition.

Cooktops & Ovens: Electric Wins over Gas

Cooktop efficiency is difficult to measure, and relatively little attention has been paid to it, primarily because stovetop cooking accounts for a small percentage of household energy use—about 5%, according to the American Council for an Energy Efficient Economy. My research shows that electric cooktops are the most efficient, and gas the worst. The section below ranks the most common cooktop technologies in order of efficiency based on the energy factor, which is the ratio of the amount of energy conveyed to an item being heated to the device's overall energy consumption. Expressed as a decimal, it reflects the proportion of energy used that actually contributes to the cooking of food.

COOKTOP TYPES

Induction Although induction technology initially failed to take off when introduced a decade or so ago, it's back, with more high-end induction cooktops entering the market. On an induction cooktop, electrical energy is transferred directly to ferrous-metal cookware through magnetic induction. Efficiency is the highest of any cooktop (about 84%) because the cookware is heated directly. It's also a safer way to cook: The cooking surface does not heat up, enabling photos like the one at top left on facing page, where water boils in a cutaway pan while ice cubes rest intact on the "burner's" surface. Induction

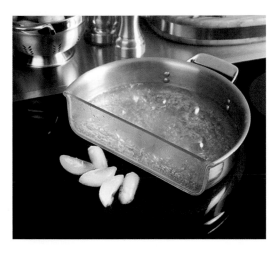

INDUCTION
Energy Factor: 0.84

ELECTRIC COIL
Energy Factor: 0.737

RADIANT
Energy Factor: 0.742

GAS, NO PILOT
Energy Factor: 0.399
GAS, PILOT
Energy Factor: 0.156

cooktops also heat up and cool down quickly, providing precise controllability. Downsides include high cost and the fact that only certain cookware can be used. Cast-iron, enameled cast iron, and some stainless-steel cookware work. Test yours to make sure a magnet sticks to it, or look for a label.

Radiant ceramic The most common mid- to high-end electric cooktop today, it has relatively fast-heating radiant elements under ceramic glass, providing a sleek, easy-to-clean stovetop surface. Flat-bottom cookware is needed for good surface contact; older-style cast-iron pans are not recommended because burrs on the metal can scratch the glass surface. Radiant-ceramic cooktops heat faster than electric coils and are nearly equal in energy efficiency.

Electric coil Available on low-cost ranges and cooktops, these old-fashioned open-coil elements are slow to heat up and difficult to clean, but fairly efficient at transferring electric energy to the pot.

Gas (natural or propane) Cooks prefer gas burners for speed and controllability, but indoor-air-quality experts often recommend against gas for health reasons. Although gas cooktops rate worst in terms of energy efficiency, they are usually more cost-efficient because the price of natural gas is typically a lot lower than electricity. Gas cooktops use only about 40% of the energy produced, and if there's a continuously burning pilot light, the overall efficiency is far lower (about 16%). In some areas, propane is nearly as expensive as electricity per unit of delivered

Ovens and Oven Fans

Self-cleaning ovens typically have more insulation than standard ovens, so if you have a choice, go for a self-cleaning model. The extra insulation keeps the outer surface of the range from becoming too hot during the self-cleaning cycle, but it also helps the oven to operate more efficiently.

Oven fans

Convection ovens have a fan in the back that circulates air to maintain more-even temperatures. As a result, either the cooking time or the temperature can be reduced. The energy savings from reduced gas or electricity use for cooking easily outweigh the fan's electricity use.

OVEN EFFICIENCY BY TYPE	
Oven Type	**Energy Factor**
Microwave	0.557
Electric (self-cleaning)	0.138
Electric (standard)	0.122
Gas (self-cleaning)	0.054
Gas (standard)	0.030

energy, making electric cooktops a more economical option. The efficiency of natural gas and propane is essentially the same.

Microwave Ovens Are Tops in Efficiency

First introduced as a practical kitchen appliance in 1965, microwave ovens have revolutionized cooking and offer substantial energy savings over standard ovens (They are 5 times as energy efficient as a standard electric oven). They work by producing non-ionizing microwave radiation (a certain frequency of radio waves) with a magnetron and directing that radiation at the food. The microwave radiation is absorbed by water, fats, and sugars, producing heat. Because the microwaves penetrate the food, heating is more rapid and requires less energy than in a conventional oven. Microwave ovens are about 5 times as energy efficient as standard electric ovens and more than 10 times as energy efficient as gas ovens.

Increasingly, manufacturers are combining cooking functions with microwave ovens to produce a new generation of "rapid-cook" appliances. These models combine microwaves with electric grilling elements so that food can be browned as well as cooked. Quartz elements are often used to create radiant heat, though General Electric's Advantium® microwave oven (www.geappliances.com) uses a halogen-lamp element. Convection is another feature offered by the Advantium and some others, such as TurboChef®'s Speedcook Oven (www.turbochef.com). In the future, most ovens likely will include multiple heating options to speed up cooking and to serve a wider range of functions, from defrosting to reheating to grilling.

Exhaust Fans Are Important to Health

Exhaust fans add to energy consumption, but their importance with regard to kitchen air quality—and the health of your home's occupants—cannot be ignored. Chemical impurities in natural gas, along with incomplete combustion, can result in dangerous levels of carbon monoxide (CO), causing headaches and fatigue at low levels and, at high concentrations, death. Because of this concern, gas ranges should be installed with quality, outdoor-venting range-hood fans, which should be operated when the cooktop or oven is on.

Exhaust fans are most efficient when placed above the cooktop or range. Downdraft fans, which are installed at the back or in the center of a range, rely on significant airflow (and power consumption) to ventilate cooking fumes effectively. Because fumes are more easily channeled into a fan installed in a range hood, fan performance is better.

If you can't vent an exhaust fan outdoors, avoid the use of gas cooking appliances. Recirculating range-hood fans can remove odors but should not be relied on to remove combustion gases.

A significant energy-saving feature to look for in a range-hood exhaust fan is a variable-speed motor. This allows the fan to operate at a lower airflow rate when full ventilation capacity is not needed, thus saving energy and reducing noise.

Dishwashers Are Shaping Up

Dishwashers have changed quite a bit in recent years. They use a lot less water, which translates into lower energy use for water heating. In 1978, water use by dishwashers ranged from 11 gal. to 15 gal. for a normal dishwashing cycle. By 2000, that usage had dropped to 6 gal. to 10 gal.

As water use has gone down, total energy use has also dropped, while the proportion of energy use for processes other than water heating has risen. In 1978, 83% of the total energy use for dishwasher operation was for heating water; 10% was for motor operations, and 7% for drying. By 1994, energy use for water heating had dropped to 56%, according to a 2003 Virginia Tech report.

However, that does not mean most dishwashers are as energy efficient as they could be. Nearly all dishwashers today have booster heaters that increase the temperature of incoming water to about 140°F to improve wash performance. An integral electric element provides this heat, and it can use a lot of electricity. Recent independent testing shows that booster heaters operate throughout the dishwashing cycle, resulting in total electricity use per cycle of 2.0 to 3.5 kwh. Used an average of 215 times per year (the frequency DOE assumes), a dishwasher could easily consume more electricity annually than a refrigerator. More research is needed to determine the significance of this electricity use.

Dishwashers vary considerably in their energy use, much more so than refrigerators. For comparison, dishwashers are rated by the federal government according to their energy factor (EF), a measurement based on the energy usage for an average number of cycles (a completely different formula than the one used to rate cooking appliances). The higher the EF, the more efficient the dishwasher: The current federal standard mandates a minimum EF of 0.46; Energy Star dishwashers must meet a minimum EF of 0.65. The most-efficient dishwashers have an EF that approaches or slightly exceeds 1.0. Although the EF is used to compute the annual energy consumption and cost estimates found on the EnergyGuide label on many appliances, the EF itself might not appear there.

Dishwashers: Less Hot Water Equals Less Energy Use

Drawerful of savings. Compact dishwasher drawers can be highly efficient (both of these models from New Zealand manufacturer Fisher & Paykel® are Energy Star compliant). An added bonus is that the integrated models, like the one pictured above, blend seamlessly into kitchen cabinetry.

WHAT TO LOOK FOR

• **The Energy Star label.** Energy Star-qualified dishwashers are at least 41% more energy efficient than the federal minimum. Keep in mind that some models exceed the standard significantly more than others; check the EnergyGuide label or the list of qualifying dishwashers at www.energystar.gov for high-performing machines.

• **Soil sensing.** With this technology, "fuzzy logic" is used to determine how dirty the dishes are. Water use and wash cycle are adjusted accordingly, saving significant water and energy.

• **No-heat drying.** Most dishwashers have an electric heating element and fan for drying dishes. Make sure the one you buy has a no-heat drying option, which can save a significant amount of energy.

Top performers. The Bosch® Evolution line includes dishwashers that exceed the minimum federal energy-efficiency standard by 147%—far more than any American-made dishwasher—using approximately the same amount of energy as a dishwasher half its size.

Easy button. The "EcoAction®" button offered on some Bosch dishwashers allows homeowners to reduce energy usage by up to 25%. Activating the feature lowers the wash temperature and extends the cycle by a few minutes.

A new way to clean dishes. Tshe LG® Steam Dishwasher™ uses only 2.8 gal. to 3.2 gal. of water in an average load.

USAGE TIPS

- **Insulate hot-water pipes** from the water heater so that water stays hot all the way to the dishwasher and doesn't cool off as much between the different wash and rinse cycles.

- **Wash full loads only**, even if it means waiting a day or two.

- **Avoid high-temperature cycles.** Many dishwashers have a setting for more intensive cleaning in which the temperature is boosted, which can significantly increase electricity use per cycle. To conserve energy, don't use this setting.

Alex Wilson is founder and executive editor of Environmental Building News *and president of BuildingGreen Inc. in Brattleboro, Vt. (wwwbuildinggreen.com). His latest book is* Your Green Home *(New Society Publishers, 2006).*

Innovations to Watch For

STEAM-CYCLE DISHWASHERS
LG has introduced a steam-cycle dishwasher that the company claims cleans dishes better. The washing cycle uses steam at over 200°F, apparently saving energy in the process because it uses a lot less water. You can choose different wash intensities for the bottom and top racks or a half-load option that cleans the top or bottom rack only.

DRAWER DISHWASHERS
The New Zealand company Fisher & Paykel and KitchenAid both offer drawer-type dishwashers. They can save energy and water by allowing you to use one smaller drawer rather than a partially loaded full-size dishwasher, or by allowing two drawers to be operated at different cycles.

CONDENSATION DRYING
While most dishwashers vent moist air into the kitchen as dishes are drying, Bosch models use condensation-drying technology, which the company claims improves hygiene and saves energy.

Solar Hot Water

■ BY SCOTT GIBSON

Unobtrusive, efficient, and energy-smart. Heating water with the sun can be almost as simple as installing a solar collector on the roof. Resembling skylights, these collectors can provide hot water for baths, laundry, and even heat.

There's nothing like a looming energy crisis to bring history full circle. More than a century has passed since Clarence Kemp, a Baltimore heating-equipment dealer, came up with the first commercial solar water heater. His patented Climax Solar Water Heater, which sold for $25, was a hit.

More-efficient designs soon came along, and by 1941, half the houses in Florida had solar hot-water systems. Roof-mounted solar collectors were common in California, too. But natural-gas discoveries in the West and a utility blitzkrieg to sell more electricity in

Florida brought the solar hot-water business to its knees.

Does the story sound familiar? It should. A spike in energy prices and short-lived government incentives created a solar hot-water boomlet in the 1970s and 1980s. The interest withered when energy prices dropped and government subsidies dried up, sticking homeowners with systems that didn't always work and couldn't be serviced due to the lack of qualified technicians. Rising energy prices are once again making solar attractive. But this time around, the industry

is offering more-dependable, better-designed hot-water systems that give homeowners in all parts of the country a reliable way to cut energy bills.

Heating water with the sun can be pretty simple. In the right climate, a 55-gal. drum painted black and perched on the roof provides plenty of hot water. Collectors like that, called batch heaters, are producing hot water all over the world. But technology has a lot more to offer these days, making solar hot water feasible for any region of the country and for just about any application, from swimming pools and hot tubs to domestic hot water and even space heating.

There Are Many Ways to Heat Water, but Keeping It Hot Is Another Story

Although solar hot-water systems vary widely in design and complexity, they share some basics. The sun heats water, or another liquid capable of transferring heat, in a collector. Specialized materials called selective coatings are made to absorb available solar radiation. They include black chrome, black nickel, and aluminum oxide combined with nickel or titanium nitride oxide.

Once water is hot, it's either moved to a storage tank or piped directly to where it's needed. That much seems simple, but the trick is making sure the water doesn't cool down too much or, worse, freeze. To cover the wide range of temperatures and solar potential that hot-water systems can encounter, manufacturers offer a variety of equipment and plumbing options.

In general, systems are either active or passive, meaning they operate with or without electric pumps. They also can be direct or indirect (sometimes called open loop or closed loop), which means the collectors heat the water that's used in the house or, alternatively, heat a nonfreezing transfer medium that in turn heats potable

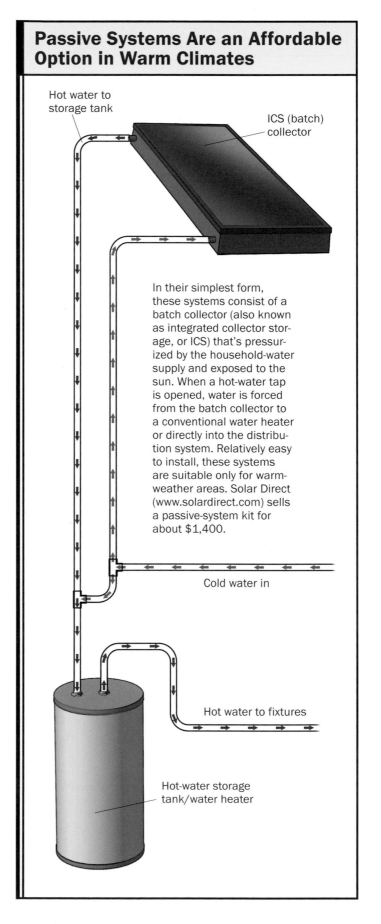

Passive Systems Are an Affordable Option in Warm Climates

Hot water to storage tank

ICS (batch) collector

In their simplest form, these systems consist of a batch collector (also known as integrated collector storage, or ICS) that's pressurized by the household-water supply and exposed to the sun. When a hot-water tap is opened, water is forced from the batch collector to a conventional water heater or directly into the distribution system. Relatively easy to install, these systems are suitable only for warm-weather areas. Solar Direct (www.solardirect.com) sells a passive-system kit for about $1,400.

Cold water in

Hot water to fixtures

Hot-water storage tank/water heater

water in a heat exchanger. In virtually all cases, solar-heated water is routed through a conventional water heater, where it gets a temperature boost (if necessary) before being distributed to its point of use.

How Much Hot Water Do You Need?

Most Americans use about 20 gal. of hot water a day, a standard industry benchmark. Most hot-water tanks are sized for a single day's consumption, so an average family of four, for example, might end up with an 80-gal. tank. Solar hot-water systems should have no trouble delivering that kind of volume, but there aren't any safe generalizations about whether it will be enough to satisfy household demands.

"The thing with hot water is that there are wide variations in demand," says Brad Collins, executive director of the American Solar Energy Society. "A 3,000-sq.-ft. house occupied by two elderly people will have substantially less demand than the exact same house next door that has five people, including two teenage girls. Their demand is tenfold what it is in the other house."

Other variables include the time of day when demand for hot water is high-

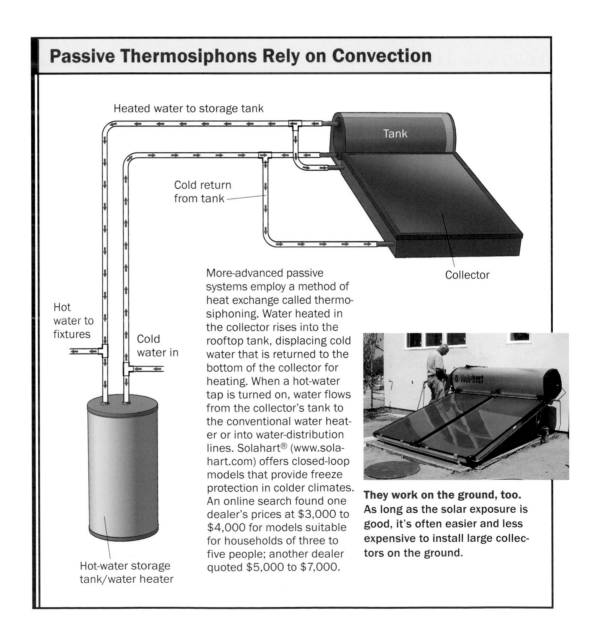

Passive Thermosiphons Rely on Convection

Heated water to storage tank

Tank

Cold return from tank

Collector

Hot water to fixtures

Cold water in

More-advanced passive systems employ a method of heat exchange called thermosiphoning. Water heated in the collector rises into the rooftop tank, displacing cold water that is returned to the bottom of the collector for heating. When a hot-water tap is turned on, water flows from the collector's tank to the conventional water heater or into water-distribution lines. Solahart® (www.solahart.com) offers closed-loop models that provide freeze protection in colder climates. An online search found one dealer's prices at $3,000 to $4,000 for models suitable for households of three to five people; another dealer quoted $5,000 to $7,000.

Hot-water storage tank/water heater

They work on the ground, too. As long as the solar exposure is good, it's often easier and less expensive to install large collectors on the ground.

est, whether use comes all at once (morning showers, for example) or is distributed throughout the day, the number of appliances in the house and when they are used, and the amount of solar potential the house has. "It's a different environment for each and every house," says Collins. "It's very much occupant-driven."

If there's such a thing as an average, the Arizona Solar Center estimates that a solar hot-water system should be able to deliver 100% of hot water in the summer and about 40% on a year-round basis. Performance varies by region. A household of four people would need 40 sq. ft. of collectors for an 80-gal. tank in Arizona, 55 sq. ft. in South Carolina, and 106 sq. ft. in Vermont.

How this translates into savings on gas or electric bills is also a wild card. Most solar hot-water systems are used to heat water before it goes into a conventional water heater, not as an outright replacement for a water heater fueled by gas or electricity. Careful consumers who are flexible about when they use hot water will see more solar benefit than a family that wants a lot of hot water all at once. Under the right circumstances, virtually all of a household's hot-water needs can be met by a solar system. But that's no guarantee.

"It's like buying a Toyota® Prius®," says Collins, likening an investment in solar hot water to owning one of Toyota's hybrid cars. "You change the way you drive because it's rewarding. You see how your involvement can impact your miles per gallon. In the same way, your involvement can impact how much energy you're going to be charged for, whether it's thermal or electrical energy. People become energy literate and smart energy consumers."

Using Solar for Space Heating

Solar collectors are commonly used for domestic hot water, but they also can supplement both forced-air and hydronic heating systems. In Europe, says Tim Merrigan of the National Renewable Energy Laboratory in Boulder, Colo., package systems that do both are relatively common. But due to heavy winter-heating loads and reduced solar potential, homeowners in this country shouldn't expect to get much more than one-third of their winter heat from solar sources with today's technology.

Elia Kleiman, the president of Synepex Energy in Cambridge, Mass., says the proportion of winter heat from solar depends on the type of heating system, the amount of insulation installed, and the tightness of the house. A best-case scenario in New England, land of snowy winters and cold, dreary springs, is that a solar system meets 40% to 70% of the heating load. That's in a well-sealed house with a radiant-floor heating system.

Radiant-floor heating is especially well suited to solar hot-water systems because it requires lower water temperatures, 120°F versus the 180°F that would be pumped through a typical baseboard hydronic system. Solar hot water also can be used for newer forced-air systems that use a technology called "hydro air." These boilers heat water forced through a heat-transfer coil, where it warms outgoing air.

For a hypothetical house of roughly 2,500 sq. ft.—well insulated and well sealed—Kleiman says Synepex would probably recommend eight evacuated-tube collectors covering roughly 400 sq. ft. of roof. That would provide 100% of domestic hot water in addition to what the system supplied to the space-heating side.

Systems like that aren't cheap. Although it's difficult to offer meaningful numbers without knowing specifics, Kleiman says that a solar-radiant floor system could easily cost $16,000 and possibly as much as $24,000 before tax credits and rebates. That's many times more than a system designed for only domestic hot water. If the collectors were tied to a baseboard hot-water system rather than a radiant floor, a homeowner

How Much Will My System Cost?

Cost is a key consideration when weighing the merits of renewable energy, not only because the systems tend to be expensive, but also because they force us to think about energy in an entirely different way. A conventional water heater doesn't cost much, but it's expensive to operate over its lifetime. A solar hot-water system is much more expensive up front but costs less to use.

Thinking in generalities isn't helpful when it comes to deciding whether solar hot water is a reasonable investment. For specifics, I went to www.findsolar .com, a website run under the auspices of the Department of Energy, the American Solar Energy Society, and the Solar Electric Power Association. It's an excellent place to get started on a hot-water system and provides a variety of other useful links.

A worksheet let me plug in a lot of specifics: my state, county, electric utility, and the number of people living in the house. In just a few seconds, the site came up with the size of the system I'd need, length of payback, annual utility savings, and even return on investment.

1. In southern Maine, I'd need one collector of about 32 sq. ft. to produce the 35 gal. of hot water my wife and I would use in a day. Having the system installed would cost about $3,500, but after a state rebate and the federal tax credit, the net cost would be less than half that. Moreover, my property value would increase by as much as $3,690, my annual utility savings would be from $224 to $335, and I would remove 21 tons of greenhouse gases from the air. That's the equivalent of 42,000 auto miles.

Years to break even? Between three and four, not including the system's impact on property-value appreciation. If I wanted estimates, a link would take me to a list of local installers, complete with contact information, services offered, and a brief summary of their experience.

2. In Tucson, Ariz., where utility rates are lower but the sun shines brighter, a similarly sized system would produce between $252 and $378 in annual utility savings.

3. In Pensacola, Fla., lower state incentives and utility rates drive the savings down to a range between $74 and $110.

4. In Dayton, Ohio, the savings are about the same as in Pensacola (about $85 per year).

If electricity rates increase more in the future than now forecast, solar hot water will become a viable option for more people. Until then, when it comes to saving money with solar hot water, it seems that if you have high utility rates, you'd be smart to get a system on your roof. If not, the decision depends on your commitment to a cleaner environment.

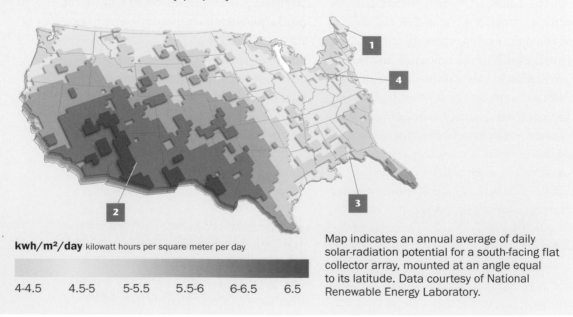

kwh/m²/day kilowatt hours per square meter per day

4-4.5   4.5-5   5-5.5   5.5-6   6-6.5   6.5

Map indicates an annual average of daily solar-radiation potential for a south-facing flat collector array, mounted at an angle equal to its latitude. Data courtesy of National Renewable Energy Laboratory.

Active Systems Reduce Heat Loss

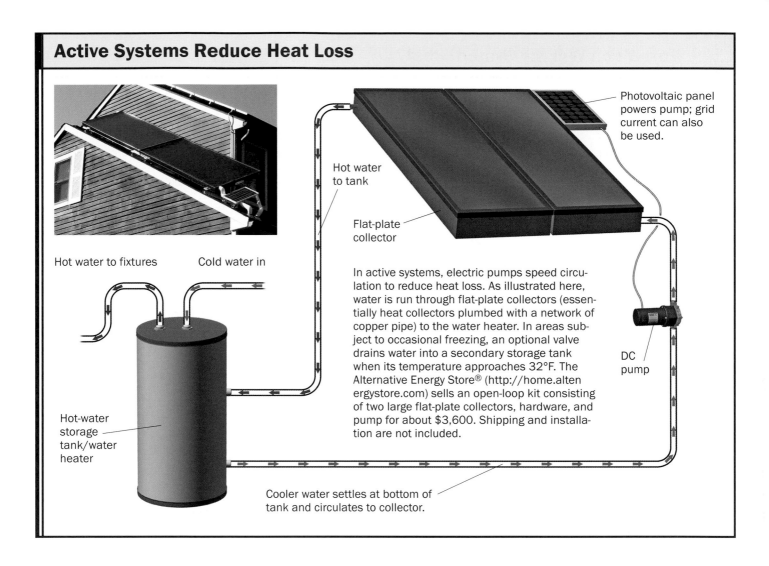

Photovoltaic panel powers pump; grid current can also be used.

Hot water to tank

Flat-plate collector

Hot water to fixtures   Cold water in

In active systems, electric pumps speed circulation to reduce heat loss. As illustrated here, water is run through flat-plate collectors (essentially heat collectors plumbed with a network of copper pipe) to the water heater. In areas subject to occasional freezing, an optional valve drains water into a secondary storage tank when its temperature approaches 32°F. The Alternative Energy Store® (http://home.altenergystore.com) sells an open-loop kit consisting of two large flat-plate collectors, hardware, and pump for about $3,600. Shipping and installation are not included.

DC pump

Hot-water storage tank/water heater

Cooler water settles at bottom of tank and circulates to collector.

might expect to see solar take care of only 20% to 40% of the heating load.

A big drawback of trying to heat a house with solar hot water is that demand is highest when the heat potential of the system is lowest. On an overcast day in northern New England, the sun is long gone by late afternoon, and the call for heat goes up accordingly. The answer is to store hot water generated during the day in storage tanks so that it can be used for heat when the sun goes down or when the days are cloudy. Tanks can be very large, 2,000 gal. or more, although Kleiman says newer systems can use much smaller tanks that hold as little as 200 gal.

Researchers are also looking down the road at promising new possibilities. Merrigan, for example, describes one experimen-

tal project in Canada where solar collectors are used to heat the ground when solar potential is abundant in summer. In winter, geothermal heat pumps can be used to extract the stored heat. This seasonal storage of heat is one idea that could make 100% solar heat possible in the future—even in Calgary, Alberta.

Rebates and Tax Breaks Could Be the Keys to the Future

What takes the sting out of the high cost of buying into renewable-energy systems is a combination of federal tax credits and state and utility rebates. The federal credit, pegged at 30% of system cost, is open to

Indirect Systems Are Most Efficient and Most Expensive

In these active systems, a pump circulates glycol in a closed loop. After running through high-efficiency evacuated-tube collectors (or flat-plate collectors), the hot glycol returns to the storage tank, where a heat exchanger warms potable hot water. Essentially freezeproof, these glycol-charged systems are able to perform in any season. ReVision Energy® in Portland, Maine, put the price of an installed system adequate for a local family of four at about $10,000.

Temperature sensor

Photovoltaic panel powers pump.

Heated glycol to heat exchanger

Evacuated-tube collectors

Hot water to tap   Cold water in

Cooled glycol to collectors

Hot-water storage tank/water heater

Heat exchanger

Controller

DC pump

Temperature sensor

Expansion tank

everyone. State and utility rebates, however, vary. Where they are generous, such as in California or Hawaii, you can expect robust growth for the solar industry.

Originally due to lapse in 2008, the federal tax credit has been extended for eight years. However, the on-and-off nature of government support is a "travesty," says Collins, and a chronic problem for the solar industry. "You can't do this with stops and starts," he adds. "It's been the history of incentives for renewables for the past 25 years."

Merrigan says that as many as 35% of all houses in Hawaii have solar water-heating systems, in part because of generous rebates. "I think it's key," he says. "It's just like for photovoltaics. PV is growing where there are incentives. The first cost of the system can

be enough to make people think about it, but to not want to make that investment. If you have incentives that can bring down that first cost, you see good market penetration."

Still, credits and incentives are available now, and they make a much bigger difference proportionally for hot water than for photovoltaic systems. "You displace roughly 2kw of energy with your water system, so it's like putting a 2kw PV system on your roof," says Collins. "But it's hot water. A 2kw system of PV might be $20,000, but a 2kw solar hot-water system might be $6000. I've often said that solar hot water is the most misunderstood bargain out there."

Scott Gibson, a contributing editor to Fine Homebuilding, *lives in East Waterboro, Maine.*

Collector Installation at a Glance

Solar hot-water systems involve a fair amount of labor-intensive planning and plumbing, but a typical collector installation is fairly straightforward. On this membrane-covered shed roof, (**1**) the first step was to erect the aluminum frames that hold the panels. The frames are adjusted to a fixed angle that maximizes the collector's solar gain and are bolted to blocking that has been integrated into the roof. (**2**) The panels, which weigh about 100 lb. each, are carried up and clipped onto each pair of frames. (**3**) Simple compression fittings connect the panels to plumbing. (**4**) The installers added two more panels and finished in about half a day. They spent another two days setting up the system.

1

2

3

4

Resources for Solar Information

Alternative Energy Store:
http://home.altenergystore.com;
Solar information and products

American Solar Energy Society:
www.ases.org;
Links, background information on solar energy

Database of State Incentives for Renewables and Efficiency (DSIRE™):
www.dsireusa.org;
Database of energy incentives listed by state and type

Find Solar:
www.findsolar.com;
Worksheets for estimating costs of solar hot-water systems

Florida Solar Energy Center®:
www.fsec.ucf.edu;
Comprehensive site on all things solar, including efficiency ratings of collectors and systems by manufacturer

Interstate Renewable Energy Council:
www.irecusa.org;
News, resources related to renewable energy

National Renewable Energy Laboratory:
www.nrel.gov;
Lots of background information on renewable energy

Solar Direct:
www.solardirect.com;
Solar information and resources

Solar Rating and Certification Corp.:
www.solar-rating.org;
Ratings for solar collectors and systems by manufacturer

Energy-Saving Thermostats

■ BY SEAN GROOM

Instead of turning down the thermostat on the way to bed and again on the way out the door, you can cut home-heating costs and count on a reliable, comfortable temperature with one of today's programmable thermostats. Basic models ($30 and up) store different settings for weekdays and weekends. More advanced models ($90 and up) store a different program for each day of the week.

Minimize Operating Time to Save Money

Whether a thermostat is manual or programmable, your savings result from the *setback,* or the reduction in temperature from the typical occupied setting. Studies by the U.S. Department of Energy have found that the energy required to raise a home's temperature to its normal level approximately equals the energy saved as the temperature falls to the lower setting. For each degree of setback over an eight-hour period, you'll reduce energy consumption by 1%; the longer the setback, the more energy savings you enjoy.

During the heating season, utility companies recommend a 68°F setting in the morning and evening and 55°F overnight and when you're not home. You can economize

on cooling costs with a setting of 78°F to 85°F when you're out or sleeping.

Check for Compatibility

A programmable thermostat has to be compatible with your HVAC system. Be especially careful when choosing one for use with heat pumps or radiant floors. A temperature setback in heating mode can cause a heat pump to operate inefficiently. And because high-mass radiant floors are slow to lose and gain heat, temperature setbacks have to be timed differently.

Finally, look for an Energy Star rating, which ensures the thermostat is capable of four daily temperature settings and is pre-programmed for efficient operation.

Installing a Programmable Thermostat

Replacing a standard thermostat with a programmable one is easy on most HVAC systems, but there are a few things you need to pay attention to that usually aren't included in the instructions. Hydronic (boiler) sys-

Choosing a Thermostat

Simple and inexpensive

Hunter®'s most basic model has four heating or cooling periods each day. It follows the same schedule for all weekdays, but you can set a different schedule for the weekend. Designed for simple installation, the device is battery-powered for broad system compatibility.

**Hunter Fan Company
Set & Save 44110, $35
(www.hunterfan.com)**

Smart and versatile

White-Rodgers®'s midlevel thermostat allows separate schedules for Saturday and Sunday, but uses the same program for weekdays. Energy Star-rated thermostats such as this one take the guesswork out of recovering from a temperature setback, automatically reaching the target temperature by the start of the programmed period. This model adjusts its call for heat by five minutes for each degree of setback. (For example, the heat turns on at 6:05 if you program a 5°F change for 6:30.)

**White-Rodgers
IF80-0471, $60
(www.white-rodgers.com)**

Easy, flexible programming

The flexibility of a high-end model like Honeywell®'s Vision Touch Screen allows you to enter a different schedule for each day. The touch screen relies on a menu-driven program similar to an ATM. A feature called "adaptive intelligent recovery system" tracks heating and cooling periods over time to "learn" how long it takes to bring your house to the programmed temperature, minimizing the system's run time. The "auto changeover" setting of thermostats in this price range switches between heating and cooling modes automatically.

**Honeywell
Vision Touch Screen RTH8500D, $109
(www.yourhome.honeywell.com)**

tems are wired differently; a professional can advise you on the best approach for your setup.

FOR A RETROFIT

- **First, cut power to the HVAC unit.** That's usually done by shutting off one or more circuit breakers: one if the unit is a heat pump, two if it's an air conditioner and furnace. The breaker for a heat pump or AC compressor is a two-pole breaker, usually two breakers with a handle tie. Most thermostats operate at low voltage (24v), which comes from the unit, and you want the power off to protect both the

transformer in the unit and the new thermostat. Remote thermostats for electric baseboards are typically line voltage (either 120v or 240v). In that case, be sure the thermostat you're installing is made for line voltage, and be sure the power is off to protect yourself.

- **Remove the old thermostat body from its base.** It will either be a press-fit unit or be held together with screws. The leads from the thermostat cable usually are attached to terminal screws on the base. Each screw has a letter next to it; often, they're molded into the plastic base and are not easy to see. If standard thermostat

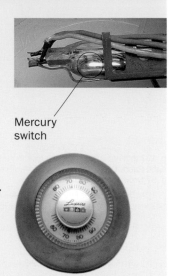
cable was used, the colors usually match up: red lead (wire) to the terminal marked "R," green lead to "G," yellow to "Y," and white to "W." By convention, the red lead is the power supply, green controls the air mover or blower, yellow controls cooling/air-conditioning, and white controls heat. The simplest programmable thermostat typically has two R-terminals: RC for power from the cool transformer, and RH from the heat transformer. If your cable has only one R lead, connect it to one of the two R terminals, and leave or install the provided jumper wire between the two. If the color of the wires doesn't match the terminal designation, use masking tape to label each wire before you disconnect it.

- **Pull out a few inches of cable, and put a clothespin or binder clip on the wire** to keep it from slipping back into the wall. If there isn't any slack, I wrap some electrical or masking tape around the cable, leaving a tail long enough to stick to the wall. If you're lucky, there'll be enough slack in the cable to cut off the bare copper and to restrip. For a clamp-type terminal, strip about ⅜ in. For a screw terminal, I usually strip about 1½ in. off each wire and cut off the excess after I've tightened the screw.

- **Run the cable through the hole in the new base,** and fix the base to the wall with a suitable anchor. Insert each wire into the terminal clamp, or wrap each wire around its terminal clockwise so that tightening the screw closes the loop. Make sure there's no insulation caught under the clamp or screw. If the cable is so short that I can't make the new connections or if I want to relocate the thermostat, I splice on a length of new cable. For low-voltage wiring like this, no junction box is needed. I use a crimp connector or small wire nuts, and I tape or cable-tie the two cables together to take the strain off the splices.

- **Before you complete the installation, plug the cable's hole in the wall** with caulk or non-hardening putty. This keeps drafts inside the wall from influencing the thermostat.

FOR A NEW INSTALLATION

- **Run the thermostat cable to an interior wall** close to the return-air location and out of direct sun.

- **Keep runs of low-voltage cable at least 2 in. away** from line-voltage cables. Use 6-conductor, 20-gauge standard thermostat wire unless you are sure that your HVAC unit and thermostat need fewer wires.

- **Run the cable into the stud bay** and through a ⅜-in.-dia. hole in a 1×6 block affixed to adjacent studs, flush to their faces. Make a service loop by leaving 2 ft. of cable in the stud bay, taped to the side of a stud.

- **Wrap 6 in. of cable around a nail** driven partway into the block. This helps to keep it from being buried under drywall.

---

*Sean Groom is a freelance writer in Bloomfield, Conn. **Mark Eatherton**, a heating contractor in Denver, provided technical information. "Installing a Programmable Thermostat" is written by **Clifford A. Popejoy**, a California electrical contractor.*

CREDITS

All photos are courtesy of *Fine Homebuilding* magazine (*FHb*) © The Taunton Press, Inc., except as noted below:

p. iii: Charles Bickford (*FHb*); p. iv: (left & right) Daniel S. Morrison (*FHb*), (center) Charles Bickford (*FHb*); p. 1: (left) courtesy © Peter Bastianelli-Kerze, (right) courtesy © Rheem Manufacturing Co.

p. 4: Every House Needs an Energy Audit by Jefferson Kolle, issue 200. All photos by Chris Ermides (*FHb*) except photos on p. 6 (left to right) Daniel S. Morrison (*FHb*), Charles Bickford (*FHb*), courtesy © John Curtis, Charles Bickford (*FHb*) and p. 7 courtesy © What's Working.

p. 12: Home Remedies for Energy Nosebleeds by Bruce Harley, issue 190. Photo on p. 14 courtesy © Kevin Kennefick; photos on p. 15 courtesy © John Curtis; photos on pp. 16 and 18 by Daniel S. Morrison (*FHb*). Drawing on p. 13 courtesy © Jackie Rogers; Drawings on pp. 14–15, 16 by Don Mannes (*FHb*).

p. 20: Can a Vintage Home be Energy Efficient? by Betsy Pettit, issue 194. All photos by Daniel S. Morrison (*FHb*). Drawings courtesy © Bob La Pointe.

p. 30: Efficient Houses Need Fresh Air by Max H. Sherman, issue 178. Photo on p. 33 by Daniel S. Morrison (*FHb*); photo on p. 35 courtesty © Aprilaire (www.aprilaire.com); photo on p. 36 courtesy © Fantech (www.fantech.com). Drawings by Don Mannes (*FHb*).

p. 39: A Practical Look at Deep-Energy Retrofits by Martin Holladay, issue 214. Photos on pp. 40, 43, 45, courtesy © Green Building Advisor; photos on pp. 42–43 by Charles Bickford (*FHb*); photo on p. 44 by Daniel S. Morrison (*FHb*); photo on p. 45 courtesy © Advanced Energy.

p. 46: Upgrade Your Attic Insulation by Mike Guertin, issue 200. All photos by Charles Bickford (*FHb*) except photo on p. 49 by Krysta S. Doerfler (*FHb*). Drawings by Dan Thornton (*FHb*).

p. 56: Beef Up Your Old Insulation without Tearing Into Walls by Justin Fink, issue 206. All photos by Dan Thornton (*FHb*) except p. 60 (left) by Andy Engel (*FHb*); p. 62 (top right) courtesy © Demilec USA; p. 62 (bottom right) Daniel S. Morrison (*FHb*); p. 63 (bottom left) courtesy © John Curtis; p. 64 (top) Courtesy © Johns Manville.

p. 65: All You Need to Know about Spray Foam by Robert Yagid, issue 204. Photos on p. 66 and p. 67 (top) by Rodney Diaz (*FHb*); p. 67 (bottom) courtesy © BASF; p. 69 courtesy © BioBased Insulation. Drawings by Dan Thornton (*FHb*).

p. 70: Making Sense of Housewraps by Fernando Pagés Ruiz, issue 177. All photos by Scott Philips (*FHb*) except magnified photo on p. 73 courtesy © Tyvek; p. 77(bottom right) by Krysta S. Doerfler (*FHb*); p. 78 (top) by Justin Fink (*FHb*). Drawing by Dan Thornton (*FHb*).

p. 79: Using Rigid Foam for an Efficient and Dry House by Martin Holladay, issue 213. Drawing courtesy © Steve Baczek.

p. 82: Basement Insulation Retrofits by Daniel S. Morrison, issue 206. All photos by Dan Thorton (*FHb*) except bottom right photo on p. 84 courtesy © Roxul. Drawing courtesy © Steve Baczek.

p. 85: Weatherstripping by Matthew Teague, issue 118. Photos on p. 85 (bottom), p. 86, and p. 88 (right) by Krysta S. Doerfler (*FHb*); photos on p. 85 (top) and left photos on p. 88 by Roe A. Osborn (*FHb*); photos on p. 87 (top right) and p. 89 courtesy © Dean Della Ventura; left photos on p. 87 by Scott Phillips. Drawings courtesty © Bob La Pointe.

p. 91: A Buyer's Guide to Windows by Sean Groom, issue 203. Photos on p. 92 and p. 94 by Rodney Diaz (*FHb*); p. 101, p. 102 (left and top right) courtesy © Marvin; p. 102 (middle right)

courtesy © Eagle; p. 102 (bottom right) courtesy © Simonton; p. 103 (bottom left) courtesy © Joseph Kugielsky; p. 103 (top right) Randy O'Rourke (*FHb*); p. 97 Maps courtesy © Energy Star; p. 97 Drawing by Dan Thorton (*FHb*).

p. 104: Do Europeans Really Make Better Windows? by Martin Holladay, issue 213. Photos on p. 104, 105, 106, and top drawing on p. 106 courtesy © Optiwin; bottom drawing on p. 106 courtesy © NFRC; p. 107 courtesy © Marvin; photos on p. 108 (top) and p. 109 by Robert Yagid (*FHb*); p. 108 (bottom) courtesy © SeriousWindows.

p. 110: Installing Replacement Windows by Mike Guertin, issue 185. Photos by Daniel S. Morrison (*FHb*). Drawings courtesy © Bob La Pointe.

p. 118: Is Your Heating System an Energy Beast? by Dave Yates, issue Energy-Smart Homes/Winter 2009. All drawings courtesy © Jackie Rogers except technical drawings on p. 120 and p. 126 courtesy © John Hartman; photos on p. 120 (top right) courtesy © Hardcast; p. 121 courtesy © Dave Yates; photos on p. 122 (top) courtesy © Owens Corning; p. 124 courtesy © York; p. 125 (bottom left) courtesy © Aprilaire; p. 125 (top right) courtesy © Danfoss.

p. 128: Finding the Sweet Spot: Siting a Home for Energy Efficiency by M. Joe Numbers, issue 93. All drawings courtesy © Malcolm Wells.

p. 136: Cool Design for a Comfortable House by Sophie Piesse, issue Energy-Smart Homes/Winter 2009. Photos on pp. 136, 140, 143, and 144 courtesy © Seth Tice-Lewis; p. 137 courtesy © Peter Bastianelli-Kerze; photos on pp. 138, 141, and 142 courtesy © Michael Sanford. Drawings courtesy © Sophie Piesse.

p. 145: Central Air-Conditioning: Bigger Isn't Better by Chris Green, issue 164. Photo courtesy © John Curtis. Drawings by Don Mannes (*FHb*).

p. 151: Low-Energy Lighting, High-Energy Design by Randall Whitehead, issue Energy-Smart Homes/Winter 2010. Photos on pp. 152, 155 (bottom), 156–158 by Dennis Anderson courtesy © Randall Whitehead; p. 153 (top) courtesy © VU1; p. 153 (bottom) courtesy © MaxLite; p. 154 (top) courtesy © LiteTronics; p. 154 (bottom) courtesy © eW™; p. 155 (top) courtesy © Randall Whitehead.

p. 159: The Bright Future of Lighting by Sean Groom, issue 205. All photos by Dan Thorton (*FHb*) except photos on p. 161 (top left) and p. 164 (top) courtesy © Cooper Lighting; p. 162 (middle left) courtesy © Kichler Lighting.

p. 165: The Energy-Smart Kitchen by Alex Wilson, issue 191. Photos on p. 166 courtesy © Maytag Corp.; p. 168 and p. 169 (left photos), p. 170 (top) courtesy © General Electric; p. 169 (right) courtesy © Whirlpool Corp.; p. 170 (bottom) courtesy © Peerless-Premier Appliance Co.; p. 172 courtesy © Fisher & Paykel Appliances; p. 173 (left and center) courtesy © Bosch Appliances; p. 173 (right) courtesy of LG Appliances. Drawings courtesy © Matt Collins.

p. 174: Solar Hot Water by Scott Gibson, issue 194. Photo on p. 174 courtesy © Viessmann Manufacturing Co.; p. 176 courtesy © Rheem Manufacturing Co.; p. 179 and p. 180 photos courtesy © Solarwrights Inc.; p. 181 photos by Charles Bickford (*FHb*). Drawings courtesy © Toby Welles/WowHouse.net.

p. 182: Energy-Saving Thermostats by Sean Groom, issue Energy-Smart Homes/Winter 2009. All photos by Scott Phillips (*FHb*) except center photo on p. 182 courtesy © White-Rodgers.

INDEX

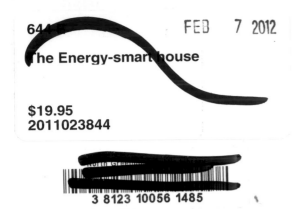
DATE DUE

FEB 2 4 2011	
MAY 3 1 2012	
NOV 2 7 2018	